WAR, MORALITY, AND AUTONOMY

To my wife, Jan, and my children Joe, Mary, Robyn, and Clare.
Thanks for the love and support.

Dan/Dad

War, Morality, and Autonomy
An Investigation in Just War Theory

DANIEL S. ZUPAN

ASHGATE

Published by
Ashgate Publishing Limited
Gower House
Croft Road
Aldershot
Hampshire GU11 3HR
England

Ashgate Publishing Company
Suite 420
101 Cherry Street
Burlington, VT 05401-4405
USA

Ashgate website: http//www.ashgate.com

British Library Cataloguing in Publication Data
Zupan, Daniel S.
   War, morality, and autonomy : an investigation into just
   war theory
   1.Just war doctrine 2.War - Moral and ethical aspects
   3.Military ethics 4.Justice
   I.Title
   172.4'2

Library of Congress Cataloguing-in-Publication Data
Zupan, Daniel S., 1956-
   War, morality, and autonomy : an investigation in just war theory / Daniel S. Zupan.
      p. cm.
   Includes bibliographical references and index.
   ISBN 0-7546-3866-9 (alk. paper)
      1. Just war doctrine. 2. War--Moral and ethical aspects. I. Title.

B105.W3Z86 2003
172'.42--dc22   2003063722

ISBN 0 7546 3866 9

Printed in Great Britain by TJ International Ltd, Padstow, Cornwall

Contents

Acknowledgements

I am very grateful to many people for the help and encouragement they have given me in writing this book. This book began as my doctoral dissertation, and I owe a great debt to my committee members, Barbara Hannan, Fred Schueler, and Aladdin Yaqub of the University of New Mexico Philosophy Department, and Clif Perry of the Auburn University Philosophy Department. Their thoughtful suggestions helped me immensely. I especially want to thank Sergio Tenenbaum, the chairman of the committee. Without his patient mentorship and profound philosophical insights, I could not have written this book.

I also want to thank my colleagues at the United States Military Academy. I am indeed fortunate to work with this wonderful group of people in the stimulating, friendly, and cheerful work environment they provide. I particularly want to thank Elizabeth Samet and Richard Schoonhoven for their indispensable help in every facet of preparing this work and for their friendship.

I am grateful to the many nice people at Ashgate Publishing who helped me in many ways. And I must thank John Hart for his professionalism and meticulous editing as he helped me prepare the manuscript for publication.

Daniel S. Zupan

Chapter 1

Introduction

The just war tradition represents an attempt by mankind to understand and articulate the moral parameters of war. When we refer to just war tradition, we refer to a dynamic, living, collective intellectual project. My work is a contribution to this ongoing project to impose constraints on the use of force, to delineate the character of just war and just conduct in war. I take the war convention – a term I use roughly synonymously with just war tradition – and the assumptions embodied within it as a starting point. At the same time, I challenge some of the assumptions and point out some of the tensions within the tradition, which I try to resolve. In this introduction I will sketch the problem and the project. I will outline the general assumptions with which I begin. I will say what I am trying to do, as well as what I am not attempting to do.

Everything I attempt to do in this work is influenced by a particular conception of the war convention. I will argue for a certain very plausible understanding of the purpose of the war convention (in fact, it is the most plausible understanding of it) and then offer a conceptual tool – what I will call the theory of autonomy – that we can use to enforce that purpose and strengthen the force of the war convention.

War has been a feature of human existence since time immemorial. Since time immemorial, mankind has sought to limit the horror of war. Paul Christopher writes:

> The modern concept of *bellum justum* was first compiled, refined, and formalized by Christian theologians and philosophers beginning with Saints Ambrose and Augustine in the fourth and fifth centuries. The tradition of recognizing constraints on the conduct of war is, however, much older.[1]

There has been for centuries a sense that there are some things you can and cannot do in the conduct of war. The judgments about the permissions and prohibitions have been moral judgments. I am not going to establish the propriety or validity of this way of looking at war. Along with the just war tradition, I am assuming it. That is, I am not going to try to prove decisively that there *should* be constraints in war, although it will be apparent that this is my view. My starting point is the war convention, which *is* an attempt to put constraints on war. The tradition sees war as an evil and seeks to limit the effects of that evil as much as possible, and it attempts to do this in terms of a certain way of looking at people. The war convention embodies and articulates an intuition that certain people should be immune from war's effects. These are noncombatants or innocents. Babies, for example, would represent the paradigm of those who should not be deliberately killed to further one's war aims. I note at the outset that not everyone shares this intuition. For instance, one opposing view recognizes the evil of war and concludes that the best thing to do is to end a war as quickly as possible. This view generally eschews constraints in war in favor of allowing any conduct, including the slaughter of noncombatants, that might reduce overall casualties. If we reduce casualties by using whatever means available, proponents of this view aver, we lessen the horror of war. But the war convention has been developed from a consciousness about the status of human beings and the nature of human relationships that resists this line of reasoning. Just war tradition constitutes, in many ways, an attempt to capture our intuition that when we are justified in resorting to war, we are justified because we are responding to an injustice that has been inflicted upon us. We are fighting in the name of justice when we defend our homeland against an invasion, for example. And our sense is that we cannot perpetrate injustice in the name of justice.

This way of looking at war rests upon the domestic analogy, where those who start an unjust war of aggression commit a crime on the international level analogous to robbery or murder on the domestic level. They have transgressed upon the peaceful lives of other human beings in a way similar to the transgression of a robber or murderer. And the analogous reasoning extends to the permissible response to injustice. Just as a police officer cannot do just anything to apprehend or stop a criminal, a nation cannot employ just any means in prosecuting a war. A policeman cannot threaten or kill the children of a criminal to induce him to turn himself in; a nation cannot slaughter the noncombatants of an enemy state to induce it to capitulate.

The war convention, then, embodies our notion that there are significant differences between combatants and noncombatants. There are things we can do to combatants during war that we cannot do to noncombatants. The war convention is supposed to underwrite our intuitions in this regard, but it does not always do so. My work is a continuation of this project and an attempt to clarify and make more consistent the multifarious components of this human enterprise, the quest for justice in war.

Looking back, I realize that my project began, in some ways, almost twenty years ago when I became an officer in the U.S. Army. Over the years I have received and given hundreds of operations orders[2] concerned with going to war under both training and real world conditions. Most of these operations orders included an annex on rules of engagement that specified the constraints on the use of force that we were under as soldiers. Since, as soldiers, we seem generally to automatically accept these rules of engagement and the direction of our civilian leaders with respect to the use of force, we are in many ways at the mercy of whatever is the prevalent conception of just war theory at the time. Hence, if there are any problems with the theory, those problems could manifest themselves on the battlefield in the form of the inappropriate use of force.

From 1991 through 1994 I taught just war theory at the United States Military Academy at West Point. It was here that I began to question some facets of just war theory. I was troubled by the fact that much of the orthodox just war theory was driven by rights talk. I found this intuitively compelling, a forceful argument for respecting the dignity of human beings. But it was unsettling that at some point the theory was willing to override the rights of human beings for consequentialist considerations. There seemed to be a credibility gap in the theory, especially with regard to noncombatant immunity since it was usually the rights of noncombatants that theorists justified overriding under certain circumstances.

I was further troubled by the notion that soldiers lose their right to life because they have chosen such a profession. This seemed to be conceptually problematic. I did not see myself in this way. And certainly the respect I felt for my soldiers prevented me from seeing them in this way. Furthermore, it struck me that the American people do not send their sons and daughters into the military with the conviction that their children have now forfeited the right to life.

Now I have been given an opportunity to resolve some of these issues. My effort is driven by a conviction that humanity is unconditionally valuable. An unrelenting respect for human dignity grounds my theory. I deny the consequentialist view that the point of morality is to bring something about; rather, on my view, morality has to do with how we relate to each other and respect each other as human beings. I contend that this view of morality, this conception of the value of human beings, captures our real moral outlook. We are not troubled by images of atrocities because of a sense that somehow the general welfare is not maximized through ethnic cleansing, for instance. Rather, we are appalled when human dignity is trampled. We cannot remember Auschwitz and think that the trouble with the Nazis is that consequentialist calculations did not work out quite right. We cannot think about My Lai in this way.

It is important to note that I am not trying to ground morality or establish the propriety of the war convention. I assume a certain moral framework and enter at the level of the convention. The convention already exists, and it both drives and reflects some of our most firmly held beliefs about war and the way it should be fought. I am attempting to find the best way to understand and support the purpose of the war convention. I have come to discover that the war convention is in need of revision because it lacks reasoned principles that are adequate to consistently make the distinctions required for a credible just war theory.

When I first began this project, I tried to use and manipulate the same old concepts that had held sway in orthodox just war theory. As a result, I ran into the same enduring problems in just war theory, though sometimes they took different forms. I found myself, like virtually every other theorist, embracing positions that were untenable or even, ultimately, contradictory. But a way out of this conceptual impasse was revealed when I came to a clearer understanding of the nature of violence and the justification for self-defense.

It turns out that if we conceive the use of violence and the response to violence in terms of maxims, we can generate the sorts of reasoned principles that provide consistent, clear guidance on the use of force. The theory of autonomy provides guidance that accounts for and is compatible with our considered judgments and which supports the purpose of the war convention better than other approaches to just war theory.

I should make a preliminary remark about my focus. I will be concerned primarily with issues about justice *in* war, not the justice about going to war. My main concern is to find a way to distinguish between combatants and noncombatants, between those we can legitimately target and those we cannot. There are those who think that we should be able to target the civilians of a country that has started an unjust war. The reasoning is that since they support the unjust war, they are somehow guilty and deserve the harm that befalls them. We witness a typical example of this attitude when we consider that many people felt that the Iraqi people deserved the hardships they suffered during and after the first Gulf War: they were deemed guilty simply by continuing to reside in their country.[3] But this is clearly a problematic approach to the issue. Surely not every citizen supports the war; babies, for instance, must be considered innocent of any sort of complicity with the evil perpetrated by their country's leaders. And we do not seem to have a way of being able to determine the "guilty" civilians from the "innocent" ones. What we need are reasoned principles to guide us so that we can use force in a discriminate manner, and no such principles seem to be available by appealing to the justice *for* war.

In Chapter 2, I describe the war convention and argue for a particular understanding of it. I will introduce many standard terms of the just war tradition, terms that figure importantly in any just war debate. I start with the assumption that some wars are just and that it follows from this that some killing in war is justified. My main focus in this chapter is to argue that one of the primary purposes of the war convention is to delineate the distinction between combatants and noncombatants and to outline the permissible conduct in war with respect to these classes of people.

I will also survey some standard objections to the war convention that question either the purpose or the legitimacy of the war convention. By examining these objections, I further support my argument about the purpose of the war convention. It also gives me an opportunity to compare the theory of autonomy with other positions in terms of their relative support of the war convention. Although it is not possible within the scope of this work to defeat in detail every objection to the war convention, I must make clear that I recognize those objections. I show some of the troubles with these objections and with the forms they take. One of the main points I want to make is that the moral motivation behind the war convention has been with us for a long time and has dictated in large degree the terms of the debate even among those who would deny its force or legitimacy. I want to show that the assumption that there should be constraints in war enjoys a long history and that many of the constraints involve the distinction between combatants and noncombatants.

I will turn at the end of this chapter to tensions within the convention itself and offer autonomy as a means of easing these tensions. By the end of this chapter I will have established the general purpose of the war convention. And given this understanding of the war convention we will begin to see how it is that understanding just war issues in terms of autonomy helps us attain the goals the war convention has been developed to attain; autonomy will prove more adequate for this aim than either consequentialist or rights-based theories and will make consistent that which had hitherto seemed contradictory.

Chapter 3 discusses autonomy. This is the theoretical foundation for the rest of the work. Although I will argue from a Kantian point of view, my conception of autonomy is not strictly Kant's. I will emphasize certain Kantian perspectives as I develop my version of autonomy, but I am developing my view with a certain goal in mind, namely, the development of a concept that will be particularly useful for just war theory. I am assuming a view of humanity as absolutely valuable, unique among earthly entities. I pick our certain features of human beings that, when viewed in the context of just war issues, will help us resolve many enduring problems in just war theory. I am not trying to ground Kant's theory of autonomy or Kant's moral system. I am interested in establishing the implications of the concept of autonomy that I develop for just war theory and in arguing that it gives us a plausible and consistent account of the war convention. As such, my view, in virtue of its Kantian roots, is decidedly nonconsequentialist.

Consequentialism holds, in general, that the moral character of an action is determined by the results it produces. Consequentialism poses the greatest challenge to the war convention, both from within and without the convention. That is, some consequentialist perspectives deny the very premise of the war convention. On the other hand, there are those who accept the legitimacy of the war convention, but reason about it from a consequentialist perspective. I do not try to defeat consequentialism in this work, just as I cannot provide definitive proof of the superiority of Kantian ethics over other ethical theories. What I do is show how my theory of autonomy, grounded in a Kantian view of humanity, gives us results that are more in line than other views with our considered moral judgments about just war. Also, these results are more consistent with the aims of the war convention. If I am successful on these two accounts, then my project will have been successful. I am offering a way of looking at just war issues that, if you accept, will provide very appealing results in terms of the purpose of the war convention. And although I will not defeat consequentialism, I will show how in principle consequentialist reasoning about just war issues renders results that are unacceptable both in terms of our moral intuitions and in terms of the motivations behind the war convention.

Throughout most of this work I will mainly juxtapose the theory of autonomy with consequentialism as the point of view with which it is most at odds. However, occasionally I will indicate where the theory of autonomy competes with certain rights-based theories, even though my theory has much in common with them. The way I understand rights-based theories is that they posit certain irreducible rights and have various ways of dealing with problems when these rights come into conflict. In the arena of just war theory, conflicts of rights loom large from this perspective. Some of the more intractable problems have to do with competing rights between groups of people who stand in harm's way.

Sometimes these problems do not seem to have resolutions, or the resolutions are very unsatisfactory, when dealt with solely with the conceptual machinery of rights theory. I will argue that the theory of autonomy offers more satisfactory answers because it provides a better conceptual understanding of the issues involved.

I must recognize up front, however, that in general, it is hard to assess rights-based views as a whole. One cannot know in advance how any given rights-based theory will resolve the conflicts or how the resolution will match our considered judgments or the mandates of the war convention. So it is not possible to respond in advance and challenge every rights-based theory. The only thing I can do is to examine how particular theorists apply their vision to just war problems and show the difficulties, if any, that result.

I want to be clear about terminology. I will refer to the theory of autonomy. This is merely shorthand. The only full-fledged theory in this work is just war theory; my work is a part of the just war tradition, an attempt at revising the theory to make it more consistent and further empower it to achieve its purpose. When I talk of the theory of autonomy, I refer generally to just war theory understood in terms of certain principles generated by my conception of autonomy. I look at human beings and human relationships in a certain way and then examine what this view implies in terms of a just war tradition that assigns roles to human beings, roles that in large measure determine the extent to which these human beings are considered legitimate targets in war. I examine old distinctions in a new light. The theory of autonomy is a conceptual tool that helps the war convention do what it is supposed to do. The theory of autonomy, then, is just war theory revised in accordance with new principles that embody more fully and consistently the moral intuitions that just war theory has meant to capture.

The perspective that autonomy will help me illuminate, in a way that is instructive for just war theory, is the following. Human beings are uniquely precious. There is something morally problematic in any use of force against them. Even in war, the maiming or killing of a human being constitutes some kind of crime. So when we fight a war, even a just war of self-defense, there are things we cannot do lest we ourselves commit a crime. Even in war, the sanctity of humanity imposes limits upon our actions. The theory of autonomy will articulate this point of view in a way that goes beyond our intuitions and provides definitive principles that can guide our thinking about just war theory.

In Chapter 4, I provide an argument for the best way to understand the distinction between combatants and noncombatants. I build upon the traditional understanding of the distinction, revise it in terms of autonomy, and argue for a stricter definition of combatant than traditionally has been acknowledged. I also argue that we are all intrinsically noncombatants and all the justificatory work of just war theory should be geared to explaining how one becomes a combatant. This, as will be shown, reverses the order of explanation as conceived in much of orthodox just war theory.

In Chapter 5, I examine problematic cases where noncombatants traditionally have been understood to have lost their immunity from attack. I explore the tensions and contradictions within the war convention, noting how various aspects of the convention seem to conflict. I then go on to analyze these issues in terms of principles generated from autonomy and show how many of the problems can be resolved in a more satisfactory way than has heretofore been the case.

In Chapter 6, I explore the Doctrine of Double Effect (DDE). I assume its importance and legitimacy in just war theory, but explain how it must be understood in the proper terms in order for it to provide the moral guidelines for which it is intended. We must understand the distinctions it tries to make in terms of the distinction between combatants and noncombatants. Since this latter distinction rests on our conception of autonomy, we can see that autonomy must guide our understanding of the content and purpose of DDE.

Chapter 6 also examines the status of combatants in terms of their autonomy and examines Walzer's claim that soldiers lose their right to life. I argue that even the death of a soldier constitutes an injustice and is a violation of principles generated by autonomy. I examine the relevance of *jus ad bellum* considerations for the purposes of understanding the justification of *jus in bello* actions, and for the purpose of assigning blame for the crime of war and the violations of autonomy that occur in war. These terms, *jus ad bellum* and *jus in bello*, discussed in Chapter 3, are standard terminology in Just War Theory. *Jus ad bellum* refers to the justice for going to war, generally a political decision made by the leaders of a country. *Jus in bello* refers to justice in war and addresses the responsibility of soldiers to fight justly during the conduct of war. Both concepts bear on the issues discussed in this chapter.

Chapter 7 concerns what Michael Walzer calls supreme emergency, which represents perhaps the greatest challenge to any just war theory that argues for constraints and the immunity of noncombatants. Faced with possible defeat by an enemy whose evil is of a certain magnitude, will it be permissible to break the constraints we have imposed upon ourselves? Will we be justified in doing the unjust in the name of justice? In the name of autonomy, can we violate principles generated from autonomy, or does our theory prohibit us from doing evil under any circumstances?

The case Walzer examines and proposes as a supreme emergency comes from World War II. Great Britain appeared on the verge of defeat by Nazi Germany. Nazi Germany represents abject evil. Great Britain's defeat would have signaled the beginning of virtually complete Nazi domination over all of Europe, a domination that promised to endure for a long time. Walzer argues that, faced with such a horrible threat, we are justified to override the war convention and deliberately target the innocent if doing so would save us – humanity – from the threat.

I will examine the notion of supreme emergency and argue that if we ever are justified in deliberately targeting the innocent, it will only be under very rare conditions where the innocent themselves should accept the principle that permitted their being killed.

In the epilogue I address concerns about just war theory and terrorism that have emerged since the September 11, 2001 attacks. I focus primarily on *jus ad bellum* criteria in an effort to achieve a reflective equilibrium between principles of domestic law enforcement and principles of just war theory. I show that the theory of autonomy, by illuminating the deep principles that justify the use of force in general, helps us achieve conceptual clarity with respect to the morality of the war against terrorism.

Notes

1   Paul Christopher, *The Ethics of War and Peace* (New Jersey: Prentice Hall, 1994), p. 7.
2   Operations orders are the formalized plans that detail how we propose to conduct a given military operation. They cover every facet of the mission, from tactics to logistical support.
3   Of course, we were not technically at war with Iraq during the period between the first and second Gulf Wars, and the suffering of the people resulted from economic sanctions. Nonetheless, the reasoning that justifies in this case the imposition of hardship on civilians through economic sanctions is the same sort of reasoning that justifies the targeting of the civilians of a country that starts an unjust war.

Chapter 2

The War Convention

In this chapter I will establish the purpose of the war convention, particularly with regard to *jus in bello* issues. I will then consider and argue against consequentialist and realist challenges to the convention. This in turn will lead to an examination of the tensions and inconsistencies that reside within the convention. I indicate the problems with orthodox just war theory and set the stage here for the development of the theory of autonomy; I express my conviction that the theory of autonomy can resolve many enduring problems in just war theory.

Michael Walzer describes the war convention as "the set of articulated norms, customs, professional codes, legal precepts, religious and philosophical principles, and reciprocal arrangements that shape our judgments of military conduct."[1] The war convention is not a single document, a completely formal system of tenets and axioms. Just war theory uses the term "war convention" to describe the collective historical striving to delineate the conditions that must obtain to make war just. So we can talk in terms of the war convention, the just war tradition, or just war doctrine: they are roughly synonymous terms that represent the various forms our efforts have taken to impose moral limits on the use of force in war. The convention is not a loose collection of ad hoc opinions devoid of consistency. There is a great body of philosophical and theological literature, codified law, and historical precedent that make up the war convention. Furthermore, there are some principles and ideas that form the core of the tradition and act to define its essence: "the recognition of a set of criteria calculated to measure with some clarity and objectivity when it may be held to be the case that the evil of war is justified because the other evil which it prevents is greater."[2] We must understand from the outset that the just war tradition is not an endorsement of war per se. Rather it recognizes the inherent evil attached to an endeavor characterized by the deliberate killing of human beings and seeks to limit that evil.[3] But the tradition assumes, and I begin with this assumption, that some wars are just and that some killing in war is justified. This implies, of course, that not all wars are just and that a lot of the killing in war, even in a just war, is not justified. The purpose of the war convention is to articulate the conditions and considerations that designate a war and its means just or unjust.

A note about technical terms will facilitate discussions that will follow. Just war doctrine is traditionally divided into two parts. The first, *jus ad bellum*, concerns justice *of* war and addresses the justification states have for resorting to war. At this level, it is concerned with which side of a given war is just; that is, which side committed an unjust act of aggression, and which side is the just side responding to that aggression. The second part of just war doctrine is *jus in bello*;

it concerns justice *in* war. Here our concerns are with the means we employ, the targets we choose.[4] We examine the conduct of war once it begins and make judgments about the justness of the means used by all involved. Michael Walzer says:

> The moral reality of war is divided into two parts. War is always judged twice, first with reference to the reasons states have for fighting, secondly with reference to the means they adopt. The first kind of judgment is adjectival in character: we say that a particular war is just or unjust. The second is adverbial: we say that the war is being fought justly or unjustly. Medieval writers make the difference a matter of prepositions, distinguishing *jus ad bellum*, the justice of war, from *jus in bello*, justice in war. These grammatical distinctions point to deep issues. *Jus ad bellum* requires us to make judgments about aggression and self-defense; *jus in bello* about the observance or violation of the customary and positive rules of engagement. The two sorts of judgment are logically independent. It is perfectly possible for a just war to be fought unjustly and for an unjust war to be fought in strict accordance with the rules.[5]

Jus ad bellum and *jus in bello* are the standard terms used in just war theory to talk about these two types of concern. I am primarily concerned in this work with *jus in bello* issues. I look at the way we fight wars, with particular emphasis on gaining a deeper understanding of who can be considered legitimate targets. I will have occasion to discuss *jus ad bellum* issues as they pertain to particular issues in *jus in bello*.

The Purpose of the Convention

Walzer says that the first principle of the war convention is that, "once war has begun, soldiers are subject to attack at any time (unless they are wounded or captured),"[6] and that the second principle is that "noncombatants cannot be attacked at any time."[7] He is correct: although not always articulated expressly in these terms, these two principles address what is at the heart of the convention. The major thrust of the convention is to delineate legitimate from illegitimate targets; that is what the convention is for, and in what follows I will provide sufficient evidence and argument to support this understanding of the convention. This is how just war tradition sees itself: "The notion that force ought to be morally justified only if it can be employed in a discriminate manner lies at the heart of *jus in bello*."[8] The purpose of just war theory and the war convention is to impose restraints on the use of violence. I will quote from a U.S. Army publication. This passage will reinforce our understanding of the purpose of the war convention and will give a good first characterization of the distinction between combatants and noncombatants.

> All persons participating in military operations or activities are considered combatants. *All others are noncombatants*. This distinction is not always easy to make. Uniformed, armed soldiers are easily recognizable. However, guerillas

often mix with the civilians, perform undercover operations, and dress in civilian clothes. *Alertness* and *caution* must guide you in deciding who is a combatant.

Noncombatants include civilians, medical personnel, chaplains, and other persons captured or detained. This category also includes soldiers who are captured, sick, or wounded or soldiers who surrender....

Only Combatants Are Proper Targets[9]

This passage tells us a lot. We learn that the paradigm of a combatant is a uniformed soldier, openly bearing arms, and we learn that the presumption is that everyone else is a noncombatant. Noncombatants are not legitimate targets. We also learn that we are not always faced with the paradigm; there are gray areas. And we learn that we must, therefore, use discrimination and caution. Whether it is easy or not, whether we can always tell the difference between noncombatants and combatants, we are always morally required to recognize the distinction and react to it properly: the distinction does not go away. John Howard Yoder talks about the moral debate about WW II obliteration bombing of German cities:

> In all of this renewal of just-war concern the focus was on only one of the many classical criteria: the immunity of noncombatant personnel. It was held that this one criterion was sufficiently powerful to eliminate one particular kind of strategy. This argument was never seriously refuted in its claim to be the imperative application of the tradition. Those who chose not to be bound by it recognized that they were choosing not to be bound by the constraints of the tradition.[10]

The tradition seeks to identify and protect noncombatants and thereby limit the horrors of war. I am concerned with the war convention itself, and it is clear that it is concerned with limiting a particular type of horror, namely the direct, deliberate targeting of noncombatants. Just war theory seeks to fence off a certain class of people from war's direct effects by defining and insisting upon noncombatant immunity. Throughout this work, then, when I talk of limiting the horrors of war, it is this particular species of horror to which I refer.

I have made the assumption that some wars are just and some killing in wars is justified. I assume that the war convention explains, to a large extent, the types of killings that are justified and the types that are to be condemned, and it does so largely in terms of the distinction between combatants and noncombatants. And this distinction seems to capture our deepest moral intuitions. We are more confident about the distinction between combatants and noncombatants than perhaps any other facet of just war theory. We feel there are innocents who should remain immune from the direct effects of our wars (almost every one will suffer some effects: the loss of loved ones, anguish, economic adversity, etc.). These innocents cannot be targeted intentionally. But if, as I maintain, this notion of noncombatant immunity is so central to the just war tradition, how does it become an issue? That is, if we are committed to this restriction, how does it come to be challenged? The objections to the war convention and its injunctions take various forms.

Challenges to the Convention

The first objection concerns whether in fact recognizing and respecting the war convention, particularly the prohibition against deliberate killing of noncombatants, does in fact limit the horror of war. There are those who take the stance that the best thing to do is to employ the means that will end the war the most quickly, even if this requires targeting noncombatants. This, it is said, will best limit the horror of war. Since the war ends sooner, war's effects will end sooner: in the long run, fewer people will suffer, and whatever suffering there is will be of shorter duration.

The force of this argument derives from calculations and estimates of damage. It involves a certain form of consequentialist reasoning that, for instance, if we starve to death the inhabitants of a city, we end in six months a war that might have taken six years. Surely, the reasoning goes, fewer people will suffer in six months than in the alternative six years. It is not my purpose to debate the credibility of these calculations, although I believe a study of the history of war and the results of such reasoning renders the thesis very dubious. I am not arguing about the empirical claim that the horror of war will be reduced if we deliberately target noncombatants. But it is clear that those who adopt this stance recognize the existence of the tradition, and to an extent, its moral force. They recognize that there is a horror to be dealt with and that the right thing to do is to limit it. But according to the war convention, the means they are ready to adopt are evil.

Lest I be uncharitable to the position, I must point out that those who reason in this way do not necessarily see what they are contemplating as evil. They recognize the horror of war and the suffering it imposes on human beings, and they seek to limit it. To this extent, consequentialism agrees with the war convention. But by employing this sort of consequentialist reasoning, they will justify things that the war convention says are impermissible – even if the greatest good results. In Chapter 3, I convey the nature of the moral problem with attempting to secure our safety by sacrificing the well being or lives of others. The war convention embodies our moral convictions in this regard and therefore sets limits on the violence we can employ, even in self-defense. The combatant/noncombatant distinction is one of the most important means of setting the limits and to be prepared to ignore it is, in this respect, to be prepared to do evil. I will provide the theoretical justification for the distinction in Chapter 4, for clearly killing another human being, even if he is a soldier, is morally problematic. At this point, though, I just want to be clear about the purpose and substance of the war convention. It will become clear how the theory of autonomy, by imposing certain restrictions against using people as means, agrees with the war convention where at least some forms of consequentialist reasoning depart from it.

The other form of the objection is the position Walzer calls "realism."[11] This is the view that: "*Inter arma silent leges*: in time of war the law is silent."[12] This objection itself has various forms.

The first is a claim of a sort of moral skepticism: moral claims are irrelevant in war: "Anything goes." I cannot defeat this skepticism here, but there is a response that challenges its claims. Walzer points out,[13] correctly I believe, that even this skeptical claim is an attempt at justification. The language employed by its purveyors throughout the history of war is fraught with terms that are richly, compellingly, normative. They (we) distinguish between a battle and a slaughter, a victory and a massacre, between justified killing and murder. But these realists argue that they are driven to the courses of action they adopt; they are driven by military necessity and the harsh realities they face in the quest for victory. Once a war begins, the reasoning goes, everything is justified.

However, the realist, as long as he is not advocating general moral skepticism, has the burden of proof to explain what is special about war that makes everything justified. Furthermore, one of Walzer's points, which the history of war reflects, is that this claim is suspect on two counts. First, as the war convention testifies, we do find some actions in war impermissible. At least much moral criticism about war has taken place and many people do condemn or condone certain actions in war on moral grounds. In this respect, realism is not a common view; at least it is not the overwhelmingly accepted one. Hence, it cannot be regarded as the default view.

Secondly, the claim itself is a plea for justification, denials of this by realists notwithstanding. Walzer examines the dialogue that occurred between Athenian generals and the leaders of Melos concerning the Athenian intention to attack Melos. When the Athenian generals tell the Melian magistrates that they (the Athenians) must lay waste the island state of Melos, they claim that their security demands it:

> The Athenians are driven...they must expand their empire...or lose what they already have. The neutrality of Melos "will be an argument to our weakness, and your hatred of our power, among those we have rule over." It will inspire rebellion throughout the islands, wherever men and women are "offended with the necessity of subjection" – and what subject is not offended, eager for freedom, resentful of his conquerors? When the Athenian generals say that men "will everywhere reign over such as they be too strong for," they are not only describing the desire for glory and command, but also the more narrow necessity of inter-state politics: reign or be subject. If they do not conquer when they can, they only reveal weakness and invite attack; and so, "by necessity of nature"...they conquer, when they can.[14]

This describes a state of affairs where communities are in a constant state of war, or constantly under the threat of war. In such conditions, the generals, arguing from a realist point of view, contend that there is no morality. But Walzer points out, again, correctly I believe, that they are appealing to this state of war as a means of *justifying* what they intend to do. There is at least a tacit acknowledgement that moral claims still hold, even in this state of war. Walzer explains:

> In fact, definitions are not at issue here, but descriptions and interpretations. The Athenians shared a moral vocabulary, shared it with the people of Mytilene and Melos; and allowing for cultural differences, they share it with us too. They had

no difficulty, and we have none, in understanding the claim of the Melian magistrates that the invasion of their island was unjust.

In any case, the possibilities for manipulation are limited. Whether or not people speak in good faith, they cannot say just anything they please. Moral talk is coercive; one thing leads to another.[15]

People have always thought that morality plays a role in our judgments about war, even though at first it might seem that we feel anything goes. The generals, the realists in this scenario, share this moral heritage and are somehow bound by it, even if loosely or reluctantly, and even if they do not acknowledge it. It should be noted, however, that even if in fact this does show that people feel a need for justification, it does not necessarily mean they in fact do need a justification. This would be to commit the is/ought fallacy. Nonetheless, we should realize that the war convention, the notion that morality plays a role in our judgments about war, has a long and influential history.

It was not my purpose here to defeat true skepticism. Perhaps I can say nothing to the true moral skeptic or the person who is sincerely committed to the view that talk of morality in war is "idle chatter."[16] But I wanted to show at least the possibility that what poses as true skepticism is a façade; in the actual history of man engaged in war, morality plays a large role. Even the professed skeptic never completely escapes the demands of morality. It intrudes pervasively into the dialogue about war, even the dialogue of those who would fain deny its force. That the convention corresponds in large part to the collective human moral judgment adds weight to its claims to legitimacy as a morally relevant feature of human discourse. It lends credence to the assertion that even in war there are moral constraints, and these constraints reflect our considered judgments about what constitutes innocence, self-defense, coercion, and murder. That the theory of autonomy will be shown to support, strengthen, and further clarify the convention lends credence to claims that it should gain membership in the organon of the convention.

There is an even stronger version of this realist position. It too embraces an "anything goes" attitude, but calls on a different kind of justification. There is an attempt to say, "the principle of force forms a realm of its own."[17] Actions that in normal times would be crimes are, in times of war, morally acceptable. These realists do not say that war justifies the wrong they do. Rather, they contend that a different morality obtains during war and that what in other times is wrong is, in time of war, simply not wrong. Or the position might be rendered in a different way. One could say that the same morality obtains in peace and in war, but that the conditions of war are so radically different from those of peacetime that new rules are required. The demands of morality would change when the conditions of their application change sufficiently. This is the strongest claim of *inter arma silent leges*.

But this claim is suspect. It is plausible to see it as expressing the view that, for instance, murder is wrong in everyday life (the realists, after all, bank on this distinction between everyday life and war), and we have an obligation to refrain from it. But in time of war, because we are going to kill on such a wholesale level and immerse ourselves in such extreme, extended, unbridled violence, the normal proscriptions no longer hold sway. When the violence, coercion, and killing reach a certain ill-specified level of complexity and intensity, either a different moral outlook is required or new rules must be invoked for the application of standard morality.

But it seems to be the case that the very existence of the war convention disabuses this view. What is deemed an atrocity in war is deemed so within the rubric of our common moral outlook. It is precisely their affront to our ordinary morality that earns our condemnation of acts of evil committed in times of war. Our normal convictions about morality, expressed by the war convention, obtain in war and peace. The realist might offer the rejoinder that his notion *does* capture our normal moral convictions. After all, we condemn killing in day-to-day life, yet are ready to condone killing by the thousands in war. We condemn lying yet condone the use of ruses and deceptions during war. They contend that these observations indicate that we do, in fact, embrace a different ethic in war than we do in peace.

But this is to misunderstand the nature of these actions. In peace, in our day-to-day lives, we do condemn most killing. But we do justify it in legitimate cases of self-defense, when our only recourse is deadly force, as when a police officer shoots a criminal who, with murderous intent, is attacking someone. We do condemn lying, but do not condemn the young woman who frightens off a would-be assailant by lying about a gun in her purse: this is just another form of self-defense. It would be absurd to justify killing but not lying when we understand them both as means of justified self-defense.

The killing in war, the ruses and deception, are forms of self-defense, justified in similar ways by similar moral reasoning, as those that inform our usual moral judgments. They neither fall under the rubric of a new and different morality, nor do the extreme conditions of war compel us to devise new rules for our common morality. And although the choices in war might often times be harder because the issues are less clear and the circumstances more demanding than they usually are in our day-to-day lives, the choices remain nonetheless moral choices. Anything *does not* go, as Malham Wakin says: "War is a physical evil, but the reasoning process which permits its use in the name of justice is bound by consistency to insist on making moral judgments concerning the means used in the pursuit of justice."[18]

This last point brings us back, as it were, to the beginning of the discussion about just war. I am assuming, along with the tradition, that at least some wars are just. When we feel we are justified to go to war, we feel so because we feel we have been wronged, or that somebody else has been wronged, as in the case when we intervene to help a weak ally defending itself against invasion by a powerful, malignant regime; or when we intervene to stop ethnic cleansing – the attempt by one ethnic group to destroy or drive away another ethnic group by means of force and terror – by a powerful majority of a defenseless minority.

Let us take the case of intervening militarily to stop ethnic cleansing. Suppose the regime we plan to attack is conducting unjust warfare against civilians. In such a case, it seems that at least part of our justification for intervening will be our conviction that it is wrong to kill the innocent. I will examine the concept of innocence in the next chapter, but I take it to be uncontroversial to condemn the violence perpetrated upon, for example, the Kosovar Albanians by Serbian forces, and that it is acceptable under at least some circumstances to use force to stop such a horrible crime. But if, in the conduct of our intervention, we deliberately target and kill noncombatants, what is the status of our justification?

The value we had been defending has been devalued. If it is wrong for the Serbian forces to do what they did, if their action is unjust, it is wrong for us to do it; if we can be justified, then we can also be unjust. If at least part of our justification is that it is wrong to kill the innocent and we are acting to stop the killing of the innocent, then it will be wrong for us to kill the innocent. The reasoning that justifies us if we defend the innocent should, and does, at the same time condemn us if we kill the innocent.

There is a related view that if our cause is just, we are justified in any means we use: *jus ad bellum* justification overrules *jus in bello* considerations. Somehow the justness of our aims changes the nature of our means: murder committed by the just side is not murder. Once the war begins, the enemy has no rights; once the enemy attacks, he loses his moral claims. Paul Christopher writes:

> As General Sherman, a senior military leader during the American Civil War put it, "War is cruelty, and you cannot refine it; and those who brought cruelty on our country deserve all the curses and maledictions a people can pour out."[19]

There are really two claims here. One is explicit: the bad guys lose their rights. The other is implicit. We (the good guys) have a duty to our own people, to our side. We must overcome injustice. This is a moral claim: in war, you must do whatever you can to win. All moral complaints become subordinate to this.

Certainly governments have an obligation to their people. So much is at stake whenever people resort to force to settle their differences that there are certain presumptions in favor of one's people. It is their safety, in large measure, that is being sought. But since the position under consideration argues for license to do anything in the name of justice, or our side, it is an implausible view, one that the war convention denies expressly. I do not say much about it other than that I assume that the end does not justify any and every means. In domestic life, the police officer who deliberately drives his vehicle through a crowd of innocent bystanders to apprehend a criminal, even a very vicious one, has done something terribly wrong, even though his ends were good. Likewise, we can employ either moral or immoral means in conducting a just war; the soldiers on the other side can fight their rulers' unjust war either morally or immorally (here is a point of disanalogy with the above: the criminal cannot commit his crime either justly or unjustly). I assume, in short, along with just war tradition, that *jus ad bellum* does not carry the day. As Barbara Herman says: "Where there is a moral convention, we cannot both use it and legitimately exempt ourselves from its requirements."[20]

Some might question the meta-ethical status of my claim that justification is really morally required. They might contend that the fact that we seek moral justification says something about our nature, not about the nature of morality. Perhaps moral justification is not really required and our seeking it merely reflects something very contingent about our conception of certain social conventions. But I am going to assume that, whatever the metaphysical status of my claim is, there is a right and a wrong and that we have a shared understanding of the core of morality, about what is morally correct or incorrect. So mine need not be a meta-ethical claim; rather, it is a claim about the facts of human existence and human affairs. At least it has been a feature of human experience since time immemorial and promises (a bleak promise) to be so for the indefinite future that humans will fight wars and try to justify the fighting of them. This work concerns the acutely human enterprise of war. I claim, and the war convention exists as testimony, that human beings do not see war as outside the moral realm. Wakin compellingly writes:

> If we combine our evaluations of classical just war theory with considerations of international law as it relates to warfare, we can readily discern a common purpose underlying the reflections of all serious proposals: to limit the human suffering caused by war and to protect those who are not implicated in the struggle.... If nations are morally permitted to wage war in response to unjust aggression, then the means employed must be judiciously selected in order to contain violence at the lowest level possible....
>
> Any cursory examination of the pronouncements of our representatives at the Nuremberg tribunal after World War II, of the agreements reached at the various Hague and Geneva Conventions, of the Kellogg-Breand Treaty, and of the court martial trials of military men accused of war crimes should clearly and unambiguously conclude that we do not believe that all is fair in war.[21]

In spite of concerns about the meta-ethical status of moral claims, in spite of skepticism about the ultimate ground of the war convention, it is undeniable that there has been a strong, persistent movement throughout human history to understand war in moral terms, make moral judgments about war, and impose restrictions in the name of justice upon the conduct of war. My work supports and is a part of this movement whose form is the war convention. Throughout this work, I will demonstrate that the theory of autonomy supports the aim of the war convention better than other competing theories and lends credibility and consistency to just war theory.

The Status of the Consistency of the Convention

The war convention needs to be made more credible, more consistent. I have been considering challenges to the war convention. I have rejected them on various grounds, and more forceful grounds for rejection will emerge throughout this work. But now I want to turn to a much more pressing problem. This is the problem that arises when those who believe in the war convention nonetheless feel pressed at times to disregard it, or perhaps use it in inconsistent ways. How do we assess the value and validity of the convention when even its supporters subvert it? John

Yoder argues that we apply the restraining criteria of the convention in such a way as to weaken them beyond a point where they are meaningful. The express purpose of the tradition is undermined by the flawed and inconsistent way we employ it. Yoder puts it this way:

> What had looked like a line that could be defended is now becoming a spectrum of degrees of concession to whatever recourse the most pessimistic picture of the conflict enables someone to claim is necessary. What initially looked like a firm structure for moral discernment has turned spongy. What claimed to be…an instrumentarium of resources for fine-tuned discrimination turns out in the majority of cases we can find in the literature to have been special pleading.… When we give the just-war system a chance to prove its integrity…it fails to deliver.[22]

The reasons to violate the war convention are usually given in consequentialist terms: we will do evil, say by deliberately targeting innocents, in order to prevent a greater evil, say the death of even more innocents. The best overall results will obtain if we violate the convention. Usually military strategists and civilian leaders cite military necessity to justify violations of the war convention. As Walzer says of military necessity: "(the) plea takes a standard form…. (T)his or that course of action…is necessary to compel the submission of the enemy with the least possible expenditure of time, life, and money."[23]

Essentially, military necessity makes the distinction between those actions that contribute to victory and those that do not; it is not its purpose to make the distinction between combatants and noncombatants. Most strategies will try to avoid excessive harm to civilians and needless expenditure of life and resources. But there will come a time, or at least the option remains open, that faced with sufficient threat, most strategists are willing to disregard the immunity normally granted to noncombatants. Christopher notes:

> …military necessity has been used to refer to a justification for setting aside or overriding the *jus in bello* principles found in the laws of war for the sake of military objectives…expediency receives considerable emphasis under the rubric of military necessity as a justification for violating the sanctity of innocents.[24]

Consequentialists will make the calculation early: if targeting civilians will end the war sooner and cost fewer casualties, then we should target civilians. This should not seem surprising. If targeting civilians produces the best overall results, then we are morally permitted, perhaps required, to do so.

There are two preliminary points I want to make here. The first point is that appeal to military necessity and consequentialist reasoning begins to erode the strength of the war convention, making the restriction against targeting noncombatants contingent, ultimately a matter of expedience. I do not provide my full argument here, but will set the stage for what comes later. As I have stated, the purpose of the war convention is to protect the innocent. Yet, from the perspective now under consideration, it appears that we will sometimes lift that protection. It does not necessarily follow from this that we have therefore eviscerated the strength of the convention. Those who reason this way might argue that the convention is not weakened if, under special circumstances, we grant exceptions and take actions that would normally be proscribed but are permissible because of the circumstances.

But I will argue that whatever justification we have for insisting on the immunity of noncombatants in any case should apply in every case and that the extent to which we grant exceptions is the extent to which we weaken our convention. Nonetheless, we must understand that there might be very special circumstances where it *would* be justifiable to deliberately target noncombatants. But the justification will not constitute an exception to the reasoning that calls for noncombatant immunity. Rather, it follows from that very sort of reasoning. I will examine this issue in Chapter 7.

The other point is that when we invoke military necessity and consequentialist reasoning to justify the deliberate targeting of noncombatants, we begin to undermine the very distinction between combatants and noncombatants. If part of the calculation as to whether to deliberately harm civilians is the extent to which doing so limits the casualties of our soldiers, then the status of the two heretofore radically distinct groups seems to be pushed towards equality. Up to a certain point in the war, certain actions are prohibited because they would target civilians; we should only aim at soldiers since they are always legitimate targets, the standard reasoning goes. But past a certain point of danger, we can kill civilians to save soldiers, or our country, or our civilians. Whatever the ultimate justification, the protection offered by the distinction has disappeared. And if the point of the distinction was the protection, in effect and in theory, the distinction has fled with the protection.

The conception of autonomy that I will develop rearranges the moral landscape of just war theory. Even the death of the soldier will be viewed as an instance of murder. And even in supreme emergency, the numbers never win out: consequentialist calculations alone are never sufficient to justify the deliberate targeting of noncombatants. There is a line we cannot cross, even in the face of calamity, lest we lose our humanity, unless it is respect for humanity itself that permits the crossing.

These are controversial claims, and I will unpack them in the following way. I will articulate the theory of autonomy and generate principles to guide our moral deliberations about just war. Then I will discuss the theoretical foundation for the distinction between combatants and noncombatants. Next I will examine certain so-called gray areas, where noncombatants are perhaps thought to be assimilated into the ranks of combatants. This will lead to a discussion of the Doctrine of Double Effect (DDE). Then I will apply the theory of autonomy to two real-world cases involving the Gulf War and the recent intervention in Kosovo. I will then look more closely at the status of combatants, then discuss supreme emergency.

As we proceed, it is important to bear in mind that we must assess the tradition on two levels: from the perspective of the way human agents employ it, and internally, from the perspective of the consistency of its varied components.

I will look at the way we employ it, examining historical cases and the dialogue of theorists. Sometimes we have failed to fully understand what the tradition enjoins us to do or not do. Sometimes, dishonest people cynically, knowingly, and purposely misuse or misapply the tradition to hide their crimes. In either case, the problems, abuses, and crimes that occur are not owing to the intrinsic shortcomings of the tradition, but to the human failings of those who use it. I will enlist the services of the theory of autonomy to give clearer guidance to those who conscientiously follow the mandates of just war theory. And the theory of autonomy will make it harder for the liars to be convincing; it might make them more hesitant to perpetrate their crimes, and it will make it easier for the rest of us to condemn and prosecute them if they are not deterred in their villainy.

I will also examine features of the convention that might be at odds with each other. For instance, certain formal parts of the convention, codified under international law, might conflict with the prohibition against targeting noncombatants. The justifying of reprisals might be an example, especially as it has been practiced historically and justified in certain cases as consistent with the convention. Autonomy will further the cause of consistency here in two ways. First, it will illuminate the directly conflicting movements within the theory and provide resolution. Second, the resolution in turn will influence decisions on the first level, namely application, since at least some of the confusions in understanding the tradition and applying it to just war issues arise from inconsistencies within the tradition itself.

Notes

1   Michael Walzer, *Just and Unjust Wars: A Moral Argument with Historical Illustrations*, 2nd ed. (USA: BasicBooks, 1977), p. 44; hereafter cited "Walzer" with page number.

2   John Howard Yoder, *When War is Unjust: Being Honest in Just War Thinking* (Minneapolis: Augsburg Publishing House, 1984), pp. 17-18; hereafter cited "Yoder" with page number.

3   I will explain later that although there is evil inherent in war, it is not the case that *we* are necessarily implicated in an evil activity when we fight a just war. When we resist the evil that is aggressive war, for instance, it does not seem right to say that we are committing an evil act. Rather, the responsibility for the evil rests with the leader of the regime that started the war.

4   This is the level of primary importance to soldiers since they are the ones who must employ force. It is important to note that the rules of war under *jus in bello* apply equally to generals and privates. Generals, since they are often intimately involved in decisions at the political level and have a different sort of knowledge about the war than privates, might also be held responsible for *jus ad bellum* issues.

5   Walzer, p. 21.

6   Ibid., p. 138.

7   Ibid., p. 151.

8   Robert L. Phillips, *War and Justice* (Norman: University of Oklahoma Press), pp. 29-30.

9   Field Manual 27-2, *Your Conduct in Combat Under the Law of War*, Department of the Army (U.S. Government Printing Office, 1984), p. 5.
10 Yoder, p. 50.
11 Walzer, p. 3.
12 Ibid., p. 3.
13 Walzer, pp. 4-13.
14 Ibid., p. 5.
15 Ibid., pp. 11, 12.
16 Ibid., p. 4.
17 Ibid., p. 7.
18 Malham M. Wakin, ed., *War, Morality, and the Military Profession* (Boulder: Westview Press, 1979), p. 242; hereafter cited "Wakin" with page number.
19 Christopher, p. 3.
20 Barbara Herman, *The Practice of Moral Judgment* (Cambridge: Harvard University Press, 1993), p. 119; hereafter cited "Herman" with page number.
21 Wakin, p. 241.
22 Yoder, p. 71.
23 Walzer, p. 144. I discuss the doctrine of military necessity more extensively in Chapter 4.
24 Christopher, p. 158.

Chapter 3

Autonomy

I intend to define a particular conception of autonomy and establish this conception as a guide for the just conduct of war. The notion of autonomy is not self-explanatory; there is a lot of disagreement as to what the concept entails. So to get my project going, I explain how I understand autonomy. What we require for just war theory, and what I think is available, is a particular conception of human beings, in virtue of their autonomy, that picks out certain features of them which instruct us forcefully and clearly how they should be treated. Such a conception will provide the justification for the constraints and limitations we must observe and the permissions we must grant during the conduct of war and will promote the purpose of the war convention. I will examine the notion that human beings have absolute value and then will generate principles of autonomy that follow from this conception of human beings. These principles form the core of the theory of autonomy and will provide the guidelines we will use to examine just war issues.

Absolute Value and Agent-Centered Restrictions

The notion of autonomy that I will describe and advance is Kantian. The Kantian way of looking at human beings offers the greatest hope of achieving the sort of results aimed at by the war convention. This notion of autonomy conceives human beings as having dignity and incomparable worth. They are priceless and thereby distinguished from all other entities on this earth, which are merely things and have price. The value or worth of humanity is not relative or contingent. Kant considers human beings to be absolutely valuable and "the ground of a possible categorical imperative."[1] Humanity is the ground, that is, of the "supreme principle of morality."[2] I want to emphasize that this is the fundamental conviction informing my approach to just war theory and is the motivation behind my choice of autonomy as the central concept generating the revisions to the war convention for which I will argue. That each and every human being has incomparable worth is the foundation of our moral reasoning. The theory of autonomy that I will use is predicated on this conviction. If humans did not have absolute value, then "nothing at all of absolute value would be found anywhere. But if all value were…contingent – then no supreme principle could be found for reason at all."[3] At least we can infer from this passage that Kant claims that mankind would grope futilely for meaning if he could not ground his reason in something that he considered a final touchstone of value. In any case, I take it that mankind is that ultimate, absolute value.

This is at the heart of my approach to moral reasoning about just war theory. To have absolute value in the sense I am arguing for means, for instance, that we cannot compare the worth of one human being to the worth of, say, one thousand human beings. That is, for instance, in deciding on a course of action in the conduct of war, we might decide on the one that exposes only one innocent person to harm over the one that poses the same threat to five innocents. But the justification for our choice cannot be that the value of the five exceeds the value of the one. Such a calculation is flawed and is inconsistent with the notion of autonomy I embrace, for it would imply that we could make a quantitative comparison among things with absolute value. I will argue that human beings cannot be compared in this way, that it does not make sense to say that a group of three people is *more* absolute than one person. A criterion for decision-making based on these sorts of comparisons leads to the central problems of just war theory, and I argue that the theory of just war I propose, informed as it will be by a particular conception of autonomy, will avoid or solve many of these problems.

Informed by the conception of humanity as an absolute value that cannot be overridden or profaned for the greater good, I generate principles to serve as guidelines for the use of force in war. As such, I consider the principles inviolable. It will never be a matter of minimizing or maximizing violations of the principles that guides our moral decision making. Rather it will be a question of violating them; any violation will be impermissible.[4] My view thus has a different logical structure than consequentialism. In accordance with my view, we should be guided by certain rules or principles, generated by autonomy, that can never be overridden, rather than being guided by attempts to maximize certain values.

When we incorporate the concept of autonomy as an integral part of our process of moral reasoning, it imposes agent-centered restrictions upon us. This is extremely desirable for our purposes: we gain an immensely powerful guiding principle in resolving just war issues. Agent-centered restrictions are:

> restrictions on action which have the effect of denying that there is any non-agent relative principle for ranking overall states of affairs from best to worst such that it is always permissible to produce the best available state of affairs...[5]

Autonomy generates agent-centered restrictions that are, essentially, protections for autonomous human beings from being used simply as means for the attainment of some good. They shield us from being sacrificed for the greater good. Since these agent-centered restrictions are generated by autonomy, nothing counts against them, and they will figure quite prominently in the theory of just war I will advance.

For example, the immunity of noncombatants from being deliberately targeted is an agent-centered restriction, and it should not be overridden; we cannot morally justify overriding it.[6] I understand that it is not necessarily the case that all agent-centered restrictions are ones that cannot be overridden. But I will argue below that the logic of the agent-centered restrictions having to do with the immunity of noncombatants follows from autonomy. And insofar as principles generated from autonomy underpin these agent-centered restrictions, they are the type of restrictions that cannot be overridden. That they cannot justifiably be overridden is the key to the force of the restrictions generated by autonomy. Since one of the main purposes of the war convention is to erect protective barriers around noncombatants, that autonomy greatly facilitates this cause is a factor greatly favoring its adoption as a tool for enhancing and revising – in the relevant ways – the war convention. If we conceive the protections afforded certain classes of people as deriving from their autonomy, we can more consistently apply the rules of war and the logic and reasoning that underpins them. One of the most attractive results of informing just war theory by a theory of autonomy is that it will more consistently enforce the war convention and more efficaciously limit the horror of war, which is what just war theory is meant to do. The theory of autonomy eases the internal tensions and inconsistencies prevalent in current just war theory.

Before I fully articulate my conception of autonomy and generate principles from it to serve as moral guides in just war reasoning, I am going to provide some preliminary discussion to set the stage. I want to show how it is that our autonomy gives us our status as beings of unconditional worth and how principles about the use of force can be generated from autonomy. Furthermore, I want to talk about just what type of value autonomy is. I will do this primarily by juxtaposing a perspective informed by autonomy to consequentialism and by drawing on an analogy with friendship. I want to establish that autonomy is a value that guides our actions insofar as it is something to be *respected*, not something to be *maximized* or *brought about*. I will also point out how conceptually the theory of autonomy differs from rights-based theories and the manner in which I propose to treat the differences.

Autonomy as conceived by Kant is a complex property of human beings involving rational agency, willing, and freedom: I will focus on rational agency.[7] Autonomy is ours in virtue of our status as human beings and our rational agency: it is an essential part of us, not something that can be either granted or taken away. So the notion of autonomy that I will develop conceives it as an intrinsic property of human beings whereby they are ends-in-themselves, absolutely valuable, rational agents. I will develop these notions in a more technical sense in what follows, but before I do that, it will be helpful to give an initial explanation as to how it is that this rational agency, the central feature of autonomy for my purposes, imbues us with unconditional worth. This will help us show how the principles put forth below follow from autonomy.

The view that I will develop is that it is our rational nature that confers value. That is, whatever is deemed valuable is deemed so in virtue of our rational choice; in this sense the value of whatever we deem valuable is conditional, that is, on its being valued by rational agents. Given this, then, the capacity for rational choice itself, as the source of value, is viewed as unconditionally valuable. To make this clearer, let us contrast my view with a view that sees something else, say pleasure, as absolutely valuable. Under such a view we would be enjoined, it seems, to maximize pleasure or promote conditions for it, etc. Everything else's value would be conditional to its function in promoting pleasure. Even the value of human beings, for example, would be conditional; their value would be subordinate to, say, the overall maximization of pleasure. Pleasure, as the value to be promoted, would dictate the moral constraints to be imposed upon our actions since we would have to act within parameters that are most conducive to the production of pleasure.

But on my view, pleasure would have only a conditional value, again, conditional on its being valued by rational agents. The rational agents, then, would be the value to which everything else would be subordinated. As such, *their* existence would impose the moral constraints upon our actions. Hence, there cannot be a value one would promote at the expense of the absolute value; as the source of value, there could be no value greater than rational agents such that we would be justified in undermining them in its pursuit. From this it follows, on the view I am advancing, that there is a presumption against any actions that undermine the conditions under which rational agents can exercise their rational capacity. The reason this follows is roughly this. In a normative theory, right and wrong actions are determined in some respects by the way in which they either promote or degrade whatever value the theory sees as primary. A theory that saw pleasure as primary would judge the moral rightness or wrongness of an action somehow in terms of its relation to pleasure; for example, an action that produced the most pleasure would be condoned. One that saw autonomy as primary would judge the morality of an action somehow in terms of its relation to autonomy; in this case, since autonomy is a value to be respected (I explain this below), an action that showed respect for autonomy would be morally correct.

Again, these are very rough descriptions of the mechanisms working within normative theories, but I am trying to show how it follows from a view of autonomy as unconditionally valuable that we have a presumption against actions that undermine the conditions under which human beings exercise their rational agency. Rational agents confer value: it is morally impermissible to choose to act in ways that is impossible for rational agents to choose since we presume that rational agents cannot confer value on actions that would undermine their capacity to confer value. Korsgaard puts it this way: "If one's end cannot be shared, and so cannot be an object of the faculty of desire for everyone, it cannot be good, and the action cannot be rational."[8] If you have this picture about autonomy and the status of rational agents, there emerges a presumption against directly harming them, against using force to undermine their agency. In contrast, a view that saw pleasure as the ultimate value, for instance, might permit harming particular rational agents as long as a general increase in overall pleasure resulted.

Given the conception of autonomy I have outlined, we can begin to see how it might work as a guiding moral principle in just war theory. Presumably, when we fight a just war, we do so to protect human beings, their rights, and their freedom. Assaults upon them constitute a wrong against them. Even those who do not conceive the wrong committed against them in terms of a violation of their autonomy at least usually view the recourse to war as undertaken to protect the rights or happiness of human beings. Those who are involuntarily submitted to an unjust war of aggression, for example, are viewed as innocent victims of some sort of crime. In fact, on all sides of any conflict, we consider that there are innocents, people who are not legitimate targets, the protection of whom, at least putatively, is the reason we fight the war. The perspective provided by autonomy will give us a clearer understanding of the status of every human being involved in the hell of war. We should examine the use of violence in war in terms of its effect upon autonomy in order to resolve some of the enduring problems within the just war tradition. Autonomy provides a carapace, always shielding the innocent, at least providing a presumption in their favor in the form of agent-centered restrictions.

Consider, for instance, the following example. Suppose there were a horrible criminal whom we were unable to capture but whom we knew we could induce to surrender if we kidnapped his child. Even if we could end a terrible crime spree and prevent the victimization of many other people by resorting to kidnapping, agent-centered restrictions would not permit such a course of action. We cannot violate principles of autonomy in the name of autonomy. That is, presumably we consider kidnapping the child to prevent the criminal from harming other human beings, from violating agent-centered restrictions with respect to other people. We are permitted to resist his evil, but not in just any way. It is impermissible to violate principles of autonomy, even if we claim[9] that we do so in the name of autonomy. If autonomy generates the restriction, it does not even seem legitimate to claim that it was for the sake of autonomy that we violated it.

Or consider another example. Suppose a police officer were chasing a serial killer. If he does not apprehend the killer, untold many will doubtless die. In spite of the undeniable benefit that would accrue if he can catch the killer, he is nonetheless precluded from driving through a playground and killing several children, even if so doing would allow him to catch the killer.

But there are those who might oppose such a view. They adopt a consequentialist position and contend that we should always be *permitted* to produce the optimal state of affairs, the optimal state here being defined in terms of the number of people killed – the fewer, the better. A stronger position says we should be *required* to create the best possible state of affairs, even if it involves actions such as those described above. And considering the way I have described autonomy, there are some initial attractions to such views, and they might lead one to believe that my theory tends towards these consequentialist conclusions. If autonomous beings are absolutely valuable, do we not have an obligation to save as many as we can? Or are we not at least permitted to do so? Since they are the conditions of value, should we not promote conditions that preserve the existence of as many of them as possible? That is, should we not *maximize* autonomy?

Autonomy: A Value to be Respected

There are certain things we do not maximize; autonomy is one of them. Autonomy is a value that, like friendship, cannot be maximized in the way consequentialism might envision. Rather, it is a value to be *respected*. And if the nature of a certain value is such that it motivates or enjoins us to respect it as opposed to promote or produce it, it imposes different sorts of moral constraints upon us than the latter type of values. For example, if we were to consider pleasure as the corner-stone of our moral theory, and if we understand it as a value to be promoted, it makes sense to say that we are morally enjoined to produce the maximum amount of pleasure. We might, for instance, be permitted or even required to cause pain to one innocent person if doing so would increase the overall amount of pleasure for certain other persons.

Now consider friendship,[10] which seems to be, like autonomy, a value to be respected rather than promoted or produced. We do not show respect for friendship by betraying one friend in order to make two new friends. If friendship were like pleasure, a value to be maximized, it might make sense to talk about promoting it by betraying a friend to gain even more friends. But this does not seem to be the correct attitude about friendship. One cannot produce more friendship in this manner because the tradeoffs are incompatible with the idea of friendship.

We can draw an analogy between friendship and autonomy. I contend that the value of autonomy is built into the value of all other human values. We do not devalue autonomy if we refuse to violate principles of autonomy in order to save lives. We can paraphrase Scanlon and say that no sacrifice of autonomy is involved if we refuse to violate principles of autonomy with respect to a few people in order to promote the autonomy of a larger number of people.[11] We do not show reverence for autonomy if we murder one autonomous being to save two, any more than we would show respect for friendship by betraying one friend in order to gain two. The point is that the value involved in friendship – as with autonomy – is not the sort of thing to be promoted in this way. Its importance does not lie in the fact that the world is better if there is more friendship. We do not seek friendship or value it because the state of affairs that obtains when there is friendship is better than one without friendship, even if in fact that is true. Scanlon says:

> When we consider the things that are generally held to be intrinsically valuable, however, it becomes apparent that in most cases taking them to be valuable is not simply, or even primarily, a matter of thinking that certain states of the universe are better than others and are therefore to be promoted.[12]

We do not value friendship because it produces a better universe. We do not decide that the world would be a better place if there were more friendships, then set about achieving that goal by making friends. To proceed in this way would certainly be to misunderstand the nature of friendship. I doubt that anyone who proceeded from this conception would ever really attain any friends. If one approached friendship in such a fashion, it would be plausible to argue that one would be treating any so-called friends that one acquired simply as means only (a notion I examine in detail below) – means to the attainment of a better universe. And, we could continue to argue, what is distinctive of true friendship is that friends do not treat each other as means only. If we see this approach towards friendship as wrong, we will see the merit in analogous reasoning about autonomy.

But to understand how this concept operates in our normative theory, consider what Christine Korsgaard has to say:

> To later generations, much of the moral philosophy of the twentieth century will look like a struggle to escape from utilitarianism. We seem to succeed in disproving one utilitarian doctrine, only to find ourselves caught in the grip of another. I believe that this is because a basic feature of the consequentialist outlook still pervades and distorts our thinking: the view that the business of morality is to bring something about...More importantly, moral philosophers have persistently assumed that the primal scene of morality is a scene in which someone does something to or for someone else. This is the same mistake that children make about another primal scene. The primal scene of morality, I will argue, is not one in which I do something to you or you do something to me, but one in which we do something together. The subject matter of morality is not what we should bring about, but how we should relate to one another. If only Rawls has succeeded in escaping utilitarianism, it is because only Rawls has fully grasped this point. His primal scene, the original position, is one in which a group of people must make a decision together. Their task is to find the reasons they can share.[13]

This passage informs our theory in the following way. When we fight a just war against unjust aggression, it will be appropriate to see it as being fought out of respect for our autonomy because that is what is at stake, whether people articulate it in this fashion or not. Their reasons for fighting, ultimately, will not be given in terms of something to be brought about, but in terms of respecting certain values, respect manifested in actions rejecting a certain way they have been treated. Certainly some of the dialogue will talk about goals to be achieved, states of affairs to be attained: a war to end all wars, a better state of peace, elimination of Nazi hegemony, etc. But these are desirable ends because of the value of autonomy, only insofar as we first and foremost value autonomy. We value it – because it is valuable – independent of any consideration of some other end state. If that end state should coincide with a greater respect for the principles generated by autonomy, so much the better for it. But when asked why we fight, we can reply in a way that needs no greater grounding or justification: "Out of respect for autonomy," in the same way we can reply, when asked why we performed some dangerous or costly task to help a friend: "Because he is my friend." Because these values are basic, and autonomy the most basic, no greater justification is wanting: this is the bottom line.

These responses capture the notion that we do things for the sake of friendship or autonomy themselves, not for some consequence we wish to achieve, but because these are the preexisting ends, the values for which we act. Walzer talks about the Finnish decision to fight the Russians at the beginning of World War II. The Finns fought valiantly against overwhelming odds and gained a negotiated settlement for terms "far worse than those that had been offered to Finland four months earlier."[14] The Finns could have avoided violent conflict altogether; they could have avoided the deaths of many, had they merely acquiesced in the unjust demands of the Russians. But they were not driven by some end state to be brought about, but rather by a need to defend a fundamental value now. He writes:

> ...it is important to try to understand the moral satisfaction with which their decision to fight was greeted throughout the world. I am not referring here to the excitement that always attends the beginnings of a war and that rarely lasts for long, but rather to the sense that the Finnish decision was exemplary (as the British, French, and Czech decision to surrender, greeted with an uneasy combination of relief and shame, was not).... It has to do with the perception that underdogs are also (usually) victims or potential victims: their struggle is right...we hope for the defeat of the aggressor in much the same way as we hope for the defeat of a neighborhood bully, even if he is not a murderer. Our common values are confirmed and enhanced by the struggle; whereas appeasement, even when it is the better part of wisdom, diminishes those values and leaves us all impoverished.[15]

As Korsgaard says, the subject matter of morality concerns the way we should relate to each other. One reason we fight and are justified in fighting is if others relate to us in a way that does not respect us simply for being the kinds of creatures we are. The Finns responded this way; they responded in a way that shows us that to value autonomy is not the same as to maximize autonomy and does not equate to the mere preservation of life.

Consider that they chose to fight, knowing that they could lose thousands of lives, yet knowing they had the option for peace, or at least the option to avoid armed conflict. The Russians had offered to cede them an even greater amount of land than they (the Russians) wanted from Finland. But the Finns rejected this offer because it was given under the threat of coercion: "Do what we want you to do; either take what we offer in exchange (even if you do not like the deal), or we will simply take it by force." I believe that their rejection of the Russian offer reflects the sort of moral phenomenon I describe, namely, that resistance against unjust aggression is primarily motivated by a respect for certain fundamental human values, a sentiment captured by the theory of autonomy.[16] One does not show respect for autonomy when one meekly capitulates to injustice simply in order to save lives. To do so would be like accepting one's own enslavement to advance one's freedom. We fight out of respect for our autonomy, the condition of all other values. And our decision to fight is not, or not always or primarily, based on a calculation of a good that is hoped to be obtained in some future state of affairs. We fight even against all odds rather than sacrifice our autonomy to the rule of violence, and we decide to fight independent of a consideration of any future consequences.

Given this perspective, we might question whether it even makes sense to talk about maximizing autonomy. What is *more* autonomy? How can you promote it? I mentioned earlier that it seems implausible that anyone who sets out to make friends with the express purpose of improving the state of the universe could ever really make true friends. Friendship is not a value that can be maximized in this sense. We can reason in like fashion about autonomy.[17] Just as we do not maximize friendship by trying, at all costs, to make as many friends as possible, we do not maximize autonomy by trying, at all costs, to save as many autonomous beings as possible.

The Means Only Principle

The first aspect of autonomy I want to address is the sort of twin feature of humanity's being an end-in-itself and absolutely valuable. In *Groundwork* Kant says:

> Rational nature exists as an end in itself. This is the way in which a man necessarily conceives his own existence: it is therefore so far a subjective principle of human actions. But it is also the way in which every other rational being conceives his existence on the same rational ground which is valid also for me; hence, it is at the same time an objective principle, from which, as a supreme practical ground, it must be possible to derive all laws for the will. The practical imperative will therefore be as follows: Act in such a way that you always treat humanity, whether in your own person or in the person of any other, never simply as a means, but always at the same time as an end.[18]

To treat humanity as an end is to treat it as unconditionally valuable.[19] Humanity must not be conceived as simply a means to some other end. It is always an end, valuable in and of itself. It is never to be considered as good merely for some other purpose, relative to some other end. (This will be made clearer when I consider, below, the feature of rational agency.) Kant captures the idea in terms of a comparison between price and dignity:

> In the kingdom of ends everything has either a price or a dignity. If it has a price, something else can be put in its place as an equivalent; if it is exalted above all price and *so admits of no equivalent*, then it has a dignity...humanity so far as it is capable of morality is the only thing which has dignity.[20] (My emphasis)

We can at least begin to see why I contend that we cannot make our judgments about what course of action we might take based on the putatively greater worth of five potential innocent victims over one innocent victim: we would be putting the five in place of the one, as if they were not only of equivalent but even greater value. Unconditional value generates unconditional commands, independent of any conditions. We have described autonomy (rational agency) as the source of value and hence unconditionally valuable. We can plausibly argue, then, that if a requirement follows from autonomy, it cannot be overridden by other considerations: commands generated by our autonomous nature cannot be overridden. They are unconditional in the sense that their imperative force is independent of other considerations, just as rational agency's value is unconditional and independent of other values. There are no considerations that would morally warrant our superseding these commands, just as there are no values that supersede autonomy.

In our just war theory, we can conceive these unconditional commands in terms of the agent-centered restrictions, generated by autonomy, that protect that class of human beings depicted by the theory itself as innocents. These are the people whose protection is the very purpose of the theory. There is no equivalent, under any conditions, of an autonomous agent. In advance then, we are precluded from even including such an agent in any calculation comparing his worth against the worth of something else. He is "exalted above all price." Conceived this way, the comparison is logically impossible.

If we were to reason that the worth of five exceeds that of one, then the worth of the one would not seem to be unconditional after all. That is, if the worth of one is absolute, exalted above all price, then it would seem inconsistent to say that we found a value that was more absolute, more unconditional. The supposed unconditional and absolute worth of the one would turn out to be conditional and relative. Under certain conditions and relative to greater numbers of autonomous beings, its value would be less than absolute. Likewise, then, the worth of the five would become conditional relative to six or seven, and so on, which would bring us to some sort of consequentialist position.

Consequentialist theories ascribe moral rightness or wrongness to an action in terms of the consequences or results it produces. They provide some criteria by which to judge what results are morally desirable, usually along the lines of the greatest amount of human wellbeing produced. The worth of an individual human being is relative to the weight his personal wellbeing has in the calculation of overall good or general welfare. His standing as an individual does not have the inviolable status that the theory of autonomy recognizes. In an extreme version of consequentialism,[21] the individual's property and person would become nothing more than communal possessions to be disposed of in accordance with whatever way contributes most to the general well being.

So to adopt a consequentialist stance conflicts with the conception of autonomy I embrace, specifically by undermining the aspect of the unconditional worth of humankind. If we ascribe absolute, unconditional worth to every human being, we have a compelling reason to regard with suspicion any moral reasoning that appears to render this worth relative and subordinate to some end, say, victory. Although we might come to choose, for example, a course of action, in the conduct of just war, whose foreseeable effects target fewer as opposed to more innocents, the reasoning for making the selection will not be, cannot be, based on the difference in relative worth of the two potential groups of victims: in terms of the theory I advance, to think this comparison possible is to make a category mistake. As Kant puts it, humanity has a value that "puts it infinitely above all price, with which it cannot be brought into reckoning or comparison without, as it were, a profanation of its sanctity."[22]

I will endeavor to show that this means, for the purposes of just war theory, that we should not weigh the immunity of noncombatants against some other good to be achieved, and that respect for noncombatant immunity is not merely an expedient in this or that case. We have afforded immunity to people in virtue of their autonomy, and we are therefore morally prevented from arbitrarily revoking that immunity.

The next feature of autonomy to consider is that of rational agency, especially insofar as our rational capacity is the source of all value. This feature constitutes the heart of the theory of autonomy and grounds the principles generated by autonomy. In the following discussion, I closely follow an argument put forward by Christine Korsgaard.

Whatever has value in the world is dependent on its having value conferred upon it by rational agents who are the source of value and themselves unconditionally valuable.[23] Korsgaard argues that Kant seeks a good or value that is absolute or "unconditioned"[24] and finds it in rational agency. By unconditioned, as already noted, we mean something whose value or worth does not depend on its being good only in certain circumstances, or under certain conditions, or in relation to something else. Without some absolute value, you would have nothing good *simpliciter*: everything would always be good only for something else. It is at least plausible to assert that our moral reasoning requires the positing of something of absolute value in order to gain purchase in the world. Kant considers and rejects, as candidates for this value, objects of the inclinations and the inclinations themselves, and settles on rational beings, for whom things have value, as the source of value. Kant says:

> All objects of the inclinations have only a conditional worth, for if the inclinations and the needs grounded on them did not exist, their objects would be without worth. The inclinations themselves as sources of needs, however, are so lacking in absolute worth that the universal wish of every rational being must be indeed to free himself completely from them. Therefore, the worth of any objects to be obtained by our actions is at all times conditional. Beings whose existence does not depend on our will but on nature, if they are not rational beings, have only a relative worth as means and are therefore called "things"; on the other hand, rational beings are designated "persons" because their nature indicates that they are ends in themselves.[25]

The objects of our inclinations cannot be the unconditioned good, since if we did not desire them, they would not be good: they "are in themselves neutral."[26] And the inclinations themselves are not the source of the good. We see that at least some of our inclinations, say bad habits, are inclinations we would rather not have. If that is the case, surely "it will not be just any inclination, but one we choose to act on, that renders its object good."[27] And if the good is unconditional, it must be something that every rational will could agree on: it cannot simply be something this or that rational will could arbitrarily desire; "the good must be a consistent, harmonious object of rational desire and an object of the faculty of desire for every rational being."[28] And, finally, "what makes the object of your rational choice good is that it *is* the object of a rational choice."[29] It must be the case that, since we make choices, we suppose that "rational choice itself makes its object good." We take ourselves to be "value-conferring" in virtue of our ability to make rational choices. The main point here is that rational agency is the source of value.

Since it is the source of all value, rational nature is the unconditioned value. Anything else that has value has that value in virtue of its value being conferred upon it by rational agents: its value is conditional on its being valued by rational agency. Korsgaard writes:

> ...since we still *do* make choices and have the attitude that what we choose is good in spite of our incapacity to find the unconditioned condition of the object's goodness...it must be that we are supposing that rational choice itself *makes* its object good.[30]

It seems clear, then, how the objects of rational choice are only conditionally valuable. But it might not yet be quite clear why it is, therefore, that rational agency is unconditionally valuable. We must recall that for Kant, there must be something of unconditional valuable in order for mankind to make sense of the moral world.[31] The existence of an unconditioned value grounds the supreme principle of morality. He says: "But if all value were conditioned...then no supreme principle could be found for reason at all.... The ground of this principle is: *Rational nature exists as an end in itself.*"[32] Through a process of elimination, he considers all of the possible candidates and rules out everything but rational nature. And when you consider rational nature, its value does not seem to be conditioned by anything else. Even the value of rational nature is conferred by rational nature itself. So rational nature is valuable independent of any conditions. It is not valuable as a means to some given end, or because it produces happiness, or because it helps us satisfy our inclinations. None of these things are considered valuable unless their value is conferred upon them by rational nature. Rational nature itself is not a value at all like these: it is the source of all value, the unconditioned condition of all other values.

Korsgaard points out that once you recognize rational capacity as the source of all value, you must recognize other rational beings as having value:

> If you view yourself as having a value-conferring status in virtue of your power of rational choice, you must view anyone who has the power of rational choice as having, in virtue of that power, a value-conferring status. This will mean that what you make good by means of your rational choice must be harmonious with what another can make good by means of her rational choice – for the good is a consistent, harmonious object shared by all rational beings.[33]

Rational nature is something we share in virtue of our humanity, and in virtue of which we make value judgments. We recognize, in our shared rational nature, a deep connection amongst us. It makes sense to say that since we see ourselves as worthy of respect, others must see themselves in the same light. That is, if one sees oneself as a value conferrer *because of* one's rational agency, and sees oneself as valuable in some ways in virtue of that capacity, then one is committed to the view that others are valuable in the same way because of *their* rational agency.

From this it follows that it is impermissible to act in a way that another could not possibly accept. This follows because if one's action or choice is one that another person could not possibly accept, then that action or choice is one upon which that person has not and could not confer value. Hence, if one acts or chooses in this way, one willfully discounts the value-conferring status of the other person. To act in such a way is incompatible with seeing others as value-conferring. One acknowledges that an act can only be good because its value is conferred by rational agents, yet acts in a way that cannot be valued by other agents. One must admit that therefore one's act is not compatible with the concomitant acknowledgment of one's own and another's value deriving from a shared rational agency.

Coercion would be a typical case of not acknowledging the value-conferring status of another person. To coerce someone is to adopt a maxim that does not regard the rational agency of another person as conferring value: part of the maxim of coercion is that one will do something (to or with respect to another person) whether that person wills it or not. If we understand the nature of coercion, we understand why acts like robbery and murder are impermissible, and we acknowledge why rational agents would not accept the coercive maxims of others. We understand why we would not be acknowledging the value-conferring status of another person if we adopt a maxim to coerce that person.

The notion of autonomy that I am developing captures the sense that we all see ourselves as individuals, as unique *beings* or agents who are valuable as individuals. Because we are autonomous agents we should not be treated in certain ways for consideration of consequences or even consideration of other autonomous agents. We feel that we are owed a certain level of respect as individual human beings, not because our personal welfare somehow contributes to a general welfare, but simply because we are human beings and are important because of that. And our rational nature presses us to see that all rational agents see themselves in the same way. The principles I generate outline the appropriate limitations on the use of force towards human beings that respect for autonomy mandates.

We see here more explicitly the limitations upon what can and cannot be considered good. There is a presumption against choices that promote discord, that cannot be harmoniously shared by "all rational beings." If it turns out that it is impossible for other rational agents to consent to one's choice, one's choice cannot be good. The objects of our inclinations must be compatible with taking rational agency as valuable. Every rational agent must get the same respect. If our choices do not honor the respect owed rational agents, they cannot be rational and they cannot be good.

Furthermore, if humanity, rational nature, is the source of goodness, there cannot be a good independent of humanity that can be achieved by using humanity as a means to the end of achieving this putative good. That is, it seems absurd to arbitrarily use humanity as a means to some end that has been deemed good. This amounts to sacrificing a greater good to achieve a lesser good. More precisely, it amounts to sacrificing a good to achieve something whose goodness depends entirely on that which was sacrificed in order to attain it, thereby nullifying the good it was supposed to have possessed. Human beings are the conditions of value. In terms of informing our just war reasoning, we cannot desecrate the autonomy of human beings for the purpose of achieving some greater good: there is no greater good. There is no good at all, in fact, independent of autonomous beings. As Onora O'Neill puts it:

> Rational agents who treat one another as ends must act on maxims by which rational agency itself is subordinated to no other ends, but is made a constraint or limit on all pursuit of ends: they must treat each other as ends-in-themselves.[34]

From the preceding discussion, we can generate the first principle from our conception of autonomy.

The Means Only Principle: We are not to use humanity as a means only.

This principle accounts for the fundamental attitude we adopt towards humanity when we address issues in just war theory. It captures the conviction that since humanity has absolute value, it cannot be used merely as a means to attain some other end.

When you use someone as a means only, you adopt a maxim – a motive or subjective principle of action – that the person being used could not possibly adopt. Consider the case of a lying promise, wherein I adopt a maxim of using deception to attain something I want. If I borrow money, for instance, promising to pay it back yet never really intending to do so, I treat the person I borrowed from as a means only. I lie to him precisely because if he knew the truth, he would not accept my plan. And it is not simply that he *would not* adopt my maxim as his own, he *could not* adopt my maxim. My maxim is that he be deceived about my intentions, that he be convinced that I would pay him back. But if he knew the truth, he could not be deceived and could not be convinced that I would pay him back. So there is a sense where it is logically impossible for him to adopt a maxim that intends his being used as a means only. It is impossible for me to consent to that about which I do not know. I cannot consent to your purpose if I do not know what it is.

Beyond this, there is another perspective that can help us understand what is involved with using someone as a means only, as simply a tool for one's use. Consider what Korsgaard says about the adoption of deceptive methods:

> ...you must be using some method to achieve your end that not everyone could use to achieve that end. The efficacy of your action depends upon the fact that others do not act as you do, and that in a sense means that others are making your method work.... For example, when you tell a lie for a certain purpose, the lie works to achieve the purpose only because most people tell the truth. That is why you are believed, and so why the lie achieves its purpose. In such a case it is not just the person to whom you lie that you treat as a means but all of those who tell the truth. This is because you allow their actions to fuel your method, and that is explicitly treating their rational nature as a mere means: indeed it is making a tool of other people's good wills...you make an instrument of the rational nature of others, and treat them as mere means.[35]

I use this passage to highlight the aspect of using people as *tools* when we treat them as a means only. We use them to achieve our purposes, essentially giving no importance to their choices or attitudes towards the proposed action, in the same way we would use a shovel to dig a hole. Insofar as it is an inanimate object, we accord it no consideration whatsoever when we employ it, adopting an attitude towards it such that it exists precisely for our purposes, independent of any of its own purposes (since, of course, it has none). In like fashion, when we use people as means only, we are in many respects indifferent to their choices and attitudes, using them as if they were there simply for our use.

But as this passage also points out, in other respects, using people as mere means is more insidious than simple indifference. In many cases, we rely on their having certain attitudes in order for our plan to work. We manipulate their good will, as in the example of a lying promise. We grant ourselves an exception, knowing (or hoping) that our plan will work because most people do not treat others with such a lack of respect. We use them and their general good will, and the general good will of all truth tellers, solely as means to our purposes.

So when we speak about using people as mere means, we are talking about treating them in ways that they could not accept. We are showing a particular lack of respect for them. Recall that we see rational nature as having a value-conferring status. When we lie to someone, we see our freely chosen ends, i.e., the ends upon which we confer value, as more important than his freely chosen ends. As Korsgaard says, you: "accord to your value-conferring capacity a greater power, so to speak, than you do that of others."[36] But we had said that an end has a value just because, in virtue of our rational nature, we confer value upon it. Hence it must be possible for rational nature *as such* to confer value upon it. If this is not possible, then the action is impermissible: such is the nature of acts that are unjustly coercive. They ignore or discount the value-conferring status of other human beings.

In many respects, this discussion provides an account of our ordinary sense of violation when we have been used as a means. That is, on some intuitive level, most of us have a sense of what it is to be used merely as a means. We understand the sense of being exploited, manipulated, and violated when someone lies to us, for example. And we generally have no difficulty understanding that it is wrong to be so treated or to treat others in this way. I have tried to capture, in a more technical sense, our considered moral judgments towards treating people as means and our attitude of opprobrium towards it.

We can contrast this perspective on lying with a consequentialist perspective. A consequentialist could justify a lie. If the lie produces better end results than the truth, the lie is justifiable: at least the option of telling the lie merits consideration. For instance, we might convince a wealthy person that we were using the money he gave us to establish a trust fund so that his child can get a very expensive education. But we lie about the trust fund and instead use most of the money for charity. We help thousands of Third World children, saving them from a life of destitution. In the end, the rich man's child gets an adequate education at a state school, though not the education we promised to secure for him. Nonetheless, he is able to be successful, and no one ever finds out about our perfidy. One might argue, given the results, that the lie is not only justified, but morally commendable.

I use this example to show how the theory of autonomy would differ with consequentialism. In general, I will show how using people as means only, in a way that might be allowed by consequentialism, yields unacceptable results in terms of our considered moral judgments and in terms of the purpose of the war convention. The theory of autonomy, by proscribing the using of people as means only, conforms with the purpose of the war convention as well as our considered judgments. I understand that in this situation, our considered judgments on the matter are not quite clear. There are those who would say the best thing to do would be to lie; in fact, on some accounts, that Kantian principles might prevent our lying even to produce the allegedly optimal state of affairs, counts decisively against them (the Kantian principles). But the main purpose of this example was to show how, in principle, autonomy and consequentialism would give different guidance. I will attempt to show that, in the context of just war theory, the guidance offered by the theory of autonomy does in fact coincide with our considered moral judgments and with the purposes of the war convention, whereas consequentialism conflicts with both. Furthermore, in general, lying does offend some of our deepest moral convictions. So insofar as consequentialism might sanction lying, it might conflict with these deep convictions.

Let me make a further comment about consequentialism before I continue. I understand that many consequentialists would also condemn telling a lie to the wealthy person. They might argue that, in general, better results accrue if we obey the rule against lying. If we violate the rule, people will have less and less confidence in whatever we tell them. The wealthy might grow suspicious of any solicitation for charity, for example. Hence, overall contributions to charitable organizations will decrease, and fewer poor people will be helped. Overall good would not be maximized; therefore, we should not lie. I recognize, in short, that there are good consequentialist rejoinders to the way I have characterized this example.

Nonetheless, in principle, consequentialism leaves open the possibility for any given case that we should lie since in any given case it might be demonstrated that such action would produce better results. With consequentialist reasoning, it always seems at least possible to justify violations of some of our most deeply held moral convictions. I will show how consequentialist reasoning about just war issues conflicts directly, at least potentially, with the very purpose of the war convention. In general, then, my discussions about consequentialism will not address all of its multifarious forms and commutations. Rather, I consider what it might in principle justify in virtue of its fundamental conviction that the moral status of an action is determined by its results and note how such reasoning gives unsatisfactory results in just war theory. Then, I show that, since the theory of autonomy coincides both with our moral intuitions and the war convention, we have good reason to favor its use over consequentialism as a reasoning tool for just war theory.

I want to make a final comment about what it means to treat someone as a means only. I believe we have clear insight, in the case of the lying promise, as to what it generally means to treat someone as a means only, insofar as he cannot possibly adopt the maxim in question. But it is not always easy to articulate the maxim in question in terms that make it readily apparent that the victim could not possibly adopt it. I want to say that generally, we treat people as merely means whenever we use violence against them to achieve our purposes. The intuition I am addressing concerns cases like murder in the domestic sphere, or the slaughter of noncombatants in the international arena of war, where those who are not engaged in harming us are killed. In such cases, the murderer presumably aims at some good, at least a good for him. But the victim cannot possibly share in whatever end it is that is the good for the murderer; the nature of unjust coercion rules out the possibility of consent. Furthermore, once the victim is dead, there is nothing at all that could be good for him ever (save perhaps eternal life, a notion not germane to this discussion). The very condition for accepting any good or end is undermined if he loses his life. For finite beings like ourselves, our bodies are the necessary conditions of our rational agency and our capacity to accept anything.[37]

This discussion informs our understanding of self-defense in important ways. When I use force on a particular occasion to fend off an assailant, I might as a matter of fact be doing so to protect my life; this might be my immediate, instinctive motivation. But this cannot be our theoretical justification. The justification for defending against direct harm or aggression is that we are acting against an agent who is manifesting a certain form of willing. Barbara Herman puts it this way:

> In Kantian ethics it cannot be what happens to an agent as a result of what is done that makes an action morally wrong. That is, killing is not wrong because it brings about death, and mayhem is not wrong because it brings about pain or harm. Moral wrongness is not a function of consequences but of willings…what is wrong with the killing maxim is that the agent fails to accord proper weight to the value of life of rational agents…in what he wills.[38]

It is the lack of respect for the value of humanity to which we react when we defend against aggression. It involves a particular violent manifestation of this lack of respect, not merely an indifference to our humanity, or even a preference for our death that some might harbor. These latter attitudes might be morally odious, but they are not threatening. They do not involve a specific willing that poses a real threat. Herman characterizes the nature of the threat and our response:

> What a maxim of aggression involves, morally speaking, is the discounting of my agency. The aggressor would use me (take my life) for his purposes. This is what I resist and claim moral title to refuse. Just as I cannot agree to become someone's slave, so I must not assent to be the victim of aggression.[39]

An aggressor would undermine or destroy the very conditions of my autonomy, and we act against such impermissible maxims. And the distinction between defending my life and resisting a certain devaluing of autonomy is important to make.   It helps distinguish the theory of autonomy from consequentialism. We do not act in order to bring about the result of saving lives (our life or the life of others). We act against an agent, a certain form of willing, because that agent and that form of willing manifest a blatant disregard for the value of autonomy. It is not a result we wish to achieve when we resist aggression; rather, we act out of respect for a value, and this justifies our resistance. We do not act to bring something about.

What we must do is respect autonomy, and respecting autonomy is not a matter of bringing more of it about; it is not a matter of maximizing autonomy. We use violence to respect a value, not in order to bring something about. As such, we are prohibited from violating that value in order to protect it. If we are fighting out of respect for a value, then we would be prohibited from taking actions that violate that value. This principle prevents us from making consequentialist calculations that might justify murdering a certain number of people as long as in so doing we save an even greater number of people. We are emphasizing the respect of a value, not a state of affairs to bring about.

Another important reason for making this distinction is that it tells us that only those who pose this particular type of threat through this particular type of willing are permissible targets of our violent acts of resistance (I will refine the notion of what types of willing and threat justify our use of force below). That is, there are moral limits to what we can do in self-defense. We can expect not to be used simply as a means to stop aggression: we are not to be sacrificed, nor are we allowed to sacrifice others, to attain some goal, even if the goal is in itself good. One who would sacrifice others in this way adopts the maxim of a murderer. In virtue of our autonomy, we are not to be considered communal property to be manipulated or appropriated by others in pursuit of their ends. When we are used this way, or when we use others in this way, it involves a certain attitude towards humanity that is proscribed by autonomy: *it is to adopt the same disregard for humanity to which we had initially responded.* Autonomy introduces a "deliberate presumption against certain kinds of actions done for certain justifying reasons."[40] It presumes against harming, for any reason, those who are not engaged in harming us. Herman tells us:

> This sets the relevant principle of casuistry. It establishes a moral presumption against violence (moral devaluation of the body), putting the burden of argument on the agent who would be violent to explain why what he would do is not governed by the terms of the presumption.[41]

Violence is not ruled out; we can resort to violence in self-defense. But the burden is to show that our actions are in fact a legitimate act of self-defense justified in terms of respecting autonomy, along with the further requirement to show that the means employed in defense are legitimate, that is, morally justified. The presumption is against violence so that serious moral deliberation must precede a resort to it and subsequently govern its use.

Proceeding under this presumption will help us reinforce a certain methodology for deciding when and how to use force: we start with the notion that everyone is a noncombatant. Once a war begins, we assume there to be a class of combatants and a class of noncombatants but often spend much of our energy in attempting to decide how one becomes a noncombatant. For some theorists, in fact, it is quite problematic how anyone could gain noncombatant immunity (see the discussion of Mavrodes in Chapter 4, for example). From the perspective of autonomy, however, since it requires that we justify any use of violence, we must start from the assumption that everyone is a noncombatant, and the hard work will be to show how people come to lose their immunity. Murphy says: "I should hope that men would accept...the principle "noncombatant until proven otherwise."[42] The burden upon us is to explain why anyone has become a legitimate target.

The Means Only Principle, then, establishes a general presumption against directly and deliberately harming any human being. The key here is the notion of direct harming because I am trying to specify certain conditions that justify the use of force, and in so doing, rule out the use of force against certain classes of people. It is generally wrong for others to harm us directly if we pose no direct threat to them; to harm in this fashion constitutes a violation of this principle generated by autonomy. We are rational agents who act through our bodies: an attack on our body is an attack on the way our rational agency manifests itself. Barbara Herman explains:

> However we regard the body – as universal means, as our embodiment as causally effective agents – it is the material condition of human agency. Having a body is not a necessary condition of agency per se. There might be beings characterized by "agency at a distance": able to effect what they will through no intermediary entity or through the body of other persons. We are not such agents.[43]

We are embodied beings, and even if we conceive the value of humanity in terms of autonomy, and autonomy in terms of rational agency, we cannot discount the role of our physical body as the condition of our agency. Herman says that an argument against convenience killing, i.e. killing another human being simply because doing so helps us get what we want, "appeals to a special condition of human agency – our vulnerability."[44] It is our vulnerability that makes an attack upon us a violation of this principle of autonomy, since it threatens the very condition of rational agency. So we have in this principle a way of understanding, in terms of autonomy, the general prohibition against harming human beings. We will be prohibited from harming others who pose no threat to us, even if doing so would stop the threat to our autonomy.

The Rejection of Unjust Aggression Principle

Since we have established this presumption against harming human beings and have generated a restrictive principle (The Means Only Principle) to account for it, we need some permissive principle(s) to justify the legitimate use of force against human beings. I will state the first permissive principle as follows:

> *The Rejection of Unjust Aggression Principle*: We are justified to use force against those who are engaged in unjust acts of aggression against us.

This principle accounts for the permissible use of force in the clearest cases of self-defense. Any maxim, the intent of which is to deliberately harm one who is not engaged in harming, is an impermissible maxim. Before I continue, let me make clear that to be engaged in directly or deliberately harming just *is* to adopt a maxim to harm. Not every such maxim is impermissible, as I will make clear below. But direct harm is tied up with the notion of adopting a maxim to harm another.

In the case of unjust aggression, an assailant who attacks someone not engaged in harming him has adopted an impermissible maxim. An impermissible maxim is by its very nature one which the victim cannot accept. For instance, if someone robs me, demands my money under some sort of threat, he takes what is mine whether I will it or not. Coercion makes consent impossible. If I could consent, it would not be robbery: it might be a loan or a gift, but it would not be the case that I had been robbed. The impossibility of my consent is what distinguishes an act of robbery from one of loaning or merely giving. The robber says, in effect: "I will take your money whether you will it or not."

Self-defense is not only justified to save one's life. We are justified in rejecting any maxim of unjust aggression, because any maxim of unjust aggression is one to which we cannot consent. In the case of robbery, this is not so clear since it might appear that we resist because the robber threatens our life unless we give him our money. But consider a case where someone is merely intent on pinching my ear or breaking my nose. My life might not be at risk, but we seem clearly justified in using some force to prevent our assailant from acting on his impermissible maxim.

When we use force appropriately against someone who is directly harming us through his unjust aggression – and thus someone who violates a principle generated by autonomy – our act is consistent with the principles of autonomy. We uphold the principles generated by autonomy and show the proper respect for autonomy. We are not ourselves violating autonomy when we use violence in response to another's impermissible maxim. Since his is an impermissible maxim, it is not a maxim I could or should adopt; therefore, I can resist it.[45]

To understand the force of this principle, and how that force is constrained by the Means Only Principle, consider the following example. We can use force to apprehend a criminal. But we cannot use force against his mother to induce him to surrender. We can shoot at him if he shoots at us; but we cannot harm his mother, even if her emotional support for him enhances his capacity for doing evil. Even if we know that killing his mother would, by eliminating his source of strength, end his crime spree and bring him to justice, we cannot harm her. Since his mother is not engaged in harming us or unjustly aggressing against us, a use of force against her would constitute a violation of a principle of autonomy. When we use force against her, we are using force against one who is not directly harming anyone. As such, *we* have adopted an impermissible maxim. Furthermore, if the criminal lays down his weapon and surrenders, we are no longer justified in shooting him since he is no longer engaged in harming us.[46]

Two issues might not be quite clear. First, it might not be clear how it is that I do not violate a principle of autonomy when I use force against a criminal. Second, it might not be clear why I cannot harm his mother to stop the criminal since this would seem like a way to stop the unjust aggression.

The reason we are justified in using force against the criminal is that he is adopting a maxim that I could not adopt. Say, for example, he intends to kill me. He intends to undermine the conditions under which I can adopt any maxims whatsoever, and I cannot adopt this maxim. To adopt it would at the same time deny my capacity to adopt it. Or more strongly, I could not adopt his maxim of killing me, say, to enjoy the use of my money in the future. If I adopt this, I immediately undermine the purpose of the maxim since if I am dead I cannot use the money in the future. In this respect, I cannot adopt his maxim so I must engage in an act that prevents him from acting from that maxim. I act against his impermissible maxim, which is essentially a maxim of using me as a mere means. Herman says:

> The aggressor acts on a maxim that involves the devaluation of my agency. I do not. I am not acting to save my life as such, but to resist the use of my agency (self) by another. Acting to save my life (as something valuable to me) would be to act for just another purpose. The moral standing of my agency – what makes it the source of reasons for others to refrain from acting against me – is not the good (to me) of being alive. Acting to sustain the integrity of my agency is to act for a morally necessary end. Thus, since my maxim of resistance is not a maxim of aggression as a means, the original aggressor cannot renew his attack on morally superior grounds. I am not acting to preserve myself through violent means. In stopping aggression with force, I am asserting my status as a rational agent. It is an act of self-respect.
>
> The justification of self-defense does not devalue the aggressor because he is guilty of aggression. He forfeits no moral title; I have no claim of moral superiority. If I may act with violence against aggression, I must do so without ignoring the fact that the object of my action is an aggressing *agent*. Moreover, the fact of his undiminished agency and value grounds a proportionality of response, not because it is better that there be more agents around but because, in limiting my action where possible, I demonstrate the moral regard he is still owed.[47]

My justification for using force against a would-be murderer is that I react against his impermissible maxim. Accordingly, the maxim I adopt when I resist, "since my maxim is not a maxim of aggression as a means," is morally justified. I do not violate a principle of autonomy in this regard. The Means Only Principle constrains my use of force against one not engaged in harming me; in this case, the criminal *is* engaged in harming me. I am justified in using force, under the permissive principle currently under discussion, to reject the criminal's impermissible maxim. In resisting a principle (maxim) that hinders or rejects principles of respect towards humanity, I promote respect for humanity. Note here also that the judgments we are making about the acts in question are in terms of the maxims involved. This will turn out to be a very important notion.

Herman's passage also indicates that we must continue to recognize the criminal as an agent. We must recognize his autonomy. Hence, once he lays down his weapon and ceases to be a threat, we must accord him the respect he is due as an autonomous agent; we would no longer be justified in killing him, although, of course, we could use some appropriate force against him.[48]

Given the foregoing discussion, it is clear that I may not harm the criminal's mother since she did not adopt the sort of impermissible maxim that justifies my forceful rejection (of it). I cannot do just anything but only react to actions that spring from the impermissible maxim. I can only react to those actions resulting from the adoption of the impermissible maxim.

A consequentialist analysis might, in principle, yield a different conclusion. Suppose this criminal were a serial killer with the blood of dozens of victims already on his hands, and suppose we had every reason to believe that his reign of terror would go unchecked for years to come. Let us suppose further that his mother is an evil person, reveling in her son's crimes. A consequentialist might argue that, if we could save many dozens of people if we killed this horrible woman, it is justifiable to kill her. At least in principle, this option can be considered within the consequentialist framework. But our principle generated from autonomy would, even in this circumstance, prohibit harming this woman. She is not directly harming us and is therefore not a legitimate target. I contend that our deepest feelings in this regard prevent us from executing an old woman who has committed no crime, even if she in fact endorses crimes being committed, and even if her execution would prevent further crimes.

To see the force of our intuitions more clearly, it might be helpful to consider a different scenario. Suppose that the mother not only rejoices in her son's crimes, but actually sends him out to commit murder. Suppose, that is, that she orders the murders. In this case, it seems we would be justified in using force against this woman. She *has* adopted an impermissible maxim, one of directly harming, or at least of aiding the harm. She seems very much like a mafia boss who orders his henchman to kill someone. We can use force at least sufficient to arrest both the boss and the mother.

In terms of just war, we will use this principle to help delineate those whom we can deliberately target. There is a presumption against targeting anyone who is not engaged in directly harming us, even though they might somehow support the war effort in a way analogous to the emotional support offered by the criminal's mother.

Now I must make a critical point. So far, the discussion of the use of force has generally been in terms of defense against unjust aggression. The Rejection of Unjust Aggression Principle, for instance, accounts for our intuitive sense that we are justified to use force against unjust attackers. Unfortunately this principle does very little work for us in just war theory, even though, as I will discuss later, many theorists mistakenly use this model to justify the force soldiers use on the battlefield. That is, we have been considering the general scenario where someone attacks us unjustly, thereby violating our autonomy. But, as will be made clear, we must discuss the justified use of force against those who are *not* violating a principle of autonomy or using force unjustly against us. We need a principle that will account for our justification for the use of force in the most common scenario pertinent to just war theory.

The Threat to the Capacity to Will Effectively Principle

Consider two combatants, enemies, on the field of battle. Very roughly we can say, for reasons I explain in detail later, that they are both justified to use force against each other in self-defense. Neither does anything wrong in using force against the other; we refer to this as the moral equality of soldiers (there is a general presumption held by soldiers that their side is the just side; more of this later). So we need to justify this use of force differently than the means of justification discussed to this point.

We can have recourse to the intuitive notion that we have a right to defend ourselves, our lives, and we can do this without consequentialist undertones. Even if a soldier shooting at me is not per se devaluing me or acting unjustly against me, I can nonetheless justifiably use force against him because he is threatening the conditions of my autonomy. Perhaps a better example of the point I am driving at is the following. Suppose I am on a shooting range and I realize that the man next to me is shooting at a metal object at such an angle that the ricochet will strike and kill me. Surely I am justified in using force against him, say by shoving his arm to move his point of aim. We can gain an initial insight into this notion from something Barbara Herman describes:

> Clearly when I am asking what it can be rational to will, more is involved than is captured by the formal notions of consistency and noncontradiction. The concept of rationality in "rational will" has content: not normative content, but clearly content with normative import. There are certain things that a rational will cannot rationally will. Among them is the (systematic) undermining of its capacity to will effectively. There are thus certain things a *human* rational will cannot rationally will, given the conditions of human willing.[49]

We can enlist the idea addressed by Herman to explain our justification for the use of force even against one who cannot properly be said to be unjustly aggressing against me. The enemy soldier is nonetheless using force in such a way that he poses a threat to my life, the very condition of my capacity to will effectively; the unwitting marksman likewise threatens my autonomy by threatening the conditions of my agency. Our discussion here trades on the same notion we used in generating the Means Only Principle. We act through our bodies; our embodiment constitutes the condition of our other capacities. We cannot will that the condition of our capacities be undermined; hence, it seems reasonable to assert that we have some justification to use some means to defend the conditions of our rationality and our autonomy. We must posit a third principle.

> *The Threat to the Capacity to Rationally Will Effectively Principle*: The use of force is generally allowed as a response to a threat to our capacity to will effectively, that is, when the necessary condition of our autonomy is threatened.

This principle accounts for our use of force against one who cannot properly be said to be doing something unjust, i.e., violating principles of autonomy. For instance, if I am walking in the jungle and my companion is about to set off a trap that will kill us both, I may tackle him to prevent this from happening. Or consider that an enemy soldier fighting for his country, for a cause he has been told is just (even though, for this example, it is not – his government lied), is not considered to be personally acting unjustly when he attacks me. So my defense against him cannot be construed as a defense against unjust aggression, defense against his violation of a principle of autonomy, or as a rejection of his discounting of my agency. Nonetheless, I can use force against this enemy soldier since his actions constitute a threat to my capacity to will effectively.

This principle complements the Rejection of Unjust Aggression Principle and accounts for the theoretical difference between the way we justify the use of force against unjust aggression and the way we justify it in cases where the one threatening us might not be deemed morally culpable. I want to make clear that these two principles are independent, that is, neither follows from the other. For example, the Unjust Aggression Principle justifies our use of force against someone who wants to pinch my ear. Clearly this does not threaten my capacity to will; just as clearly, however, it is an act of unjust aggression and we can use force to reject the impermissible maxim of this action. On the other hand, the Rejection of Unjust Aggression Principle does not provide me justification to use force against an enemy soldier. He has not adopted an impermissible maxim. But clearly, he represents a threat to my capacity to will, so I am justified to use force against him under the Capacity to Will Principle.

I want to make one more point before I proceed. We face minor threats that are not instances of unjust aggression, yet against which we can use some force. For instance, suppose I am at a crowded party and someone next to me is gesturing with his arms. If I can see that he is, unbeknownst to him, about to hit me in the nose, I am justified in raising my arms and using a minimum of force to deflect the blow. His action in not unjust, I am justified in using force, yet this is not a threat to my capacity to will. There seems to be a gap in coverage, as it were, provided by the Capacity to Will Principle. But this is not a major concern here. One would hope that we could generate another permissive principle to accommodate such situations. At any rate, we do not need to concern ourselves with it here because the Capacity to Will Principle has been generated specifically for work in just war theory to account for the justification for the use of force when our capacity to will effectively *is* threatened.

Continuing our discussion of using force against threats that do not proceed from an impermissible maxim, we must note that there are limits to what we can do in response to a threat to our capacity to will effectively. With the introduction of this principle, it might initially seem that I have introduced a tension or conflict into the theory of autonomy. In order to see the tension, let us revisit the shooting range example. We do not seem to have any reservations about shoving the man's arm so that the ricochet from his shot will not kill me. But I think that many of us would have some reservations about shooting and killing him in order to save ourselves. And we would have even greater reservations about shooting a child standing nearby so that his scream would distract the man in order to alter his point of aim. Yet these are scenarios where we are using force – to resist a threat to our capacity to will effectively – against someone who is not properly doing something unjust towards us. How can we account for the very deep intuition that there are limits to the force we can use, and that the limits are different in the case of soldiers fighting one another as opposed to cases like the shooting range scenario?

We have already provided some explanation for the limits to what we can do even out of respect for autonomy. We noted that we cannot violate principles of autonomy in the name of autonomy: we are justified in using force out of respect for a value, autonomy, and are on that account proscribed from violating principles generated by the value out of respect for which we act. And we noted that we can use force generally only against those engaged in directly harming us. These proscriptions clearly preclude shooting the child in order to save ourselves. To shoot him seems to be using him as a means: there is nothing relevant in the situation that makes it the case that we would not be treating him as a mere means. The child himself has not adopted an impermissible maxim, nor is he engaged in directly harming us. To harm him would be to violate principles of autonomy. And in this instance it would seem inaccurate to say that, in using force to protect ourselves, we were acting out of respect for autonomy. It would be more accurate to say that at this point we have in fact merely acted to bring about another end, that is, the saving of our lives. We would not have acted out of respect for a value, but in order to promote a value, in this instance, life. If we find it odious to kill the child to save our own lives, then we might see more clearly the insight behind the earlier distinction between acting to defend or promote a value and acting out of respect for a value. We have indicated that the proper motive and justification is the latter, and we should see here the force and appeal of that perspective since it imposes more appropriate restrictions, ones that align more closely with our deepest intuitions on this matter.

But let us now compare the difference between what the soldier does and what the shooter at the range does. Both are engaged in acts that we could construe as directly harming. Even though the shooter does not intend to harm me, his actions are a direct threat to my capacity to will. Intentional or not, my capacity to will is threatened by both agents. Whether they are morally culpable or not, they both threaten me. (I will explain in Chapter 6 that even though the enemy soldier who shoots me has not violated principles generated by autonomy or discounted my agency, nonetheless, principles have been violated, and my agency has been discounted.) But why do we have different moral intuitions about the limits to the use of force in each instance?

What accounts for our different judgments are the different maxims involved. The soldier has adopted a maxim whereby he deliberately intends to harm me. Just as in the case of the murderer, what justifies our use of force is that we are reacting to his maxim. It is a *maxim* to which we react. In the case of the soldier, his maxim is not impermissible, but it is a maxim he has adopted – he is aware of and responsible for it as his maxim – which is deliberately directed at my harm. If we conceive our actions as a response to the maxims involved, it is much easier to understand our intuitions about the case of the soldier and the shooter on the range. The soldier is involved in direct harming and knows it; he intends it and has adopted this maxim. We can, I think, unproblematically react with force against a maxim directed at the deliberate undermining of our capacity to will effectively.[50]

The case of the shooter is different. What is the maxim to which we are reacting? Because he is unwittingly threatening our capacity to will, he has not adopted a maxim that threatens this capacity, and we are hesitant to use deadly force against him. We feel justified in hitting his arm, or even perhaps throwing a rock and knocking him out, but most of us feel it would be wrong to kill him. At least we are much more troubled by the thought of killing him than we are about killing the enemy soldier; no matter how one decides this issue, it is at least clear that there is a difference between the soldier and the shooter. And I think that the reason for this is that at this point, with respect to the shooter, we seem also to be more accurately acting to save our lives as opposed to reacting to respect a value. That is the intuition informing our judgments. Barbara Herman talks about innocent threats and says:

> (T)he argument that justifies violence in self-defense does not justify violence against innocent threats (persons whose actions, or the effects of their actions, threaten life but who do not intend any harm or violence.) Self-defense is permitted as a way of resisting a willed attack on my agency. Since the innocent threat is identified as having no agency-discounting maxim, I may not act against him in self-defense. For the same reason, I may not take the life or the organs of another to stay alive. In neither case would I be acting to sustain the integrity of my agency – only its duration.[51]

Although I am not entirely in agreement with her argument (for one thing, we have already indicated that at least some use of force is justified against innocent threats, for instance, shoving the arm of the shooter on the range), it is very helpful. It helps us understand why the theory of autonomy justifies the use of force in terms of reactions to maxims, not actions. We can extend the discussions from earlier principles to inform our discussion here.

If we conceive the notion of self-defense in terms of reactions to certain maxims or forms of willing. we can more readily bring the theory of autonomy to bear in solving this problem. Recall that we stated that our justification for using violence against aggression is that we act to resist a devaluation or discounting of our agency (we reject maxims that do not properly respect or value us in terms of our rational agency), not per se to defend our lives. As Herman says: "Acting to save my life (as something valuable to me) would be to act for just another purpose" (quoted earlier).[52] Herman further notes (quoted earlier): "Moral wrongness is not a function of consequences but of willings...what is wrong with the killing maxim is that the agent fails to accord proper weight to the value of rational agents...in what he wills."[53]

Justifying violence merely in terms of defense of life has consequentialist implications that are unacceptable in terms of the theory we are attempting to develop. Now, the enemy soldier might not devalue or discount my agency as such (insofar as his is not an impermissible maxim), but he is nonetheless engaging in a "willed attack on my agency." So it seems reasonable to account for my use of violence in terms of resisting a threat to my agency, not merely as a defense of my life. That is, he might not be devaluing my agency in terms of adopting an impermissible maxim. But he does will an attack on my person, the condition of my agency, so we can employ the language of resistance to a threat to agency rather than the language of defense of life. If we use force against a willed attack against our agency, *our resistance to that attack takes on the moral character of our resistance to a discounting or devaluation of our agency.*

Moreover, conceived along these lines we can understand the limitations to the use of force more readily. In generating the Rejection of Unjust Aggression Principle we noted that we could use force against the criminal but not against his mother, even if she were an evil person who reveled in her son's crimes. We could only react to the criminal's impermissible maxim and the actions resulting from his adoption of the impermissible maxim.

The key concept here is a reaction to maxims. And if we understand things in this way, it is easy to account for our conviction that restraint is required in the case of the unwitting shooter on the range in a way that it is not required in the case of an enemy soldier shooting at me. This also renders a surprising consequence. It turns out that we can use force against certain permissible maxims but not against certain impermissible maxims. For instance, we can use force against an enemy soldier because he has adopted a maxim directed at my harm, even though we do not consider this an impermissible maxim per se, that is, we do not see the soldier as doing something unjust. But we cannot use force against, for instance, a civilian supporter of the war even if the civilian knew the war was unjust and had adopted a maxim directed at achieving the unjust aims of the war. The types of maxims to which we can react with force must involve a certain form of direct threat to our agency. I will develop this point in Chapter 4.

Let us reconsider the case of the firing range. Let us suppose that the man next to me looks over at me and mistakenly believes I am the anti-NRA serial killer who has been going to rifle ranges and killing people. Suppose that when I pick up my rifle, he thinks I intend to kill him and so starts shooting at me. It seems now much less problematic to shoot him, even though he has not really adopted an impermissible maxim. That is, he is not trying to murder me, but in his mind is trying to stop a serial killer. Nonetheless, he is intending to harm me, and that makes a lot of difference.[54] Using force against him here is much less morally controversial than in the case of his unintended ricochet for the same reason that using force against an enemy soldier intent on shooting me is justified. Both constitute a willed, intentional attack on me; both agents have adopted maxims to which my violent response is justified.

Let us contrast this with another example. Suppose I am standing on a curb, and I slip off directly into the path of a bus. The only way to save myself would be to reach up and grab a man standing on the same curb. I could pull myself to safety, but I know that the force of my pulling would send the man into the street where he would be killed by the bus. I think in this instance, we are likely to condemn my actions. And I think the reason is that now I have merely acted for another purpose, namely, to save my life. Here the distinction between the language of resistance to threats to agency and saving of life becomes important and where insights from the Means Only Principle further inform the discussion in important ways. Here it seems that we violate the Means Only Principle when we kill an innocent bystander to save our own life: we have violated a principle of autonomy in trying to save our lives.

Even if we contend that we are trying to save the conditions of our agency/ autonomy, we said that we cannot do just anything in defense of autonomy. Autonomy is a value out of respect for which we act when we resist threats to our agency. In the bus example, it appears that in trying to preserve the conditions of our agency, we in fact violate principles of autonomy in order to save our life. That is why it strikes us as an odious action. We insist that we are not justified in violating principles of autonomy. If the use of force is not justified under a principle generated by autonomy, you cannot use it.

We might gain more insight if we consider yet another example. If someone is shooting at me, or even randomly shooting at a crowd of which I am a member, I do not think I would be condemned for ducking, even though the bullets I might have stopped may now hit someone else. But clearly we would judge the case differently if, in the same situation, instead of ducking, I grab the baby out of the arms of the woman next to me and use it as a shield. In the first instance, we might construe my actions in terms of reacting to a threat to my agency. But in the second instance, the most natural description of my action would be that of violating principles generated by autonomy in order to save my life. And this is a key point. I had said earlier, about the bus example, that we might contend that we were trying to preserve the conditions of our agency. But that contention seems specious. In that example, we would not be acting out of respect for autonomy, but to save our lives, and in so doing we would be violating principles generated by autonomy. On the other hand, even if we argued that we were merely trying to preserve our agency, we would have to admit that we were using impermissible means to do so since we would be deliberately threatening the capacity to will of those who were not threatening us.

These distinctions between resisting a threat to autonomy and defending our life, or between acting out of respect for a value and defending our life, go a long way towards capturing the moral insight behind our different intuitive responses to the cases under consideration. They help explain why we condemn using the baby as a shield, for instance, yet do not condemn ducking when shots are fired or the shooting of an enemy soldier who is firing at me. And as the case of the baby shield starkly highlights, even though we can use some force against an innocent threat, as in shoving the man's arm, there are certainly limits to the force we can use. We might say that our use of force exceeds the justified limits at the point where our actions more obviously resemble a violation of principles generated by autonomy than a respect for a value, when we deliberately threaten the capacity to will of those who are not deliberately or directly harming us.

We must recognize that in some sense I harm the man whose arm I push. We cannot go around meting out blows to another's body. He has not adopted a maxim of harming me, yet I use force against him. But it seems obvious that this indignity visited upon his person is minor compared to the threat I face, namely, the undermining of my capacity for any autonomous agency. Having said this, we should revisit the example of the child on the shooting range. It does seem that I would be justified in shoving the child so that he bumped into the man's arm. If the child only suffers a small fright and perhaps a bruise; it would seem permissible to shove him in response to this threat to our agency. Here appears one of the gaps in coverage provided by this principle, which I mentioned earlier. The child is not involved in directly harming me, yet we want to justify at least some use of force against him. We would have to generate another permissive principle, since if our shoving the child constituted a violation of principles of autonomy, the shoving would be proscribed.

Of course, we cannot just proliferate principles to accommodate any use of force we want. This would eviscerate the theory of autonomy. But the theory itself will impose the limits of proliferation. Any proposed principle must be consistent with not treating others as means. Where to draw the line with reference to these innocent threats is cloudy. How much harm can we inflict on the shooter or the child? Can we maim them to save our lives, or shoot off one of their fingers to save our hand? But these are issues related to the general problem of innocent threats and although important, their resolution is not central to, or within the scope of, this project. The primary situations we are considering concern deliberate threats to our capacity to will effectively, and in the milieu of just war theory, the threats we are concerned with are primarily not innocent threats in the sense that they have not adopted a maxim of harming.

I have given a way of understanding the relationship that obtains between enemy soldiers that clearly sets it apart from the case of the man on the shooting range and other innocent threat scenarios. The purpose of the Threat to the Capacity to Will Effectively Principle was to account for our justification to use force against those who are not considered to be acting unjustly yet are nonetheless a threat to us. And we have seen that a proper understanding of this principle, in conjunction with the other principles generated by autonomy, provides us with that justification while at the same time maintaining appropriate limits on the use of force.

I want to consider one more perspective. I have asserted that most of us would find it morally problematic to shoot the man on the shooting range whose ricochet will kill me if I do not kill him first. But there are probably those who think that it would be justified to kill him. I do not know exactly what to say to them. I have given a characterization of the justification for the use of force in self-defense and have insisted that we cannot violate principles of autonomy, even to save our lives. Those who reject my argument will reject my conclusion about the man on the range. But I would hope nonetheless that they accept my argument and conclusion when applied to the case of soldiers, which was the very purpose of this discussion. I have attempted to provide a theoretical basis for the difference between the threat posed by a soldier and the threat posed by someone not intentionally willing to harm me. In doing so, I have provided an explanation as to why using force against a soldier is unproblematic, even though the use of force against others, who might be equally threatening, is problematic. I wanted to show that there is something unique about the soldier that sets him radically apart from other types of threats.

I must make a final point about this principle. I have generally been comparing and contrasting principles generated from autonomy with consequentialism, showing how we get different results in various cases by viewing them from these different perspectives. But this principle is a little different. That is, it is not so much that consequentialism will look differently at the issue this principle addresses; rather, consequentialist-driven just war theories lack the conceptual apparatus to really account for the insights provided by this principle. Rights-based theories suffer from this deficiency also. I will give a full exposition later, but I note now that just war theorists, either rights-based or consequentialist, generally consider the use of force from the perspective of reacting to an unjust assailant.[55] At the same time, most theorists recognize the moral equality of soldiers, that is, that soldiers fighting justly are generally exonerated from blame with respect to the political decision to go to war. Soldiers fighting each other are not per se doing something unjust when they use force against one another. These views are incompatible; it is inconsistent to justify the use of force against enemy soldiers as a defense against unjust aggression while at the same time accepting the view that the enemy soldier is not acting unjustly when defending his country. And even though at some point these theorists recognize the moral equality of soldiers, when they provide the justification for the use of force between combatants, there is a slide towards justification in terms of the unjust assailant model.[56] And we should note that the idea of the moral equality of soldiers is an important facet of just war theory. Since the theory of autonomy seems to have better means for accounting for the various facets of the war convention, we have another reason for favoring it over consequentialism or rights-based theories. We gain a great deal of consistency by adopting the theory of autonomy.

The Principles We Can Reasonably Reject Principle

We need a way of accounting for our preference, all things being equal, to harm fewer as opposed to more people. Let us consider a wartime scenario. Suppose we must attack a certain objective and must choose one of two platoons – first platoon or second platoon – to send on the mission. Either platoon can accomplish the mission. If we choose first platoon, it can expect minimal losses, since it can attack along a covered and concealed route. Second platoon, on the other hand, would experience significant casualties because it must attack across open terrain, in full view of the enemy. The obvious choice, then, is to choose first platoon. We should choose the course of action that results in the least harm. Since the action had to be done (we assume the platoon's objective is a legitimate one, and since we assume some wars are just, we must justify some of the means necessary to achieve the legitimate aims of the war), we should choose the action that harms the fewer people.

But given this example, it might seem natural to ground this choice by means of an appeal to consequentialist reasoning. It might also seem that this choice cannot be required by the theory of autonomy; since everyone has unconditional value, it may seem that it would not matter whether fewer or more people are killed. But we can see how we can arrive at the decision to harm fewer people precisely out of respect for their autonomy,[57] using a line of reasoning borrowed from T. M. Scanlon. I will examine Scanlon's argument and then show how his view follows from autonomy.

Scanlon talks about the viability of moral principles in terms of whether they can be reasonably rejected by individuals motivated "to find principles for the general regulation of behavior that others, similarly motivated, could not reasonably reject."[58] And he insists that "the justifiability of a moral principle depends only on various *individuals'* reasons for objecting to that principle and alternatives to it."[59] What he offers is a way to reconcile the sanctity of the individual with the intuitive force of aggregation, while not collapsing into consequentialism. As we have seen above, there does seem to be good reason to say it is morally required to harm fewer people rather than more, all things being equal. Scanlon says that any principle that is indifferent with respect to allowing harm to either the smaller group or the larger group could be reasonably rejected.

Before we examine Scanlon's case, let us begin with the following scenario. Suppose you are faced with a situation where two people are in danger and you can only rescue one; the one you do not rescue will die. All things being equal, that is, you have no special relationship to either person, neither one did anything reckless or immoral to get himself into the situation, etc., you can rescue either one without there being any morally problematic issues. The situation, by being completely symmetrical, is indifferent. But suppose you add another person to the scenario; suppose you now face a choice between saving one or saving two. If we say the situation is still indifferent, that is, that you can save either the one or the two without any morally troubling implications, then it seems that the added person makes no difference. But that does not seem right. This is the insight Scanlon examines.

He considers a case where we must choose between saving one person or two. He argues from the perspective of "someone in the larger group."[60] Each person's fate must be given positive weight, he argues. If we choose to save the one, then the "fate of the single person is obviously given positive weight...since if that person were not threatened, the agent would have been required to save the two."[61] But then, if that person's fate has positive weight, it is unreasonable to discount the weight of each individual in the larger group. That is, if we see the person's life as valuable and as therefore a reason for saving him, we should see everyone's life as a reason for saving him. But it seems unreasonable, then, to save one instead of two because it would imply that the "presence of the additional person...makes no difference to what the agent is required to do or to how she is required to go about deciding what to do."[62] If the first person's life made a difference and provided a reason for acting in the way that the agent chose to act, then both persons' lives in the larger group should make a difference and provide a reason for acting. Scanlon says that a principle that permits an agent to save the smaller group could be reasonably rejected by a member of the larger group. Such a principle "is unacceptable, the person might argue, since his life should be given the same moral significance as anyone else's in this situation."[63]

The effect of the argument is to attach moral significance to each person's life, significance that is not dependent on its contribution to an aggregate value. Certain forms of consequentialism, like Mill's utilitarianism, also take everyone's wellbeing into consideration, but do so in order to assess its contribution to overall social utility: the relative value derives from its role in maximizing overall social good. Hence, in principle, consequentialism could justify coercing certain individuals – sacrificing their wellbeing in ways that seem unjust – in order to increase the general welfare. In terms of my theory, autonomy is the starting point of deliberation, and it carries the argument. It has value independent of consideration of maximizing some other good. We reason from the standpoint of individuals, not from the perspective of the total aggregate good resulting from some outcome. And since our reasoning revolves around the notion that people could accept the principle we are advancing, it is noncoercive. This method of reasoning will pay large dividends as we work our way through difficult issues in just war theory.

We have at least a rationale, not based on consequentialist reasoning, for preferring the harm of fewer over the harm of more. But we must show how this rationale follows from autonomy in order to deflect the charge that the theory of autonomy must appeal to consequentialist reasoning in such circumstances.

If I act on a principle you could reasonably reject, it does not seem that I am treating you as a value-conferring agent. Recall what Korsgaard says:

> ...you must view anyone who has the power of rational choice as having, in virtue of that power, a value-conferring status. This will mean that what you make good by means of your rational choice must be harmonious with what another can

make good by means of her rational choice – for the good is a consistent, harmonious object shared by all rational beings.[64]

When I act on a principle you can reasonably reject, I give my preferences unwarranted precedence over yours. You must be able to confer value upon my choice in order for it to be considered rational and therefore good. In virtue of your capacity to confer value, you have equal status with me. But I discount your value in favor of my inclinations if I act in ways you could reasonably reject. I do not give you the respect you are due as a rational agent.

We could capture this insight in another way. To say that you reasonably reject a principle is to say that your choice not to accept it rests on reasonable grounds: you have reasonable grounds not to consent. If I decide I will act on the principle anyway, then I have adopted a maxim to act in such a way whether you will it or not; thus, I coerce you. We can state our final principle.

The Principles We Can Reasonably Reject Principle: Our actions must be justifiable in terms other autonomous agents can accept. That is, they must accord with principles people cannot reasonably reject.

This principle primarily accounts for our preference, all things being equal, that fewer rather than more people be harmed by any given use of force, without our having to ground this preference in consequentialism. Although the reasoning involved in generating this principle can and will be employed in other ways by the theory of autonomy, this is one of its primary purposes. We have a rationale, derived from the perspective of autonomy, for preferring the harm of fewer over the harm of more by attaching moral significance to the life of every human being. If we have two possible courses of action for accomplishing a mission, we will choose the one that exposes fewer people to harm, all things being equal. But we do not justify our choice in terms of an overall good. This principle gives us a conceptual way to understand the intuitive appeal of aggregation without requiring consequentialist tools by considering what principles each individual would consent to such that he is not being used as mere means: consequentialism could use him as a mere means.

So the Principles We Can Reasonably Reject Principle is important for theoretical consistency. At this point it is important to note that we should consider all the principles in context of one another. They may not all apply to any given case, but they will not conflict with one another, our considered moral judgments, or the war convention. The Reasonable Rejection Principle is consistent with the Means Only Principle, and consequentialism is not. We presume that people would not consent to (would reasonably reject) a principle that permitted their treatment as mere means – if they even could; the deep point is the impossibility of consent to such a principle given the coercion it entails. Consequentialism, on the other hand, could in principle permit the treatment of people as mere means if the overall good is thereby enhanced.

I do not conceive my argument, of course, as a decisive defeat of the consequentialist position. But it does highlight reasons why my theory is preferable to consequentialism for just war purposes. For instance, the pressures about numbers – that is, the number of people to be affected by various actions or policies in war – in just war theory are always goading us to violate the immunity of noncombatants when the numbers work out right. It is important to recognize the conceptual difference between the methodology I advance and the consequentialist one. Consequentialism looks to the aggregate good from the perspective of the aggregate (a problematic notion itself). Hence, the numbers themselves, in the end, carry the argument; the principle distinction recognized is between the many and the few. For just war purposes, this has disastrous results because we want to recognize the distinction between combatants and noncombatants. When we look at the numbers from the perspective of individuals, assessing principles people could reasonably accept or reject, we recognize both distinctions, if you will: the fewer/many and the combatant/noncombatant. We are forced to look at the perspective of the noncombatant and see if he could reject a principle that treats him like a combatant, that is, a legitimate target. We recognize immediately that such a principle would be rejected on logical grounds alone. We also recognize, in fact, that people have rejected such a principle, and this rejection is the grounds for the moral force carried within just war theory by the immunity of noncombatants. The individual matters in a way that he does not matter when viewed from a consequentialist position. From a consequentialist point of view, the focus is the aggregate whole so that, in principle, the particular individuals involved in the calculation are irrelevant. So the fact that someone is a noncombatant is not an especially relevant feature of the equation, although it can be. That is, surely a consequentialist could and would attach a certain value to the maintaining of the combatant/noncombatant distinction. But, again, that value would still be subordinate to the consequentialist value to be promoted, say, overall happiness. As such, the distinction has only contingent value and could be overridden if it were expedient to do so. As I have argued, the distinction between combatants and noncombatants is the central feature of just war theory. My account of aggregation, a nonconsequentialist one, better supports the war convention. It avoids the coercive elements of consequentialism that are cause for so much of the concern about it (consequentialism). It requires us to act in ways that people could accept, rejecting as impermissible any actions that treat people as mere means.

We should also consider this issue from another perspective: do we really accept a principle that seems to devalue soldiers such that their deaths are preferable to that of civilians, even if more of them (the soldiers) face risk than do the civilians? Although I discuss this in detail in Chapter 6, it is appropriate for this discussion briefly to point out that we do not devalue soldiers when we prefer that they, rather than noncombatants, face risks. On one level, of course, we reject the principle that puts soldiers at risk in the first place: we reject the coercion that is unjust war. That is why we are fighting – to resist evil. But the blame for such coercion falls on the head of whoever started the war; he has devalued us all. On another level, however, that soldiers are put at risk rather than noncombatants represents a deep commitment to the value of humanity. Some of us choose a role that puts us in harm's way to protect the innocent. To adopt a consequentialist stance, then, on this account could render the distinction between combatants and noncombatants incoherent, since we could opt, in principle, to put noncombatants at risk rather than endanger combatants, again, if the calculations worked out right. This sort of reasoning would weaken, if not nullify, the moral force of the combatant/noncombatant distinction.[65]

Finally, we should note that much of the force of this principle comes from its forward-looking character. By this I mean that we employ it quite often in the context of deciding a future course of action or developing policy for the use of force. Can our policies meet the reasonable rejection criterion? We decide this in advance because no one who stands to be the victim of violence would willingly accept such victimization at the time. If I am a member of the fewer people to be harmed rather than the larger group to be saved, I might very well rail against the decision. Nonetheless, the principle of saving more rather than fewer is a principle I cannot reasonably reject. The principles we generate must meet the test.

We have generated the following four principles:

1. The Means Only Principle: We are not to use humanity as a means only.
2. The Rejection of Unjust Aggression Principle: We are justified to use force against those who are engaged in unjust acts of aggression against us.
3. The Threat to the Capacity to Rationally Will Effectively Principle: The use of force is generally allowed as a response to a threat to our capacity to will effectively, that is, when the necessary condition of our autonomy is threatened.
4. The Principles We Can Reasonably Reject Principle: Our actions must be justifiable in terms other autonomous agents can accept. That is, they must accord with principles people cannot reasonably reject.

We can use these principles to guide our moral deliberations about just war issues. The principles overlap each other and draw upon each other for force and meaning. Indeed, they are merely facets of the same concept. I will seek a reflective equilibrium, applying the principles where they seem appropriate, bouncing the conclusions and implications against our deepest moral convictions and the purpose of the war convention, thereby ultimately assessing the value of the theory of autonomy to just war theory. Some principles will be more germane in particular cases than others, but they all will lead us to approach problems from a particular perspective. We are called to adopt a certain attitude towards humanity, and we must adopt a willingness to live with the implications of this attitude.

Notes

1   Immanuel Kant, *Groundwork of the Metaphysic of Morals*. Trans. H.J. Paton (New York: Harper and Row, 1948), p. 428; hereafter cited "Kant, *Groundwork*." All page references to *Groundwork* are from the Prussian Academy edition.

2   Ibid., p. 392. This is where Kant explains that the purpose of the *Groundwork* is to establish the supreme principle of morality, not where he offers the argument that man is the ground of the principle.

3   Ibid., p. 428.

4   This does not rule out the possibility of formulating a principle such that it would require that you take numbers into account, at least in special circumstances. The Principles We Can Reasonably Reject Principle, articulated later in this chapter, will regard numbers as relevant.

5   Samuel Scheffler, *The Rejection of Consequentialism* (Oxford: Clarendon, 1994), p. 2.

6   There are cases where at first glance it appears that we override noncombatant immunity. In Chapter 6, I discuss the Doctrine of Double Effect, which provides justification for the unintended harm that might befall noncombatants during the conduct of legitimate military activity. One important aspect in such cases is that the noncombatants are not *deliberately* targeted: we do not deliberately override their immunity. But the most difficult issue with respect to the prohibition against deliberately targeting noncombatants has to do with supreme emergency, the subject of Chapter 7. I will argue there that if we are allowed to deliberately target noncombatants, it will only be at their consent. Their immunity is something owed to them out of respect for their humanity. If, out of respect for humanity, they have a moral obligation to forfeit that immunity, then if we target them, we are not overriding the immunity (since they are no longer entitled to it) and in this respect are not overriding the war convention. But this will be shown to be an extremely, almost unimaginably rare circumstance.

7   My thesis does not depend on its being a correct interpretation of Kant, although this is how I interpret him.

8   Korsgaard, "Kant's Formula of Humanity" in *Kant Studien*, 77 Jahrgang, Heft 2, 1986.

9   The claim itself would be illegitimate. You cannot violate a principle and claim you are doing it to uphold that principle.

10   I borrow this argument from T.M. Scanlon, *What We Owe to Each Other* (Cambridge: Belknap Press, 1998), pp. 160-68.

11   Scanlon, p. 165. Scanlon writes, making a slightly different point: "If, as I have just maintained, the conception of friendship that we understand and have reason to value involves recognizing the moral claims of nonfriends as well, then no sacrifice of friendship is involved when I refuse to violate the rights of strangers in order to help my friend."

12   Ibid., p. 88.

13   Christine M. Korsgaard, *The Sources of Normativity* (Cambridge: Cambridge University Press, 1996) p. 275.

14   Walzer, p. 71.

15   Ibid., pp. 70-71.

16   Of course one consideration under *jus ad bellum* is whether the Finns felt they had a legitimate chance of victory or at least achieving a political settlement that was more acceptable to them. If theirs was simply a lost cause, to choose to fight would be to simply waste the lives or their citizens: this would be morally condemnable.

17 David Cummiskey argues that Kantian ethics are fundamentally consequentialist and that the goal of this ethics is to promote conditions that would conduce to the flourishing of the greatest number of rational agents. Our moral task, for Cummiskey, is to maximize rather than respect autonomy. See "Kantian Consequentialism" in *Ethics*, 100 (April 1990), pp. 586-615.

18 Kant, *Groundwork,* p. 429.

19 Korsgaard, "Kant's Formula of Humanity" in *Kant Studien*; 77 Jahrgang, Heft 2, 1986, p. 197.

20 Kant, *Groundwork,* p. 434-5.

21 Of course, one can refine consequentialism to meet these objections. I am not trying to refute consequentialism. Rather, I am contrasting the radically different structures of the two views. My view embraces agent-centered restrictions generated by autonomy, and consequentialism eschews agent-centered restrictions in favor of maximizing some good.

22 Kant, *Groundwork,* p. 435.

23 Some, of course, reject this view as being excessively anthropocentric. But the problem of the status of animals is not one I can address here. In any case, my purpose is to develop a certain concept for specific use in just war theory. Whether one accepts the view in general, one might nonetheless see its efficacy in this specific role.

24 Korsgaard, p. 191.

25 Kant, *Groundwork,* p. 428.

26 Korsgaard, p. 195.

27 Ibid., p. 195.

28 Ibid., p. 195.

29 Ibid., p. 196.

30 Ibid., p. 196.

31 Some people, of course, reject the need for this unconditioned value. But it is Kant's view, at least on Korsgaard's interpretation. I agree with this interpretation and it is the view to which I subscribe. Beyond this, I am trying to establish what follows from this conception of humanity/rational nature *if* one were to subscribe to it.

32 Kant, *Groundwork,* pp. 428-29.

33 Ibid., p. 196.

34 Onora O'Neill, *Constructions of reason: explorations of Kant's practical philosophy,* (Cambridge [England]; New York: Cambridge University Press, 1989) p. 138.

35 Korsgaard, p. 199.

36 Ibid., p 199.

37 I say more about this below.

38 Herman, p. 124.

39 Ibid., p. 129.

40 Herman, p. 117.

41 Ibid., p. 117.

42 Jeffrie G. Murphy, "The Killing of the Innocent", *War, Morality, and the Military* Profession. Ed. Malham M. Wakin, (Boulder: Westview Press, 1979) p. 350.

43 Herman, p. 126.

44 Ibid., p. 122. She points out that a race of invulnerable rational agents would "be indifferent to the homicidal intentions of others;" they would not consider it rational to "adopt maxims of killing."

45 I will make this point more clearly below.

46 Of course, we can still use some force against him: we can handcuff him, for instance. But the further use of whatever force is required must be constrained by the notion that

we are permitted to do only that which is required to contain the threat. Furthermore, it is governed by certain demands of legal justice, namely, the extent to which incarceration or other punishment is mandated by the law and the responsibility to protect citizens from any further harm posed by the criminal.

47   Herman, p. 130.

48   See note 46.

49   Ibid., p. 121-22. Of course, there are circumstances where we commit acts that we know will undermine our capacity to will. Suppose we sacrifice ourselves to save our child – I jump in front of the child and take a bullet, for example. But here we are establishing a presumption against willingly submitting to a threat. The case of saving a child is clearly different from standing by passively in the face of one's own impending ruination. In fact, saving one's child – or a fellow soldier in combat – might be construed as a supererogatory act. But the discussion of the permissibility of self-sacrifice is not relevant to my project, although it seems we could generate a permissive principle that permits it: the very structure of self-sacrifice might show that it is not coercive.

50   Herman rightly points out that "justification of self-defense requires knowledge of another's maxims" on this view. She also points out that in some circumstances "we can infer an agent's intentions with great confidence" (p. 130n). Since we can infer the intentions of enemy soldiers with confidence, this is not a serious limitation of the position I am advancing here.

51   Ibid., p. 130

52   Ibid., p. 130.

53   Ibid., p. 124.

54   There are further complications that I cannot discuss, for instance, whether I am justified in using force against a policeman who is trying to arrest me after I have been framed.

55   See Murphy, "The Killing of the Innocent," p. 361; and Anscombe, in "War and Murder" seems to base her entire argument on this perspective. Even Herman in "Murder and Mayhem" uses the same model. Although she might not be appropriately described as a rights-based theorist (she is certainly not a consequentialist), we can see that the unjust aggression model is the standard model used for justifying the use of force. It is an inadequate model for most issues in just war theory.

56   Walzer is a notable exception. He recognizes the moral equality of soldiers and does not adopt the unjust assailant model to justify the use of force between enemy soldiers. His approach to the issue is to say that soldiers lose their right to life "(S)imply by fighting" (p. 136). I will argue in Chapter 5 that this view has problems of its own. For now, I note that it seems problematic to assert that one has lost his right to life simply because one chose a profession dedicated to resisting aggression.

57   Granted, there are other reasons. A commander chooses in this way to conserve his fighting strength, for example, and be prepared for the next mission. I am looking for the moral justification.

58   Scanlon, p. 4.

59   Ibid., p. 229.

60   Ibid., p. 232.

61   Ibid., p. 232.

62   Ibid., p. 232.

63   Ibid., p. 232.

64   Quoted earlier.

65 It is beyond the purpose of this investigation to pursue the issue of whether this line of reasoning holds equally for conscripts as for volunteers. I am inclined to say it does. Although I feel universal conscription as a general policy is impermissible, there do seem to be cases where a country can justifiably call on its citizens to take up arms – say when its survival interests are at stake. This seems analogous to the domestic Good Samaritan laws. We do not require people to act as firemen and policemen, but we do require them to perform police or firemen tasks to save another person if they can do so without unreasonable risk to themselves. Obviously the point of disanalogy is that the soldiers will inherently face a lot of risk. But in the scenario that I envisage as the only legitimate one to justify conscription, the conscripts already face risk. We all face risk, so their refusal to take up arms is akin to someone's refusing to be part of a bucket brigade trying to stop a fire that will engulf us all while at the same time insisting that others continue with the task so that they can save him; such behavior is indecent, a dereliction of moral duty.

Chapter 4

The Distinction

I have argued that one of the main purposes of the war convention is to distinguish between combatants and noncombatants and to define permissible behavior with regard to each class. I have indicated the pressures that lead us to override the convention or question the very legitimacy of the distinction. In the Chapter 3, I listed some principles generated by autonomy. Now I will offer the theoretical foundation for the distinction itself in order to reinforce the legitimacy of the war convention. Once the distinction is fully articulated, we will be better able to apply the theory of autonomy to just war issues.

In this chapter I argue from the point of view that we are all essentially noncombatants and that it is only the advent of war that makes some of us combatants. I develop the key notion that the best way to establish the distinction between combatants and noncombatants is in terms of the adoption of certain maxims. I will examine the phenomenon of surrender both to explain how soldiers can use force against one another while respecting autonomy and to show why it is morally wrong to attack noncombatants. I will indicate how *jus ad bellum* considerations bear on *jus in bello* issues when I discuss how it is that even the death of a soldier in war in some ways constitutes an instance of murder.

Noncombatancy is Not a Role

As I indicated earlier, it is appropriate to start with the injunction "noncombatant until proven otherwise." It is a mistake to suppose we must justify noncombatancy. The reason that aggression is a crime is because it impedes people from pursuing their peaceful purposes, and unjust acts in war are attacks upon people who are not threatening. How is it that we have come to a position where we have to justify our immunity from attack, which derives from our autonomy, that seems to be our normal condition? It is analogous to having to justify to one's assailant on the street why one is not inherently a victim, why, that is, his assault upon you is a crime. We do not have to justify why we should not be assaulted. Justification is required by those who use violence on other human beings, seeming to violate principles generated by autonomy. He who would harm me carries the burden of justification: say he is a police officer and is attempting to arrest me. He must show reasonable cause that I am suspected of wrongdoing, and he must show that force was necessary to subdue me. I, on my part, must show, if I plead self-defense against an assailant, that I was really threatened (I am not justified in thrashing the old lady who takes cuts in line at the market) and that the force I used to protect myself was proportionate. The presumption then is that we are essentially, qua persons, noncombatants; there is an initial presumption that this state of noncombatancy is not in need of justification.

Robert Phillips says: "combatancy and noncombatancy are functions or roles which people fulfill."[1] He is half-right. *Combatancy* is a role, and I explain this in detail below. But why should we characterize *noncombatancy* as a role? Often, seeing noncombatancy as a role has had the effect of letting a certain presumption dictate the terms of the debate, namely a presumption that the class of combatants is a logically prior class, and that we then bestow noncombatant immunity upon various groups based on certain criteria; immunity must be derived. George I. Mavrodes argues along these lines. He refers to the "*alleged* moral immunity of noncombatants"[2] (my emphasis) and states: "The immunity of noncombatants is best thought of as a convention-dependent obligation related to a convention which substitutes for warfare a certain form of limited combat."[3] According to this view, there is no morally compelling reason to refrain from killing noncombatants. We have no reason to unilaterally observe the prohibition, but do so only contingent on our enemy's observation of the prohibition. I cannot critique his view completely here. But since his view is in many ways representative of those that question the validity of the distinction between combatants and noncombatants, it will be instructive to examine it. Although I ultimately reject his position, he does illuminate some problems and confusions within the just war tradition with respect to noncombatant immunity. What is at issue is whether we can provide any non-arbitrary, rational grounds for the distinction between combatants and noncombatants.

Mavrodes contends that "*immunity theorists*"[4] (those just war theorists within the just war tradition who embrace noncombatant immunity) base their distinction between combatants and noncombatants on a confused conception of innocence. Immunity theorists often use the terms *noncombatant* and *innocent* synonymously. And this usage seems problematic. Consider, along with Mavrodes, the case of two people. One, a noncombatant, is an avid supporter of an unjust war and its aims. He contributes "both his savings and the work which he knows best how to do, and he may avidly hope to share in the unjust gains which will follow if the war is successful."[5] This person is nonetheless "innocent," by virtue of being a noncombatant, in just war terms. The other person is a combatant, though a reluctant one. He has been drafted into service. He may not understand the aims of the war, and he probably does not support it. At least, we can assume, he does not support it in full knowledge that it is unjust and in hopes of gain, in the manner of the "innocent" noncombatant described above. Mavrodes tells us:

> He may have no understanding of what the war is about, and no heart for it. He might want nothing more than to go back to his town and the life he led before. But he is "engaged," carrying ammunition, ...or even banging away ineffectually with his rifle. He is without doubt a combatant, and "guilty," a fit subject for intentional slaughter. Is it not clear that "innocence," as used here,

leaves out entirely all of the relevant moral considerations – that it has no moral content at all? Anscombe suggests that intentional killing during warfare should be construed on the model of punishing people for their crimes, and we must see to it, if we are to be moral, that we punish someone only for his own crime and not for someone else's. But if we construe the criminality involved in an unjust war in any reasonable moral sense then it must either be the case that many noncombatants are guilty of that criminality or else many combatants are innocent. In fact, it will probably be the case that both of these things are true. Only if we were to divest "crime" of its moral bearings could we make it fit the combatant/ noncombatant distinction in modern wars.[6]

Understood this way, Mavrodes seems correct. The notions of guilt and innocence seem out of place or even misused when applied to the soldier and the avid civilian war supporter. If the terms refer to certain attitudes or ideological commitments, then certainly their usage in just war theory is misleading at best.

But the innocence the immunity theorists talk about concerns the fact that those ascribed this property are not engaged in directly harming. There is a particular kind of threat that combatants pose, which noncombatants do not pose, that is critical to the distinction between the two classes of people. The distinction does not turn, as we will see, on one's ideological views. Perhaps if we look again at the synonymy between *noncombatant* and *innocent*, we will be less troubled by the way innocence is invoked within the theory. That is, let us just call the civilian a noncombatant: clearly he is that. He is not armed and not engaged in directly harming or aggressing against anyone. And the soldier is a combatant, armed and, even if shooting ineffectually, engaged in direct harming in a way that the noncombatant is not.

Viewed in this way, Mavrodes' concerns are less pressing. The distinction between combatants and noncombatants is still fairly sharply defined, and the term innocence used to refer to noncombatants does have morally relevant content. It does not make the two senses of innocence the same, and it is important not to confuse the two senses of the term. But if we understand the way we use the term in this context of just war theory, we can see how it helps draw the distinction between combatants and noncombatants.

Furthermore, Mavrodes' view has a very problematic feature. He feels that the notion of noncombatant immunity rests on a convention. I indicated earlier his view that:

Now the core of my suggestion with respect to the immunity of noncombatants is this. The immunity of noncombatants is best thought of as a convention-dependent obligation related to a convention which substitutes for warfare a certain form of limited combat.[7]

Given that respect for noncombatant immunity rests on nothing but a mere convention, he feels that it would be imprudent, even immoral, to observe the convention if others did not. He explains:

If one's cause is just, but the slaying of noncombatants will not advance it to any marked degree, then one ought not to slay them. But this is just the requirement of proportionality, and applies equally and in the same way to combatants. If one's cause is just and the slaying of noncombatants would advance it – if, in other words, one is not prevented by considerations of justice and proportionality – this is the crucial case. If one refrains unilaterally in this situation then he seems to choose the greater of two evils (or the lesser of two goods).[8]

One refrains from slaughtering his enemy's civilians contingent on "his enemy's similar restraint."[9] Mavrodes makes a comparison between the prohibition against killing noncombatants and conformity to traffic rules. We conform to them because they have generally favorable results: fewer deaths in war, fewer accidents on the road. He believes consequentialist reasoning would support the convention so conceived. But this is not clear at all. For example, consequentialist reasoning in any given case might indicate that fewer overall deaths would occur if certain civilian population centers were destroyed.   So we might object to Mavrodes' reasoning on these grounds.

Furthermore, it is not clear that his view allows for reciprocity or provides for any constraints. To see why this is so, consider a case where we are fighting an enemy who we know will not attack our noncombatants under any circumstances. If the enemy is committed to restraints, then it would seem that the only reason we would have for not killing his noncombatants is if it were simply inexpedient. There would be no reason to distinguish between combatants or noncombatants except questions of military necessity, proportionality, or even convenience. This is a troubling result of Mavrodes' view. And it is a view that does not seem to correspond with our intuitive understanding of the war convention, as Anscombe points out:

> For men to choose to kill the innocent as a means to their ends is always murder, and murder is one of the worst of human actions. So the prohibition on deliberately killing prisoners of war or the civilian population is not like the Queensberry Rules: its force does not depend on its promulgation as part of positive law, written down, agreed upon, and adhered to by the parties concerned.[10]

Anscombe is denying that noncombatant immunity is a mere convention. She is correct. I intend to argue that there are deep philosophical foundations for the distinction between combatants and noncombatants. The theory of autonomy can provide a clear philosophical basis for the distinction that does not reduce to a convention. Far from being the case that noncombatancy is a convention, war creates the class of combatants. Everyone starts out as a noncombatant, even soldiers. When a war begins, combatancy is imposed upon certain people.[11] How does one become a combatant, and how do we justify the violence that combatants employ? How can a theory based on the sanctity of autonomy countenance the killing of combatants?

The Phenomenon of Surrender and the Adoption of Maxims

Let us consider the case of soldiers fighting each other, employing just means. We assume the moral equality of soldiers. As long as they employ just means against legitimate targets, the justness or unjustness of their government's war is not their responsibility. Using just means generally means using tactics, weapons, and ammunition considered legal under international law. Legitimate targets are generally targets considered legitimate under international law, such as military installations or soldiers. Of course, part of the purpose of this work is to further define what constitutes a legitimate target, but for the purpose of this discussion, we can say that a soldier is considered justified when employing the appropriate means against the appropriate targets, whatever "appropriate" turns out to be. So, soldiers are responsible for fighting justly. Christopher puts it this way:

> ...the guilt for initiating the war does not necessarily extend to those who are fighting it. This is the notion of *moral equality among soldiers*...soldiers are to be respected (or punished) based on their conduct as soldiers, even when they are members of the enemy's forces. Because soldiers are judged by their actions on the battlefield rather than in terms of the political considerations of the war itself, they are protected rather than punished when their status as combatants (that is, soldiers) is terminated, whether by capture, surrender, or injury.[12]

Here is where Mavrodes' discussion is very insightful and does point to some confusion within the immunity theorist camp. He quotes Anscombe, "writing of the people who can properly be attacked with deadly force:"

> What is required, for the people attacked to be noninnocent in the relevant sense, is that they themselves be engaged in an objectively unjust proceeding which the attacker has the right to make his concern; or – the commonest case – should be unjustly attacking him.[13]

Mavrodes makes clear that the noninnocents of the immunity theorists are the "guilty" and are "fit...for intentional slaughter."[14] It is the introduction of the term guilt and the way it is used that is deeply problematic for orthodox just war theory.

Clearly Anscombe, justifying the use of force, envisions a scenario where an assailant makes an unjust attack against another person. Self-defense seems uncontroversially justified here. But given the moral equality of soldiers, when enemy soldiers engage one another on the field of battle, neither is doing anything unjust. As long as they are fighting justly, we cannot say either is noninnocent in the way Anscombe seems to intend; neither of them is guilty.[15] And I cannot use the fact that some people use the term "noninnocent" as a justifying term when they use force against a criminal; combatants are not committing a crime – they are innocent in this sense of the word. So that sort of justification is not applicable to the case of soldiers. If I say that guilty just means combatant, I have only described the distinction, or given it a different name. I must show how being noninnocent, even if innocent in the sense of having not committed a crime, makes a soldier a legitimate target in war. What I need to do is to explain the nature of the distinction and provide a justification for it that supports our conviction that noncombatants cannot be killed while combatants can be. As it stands now, the issue is cloudy.

Anscombe, for instance, justifies our use of force against one who unjustly attacks us. But this does not seem to give us any justification, given the moral equality of soldiers, to kill a soldier fighting us justly. If we cannot come to a conceptually clear justification for treating a combatant differently than a noncombatant, the distinction does seem to rest on a confusion rather than upon the solid ground we seek. The challenge for the theory of autonomy is to explain how it is that we can use force against a soldier who is not to be seen as violating a principle of autonomy/not unjustly attacking us and how our use of force against such an agent is not in turn a violation of principles of autonomy, and how all of this is different from cases involving the deliberate targeting of noncombatants.

How can it be that when a soldier kills an enemy soldier he does not thereby violate a principle of autonomy with respect to the enemy soldier? It is important to ask the question in this way because I contend that every violation of principles generated from autonomy is unjust. If a soldier violates a principle of autonomy when he kills or wounds his enemy, then he has committed an unjust act, and hence no soldier could justly employ force. But we have assumed that at least some wars are just and hence some use of force and some killing in war is justified. If we also assume the moral equality among soldiers, it would seem that we have a serious problem because it would appear that soldiers could not justly engage each other in combat.

If we carefully examine the relationship that obtains between soldiers, we can see how it is that they do not necessarily show disrespect for each other's autonomy, violate principles of autonomy, when they employ force against one another. When I fight the enemy in war, I engage him *qua* soldier, not *qua* person. And my activity is not primarily one of *killing*, but rather of *restraining*. Phillips describes the importance of these distinctions as follows:

> To those who argue that there is no relevant difference between killing in war and murder in the case of one combatant killing another, we may reply that it is possible, given a well-thought-out doctrine for the justification of the use of force, to direct forceful actions in such a way that while the death of the enemy may be foreknown it is not willed. The purpose of combats as expressed in the actions of individual soldiers is the incapacitation or restraint of an enemy combatant from doing what he is doing as a soldier in a particular historical situation; it is not the killing of a man. This is the essence of the distinction between killing in war and murder in the case of combatants, and the moral relevance of the premise is exhibited in the obligation to acknowledge prisoner immunity, an obligation not incumbent upon someone who fails to observe the central distinction between the man and the combatant in the man.[16]

This seems to be getting at a very important distinction. But without a theoretical foundation, it could be used to justify anything by coming up with the appropriate description under which you could attack a person. For example, could I justify the killing of noncombatants *qua* contributors to the war effort? And am I really "restraining" when I bomb the sleeping enemy soldier, knowing there is no chance for him to gain "prisoner immunity"? We must ground the distinctions in the theory of autonomy in order to use them effectively.

The distinction captured in the use of "qua" is getting at the maxim soldiers adopt which distinguishes them from noncombatants. In order to understand this and illuminate the theoretical foundation for the insight under consideration, let us carefully consider the phenomenon of surrender. I allow the enemy to surrender; he is willing to accept my surrender. We are both willing to engage the enemy qua person, and insofar as we are so willing, we recognize the humanity, the autonomy, in the man. (Of course, insofar as we are not willing to do this, we are simply killing; we have adopted the attitude of a murderer and have disregarded the autonomy of our enemy.) Here talk of roles is instructive. The soldier was in the role of a combatant until he surrenders. Once he capitulates, he reverts to his natural – so to speak – state as a noncombatant. Since he is once again a noncombatant, agent-centered restrictions come into play to protect him: he no longer forfeits these protections by threatening others. This coincides with the discussion of principles generated by autonomy. When we use force against the enemy, our force is directed at a certain sort of agency manifested by the enemy that involves a particular threat to our agency.

What provides the justification for the use of force is the maxim he has adopted whereby he deliberately intends our harm, as we discussed in generating the Threat to the Capacity to Will Principle: we can resist the maxim. And clearly on this account, we could not derive a justification to bomb noncombatants *qua* contributors to the war effort, for example. The only sense that can be made of the distinction is that we can use force against the appropriate maxim. Even if ideologically they support the war, even if they hoped for illicit gains from an unjust war, their maxim is not the sort of threat to us that warrants the use of force against them. We now have a precise way of understanding the insight behind distinguishing between the enemy qua soldier and the enemy qua person. The distinction rests on the maxim involved.

In our discussion of the Means Only Principle we indicated that a threat to our body constitutes a threat to our autonomy insofar as the body is the material condition of our autonomous agency. So we can engage in acts that stop the threat to our persons. This notion was further explored in the Threat to the Capacity to Rationally Will Effectively Principle, a principle generated to address just such a situation as the one now under consideration. Even though the enemy soldier is not per se doing something unjust when he attacks me, I am nonetheless morally justified in resisting a threat to the necessary condition of my autonomy. But when the threat ceases, so does our justification for the use of violence. We recognize the autonomy of the enemy when we accept his surrender; we suspend our use of force against him because he has given up the maxim that warrants our use of force against him.

So we get a picture both of the way in which we justify the use of force against someone who cannot properly be said to be violating principles of autonomy; and we see how we can employ force against an enemy combatant while respecting his autonomy. This characterization of the phenomenon of surrender is supported by our principles generated by autonomy. We can use force against those engaged in directly harming us and as a response to a threat to our capacity to will effectively. Furthermore, we must recognize the autonomy of the enemy soldier by being willing to accept his surrender, when he gives up his maxim of intending harm, lest we devalue his agency. And of course, since noncombatants never have adopted the maxim to directly harm us, and since our use of force is justified as a reaction to certain maxims, we cannot attack noncombatants.

We can now come to a clearer understanding of the nature of combatancy. It entails a particular activity, one of direct harming. When a soldier becomes a POW, he is no longer a legitimate target because he has ceased, or has been prevented from carrying on with, a certain activity. He is no longer engaged in directly harming us. Here the Means Only Principle forcefully tells us what we *may not* justifiably do, that is, use force against one who is not involved in directly harming us. Once the enemy soldier surrenders, he does not pose a direct threat of physical violence. Notice that he is still a soldier; he has a right, even an obligation, to attempt to escape, reenter his own forces, and resume his role as a combatant. But right now he is a noncombatant because he is not engaged in the role of one engaged in directly harming us.

And let us be clear about the nature of this role. It is not as if the soldier shaving or sleeping is no longer a threat and therefore not a legitimate target simply because he is not now shooting at me. It is the nature of the general role of combatant that poses a threat independent of any particular action at any given time. Anscombe puts it in the following way:

> There is an argument which I know from experience it is necessary to forestall at this point, though I think it is visibly captious. It is this: on my theory, would it not follow that a soldier can only be killed when he is actually attacking. Then, for example, it would be impossible to attack a sleeping camp. The answer is that "what someone is doing" can refer either to what he is doing at the moment or to his role in a situation. A soldier under arms is 'harming' in the latter sense even if he is asleep.[17]

What is involved is a reasonable expectation of a disposition to harm. We still count the enemy soldier as having adopted the maxim of intending our harm. We can make a comparison to a man dedicated to his profession. He adopts a maxim whereby he intends to go to work whenever it is necessary; but it is not as if he is doing so all the time. He is neither always working nor always thinking about it. But if his supervisor calls him on the weekend and says some important work needs to be done, he drops what he is doing and goes to work.

In similar fashion, the soldier is not constantly threatening me. But if his sergeant wakes him up in camp and says it is time to attack, he attacks. Not every soldier on the battlefield is in reality a threat to me: he may be a complete coward or the worst shot in the world. But I cannot reasonably be expected to discern the coward from the warrior, the poor shot from the marksman, in a firefight. Any uniformed soldier must be considered a legitimate target in virtue of the maxim to do harm we must assume he has adopted.

To understand this from a different perspective, consider our reluctance to attack the enemy on religious holidays. If we know that the enemy does not conduct hostile acts on certain holidays, we often cease or curtail our combat activities. That we do so reflects our acknowledgement that during these times, the enemy has given up his maxim of intending harm. He is no longer threatening in the relevant ways.[18]

Seen in this light, we can reconsider the distinction between killing and restraining. While it might be true that it does not seem that we are merely attempting to *restrain* the sleeping soldier when we bomb him, we can see how he nonetheless remains a legitimate target. The notion "restraint" is supposed to capture is that we must be committed to accepting the surrender of those who would relinquish their maxim of intending harm. And if there are ways short of killing to achieve our military aims, we should use them. For instance, we could use psychological warfare to induce the enemy to surrender or get them to withdraw, etc. I cannot specify the criteria we might use to decide when such courses of action would be feasible; the point is that, if we could equally attain our ends by either killing the enemy or by using non-lethal means, we must be committed to the latter.

On the other hand, since even the sleeping soldier, in virtue of his role and his maxim, constitutes a constant threat until his actual surrender (or death, or incapacitation), our bombing him in his base camp while he sleeps is a legitimate tactic that has the same moral character of killing him in a firefight. For even in a firefight, our options are limited by the enemy's actions. That is, we can limit our use of force, restrain as oppose to kill, only if the enemy surrenders. His failure to surrender in either scenario – the base camp or the firefight – maintains him in his role as a threat. Beyond this, it is extremely important to recognize that the distinction between restraining and killing is a conceptual tool meant to support the notion that we are acting against a certain sort of maxim. The incapacitation of the enemy, *either* by killing or capturing, is construed as the restraining of him in the particular role he plays in virtue of the maxim he has adopted. For surely we have no license to either kill him *or* demand his surrender if he has not adopted a maxim of intending harm. It is his status as a soldier, committed to our harm, that justifies our demand that he submit to us in any way. So ultimately, restraining is a term used to designate *any* legitimate force used against the enemy soldier to set it apart from the harming or killing of a person who has not adopted the sort of maxim that would justify a use of force against him.

Since we have been discussing combatancy in terms of roles, we should briefly examine an argument that Christopher puts forward[19] and which I think is seriously flawed. He offers what he advertises as a Kantian way to justify the killing of soldiers. He says that soldiers have freely adopted their roles; it is their choice to be members of the profession of arms, so they are not being treated as mere means when they are killed or wounded. But this clearly is to misunderstand the Kantian project and what it means to treat someone as a mere means. Soldiers might have chosen to protect innocents against evil, but they have not chosen that there be evil, that they should have to put their lives on the line. They are, ultimately, being coerced, and that is precisely what it is to be treated as mere means.[20]

Christopher draws an analogy between a soldier and a waiter and says: "When one treats a waiter as a means to getting dinner, it is acceptable because we are treating him appropriately given the end that he has chosen for himself; that is, we are treating him as an end in himself."[21] This might be an acceptable understanding of the waiter's job, but it does not capture adequately the soldier's profession. It is much more appropriate and illuminative to draw an analogy between police officers and soldiers. It does not make sense to say that because a police officer has chosen his role that it is therefore acceptable for criminals to shoot the police, that a criminal treats a police officer as an end in himself when he kills the officer. The reason this strikes us as absurd is because the police officer's role, like that of the soldier and unlike that of a waiter, is *by definition* one of resisting coercion. Thus, when Christopher says, "...soldiers deserve the respect appropriate to that profession.... In wartime, soldiers may be killed because that is treating them appropriately as soldiers,"[22] it sounds morally repulsive, as if killing a soldier in war has the same moral significance as ordering a meal from a waiter. It seems unreasonable to say that I treat the enemy *respectfully* when I shoot him. This does not seem to match our intuitions. Rather, in order to understand the way that we can conceptually respect autonomy we must recognize the implications of the phenomenon of surrender. We will not harm those who can no longer harm us. This in turn leads us to recognize that we are reacting to the maxims of enemy soldiers as manifested in their actions of direct harming. In this sense, we are not treating the enemy in any particular way, per se, but are rejecting a threat to our own autonomy; our use of force, understood this way, is an act of self-respect, as Herman has pointed out.

We can understand this insight more clearly if we contrast combat with murder. The murderer is focused on his victim in a way that the soldier is not. That is, there is no particular action that the murderer's victim can take to lose his "victim" status. The murderer is bent on killing him *qua* person. Soldiers, on the other hand, can lose their combatant status by giving up their intention to harm. As such, soldiers are focused on the *actions* of their enemies; they are bent on restraining them *qua* threats/soldiers, not *qua* persons. In this way we can delineate the actions of soldiers from those of murderers and can understand the way in which soldiers do not violate principles of autonomy when they engage their enemies.

The route to the justification for killing soldiers is not as direct as Christopher would like it to be. I have offered a different path we can negotiate; however, we will not fully grasp the moral reality concerning the deaths of soldiers until we flesh out the implications of *jus ad bellum* issues, which I will explore in depth towards the end of this chapter and again in Chapter 6. But first, I need to return to something I said earlier, namely, that we must consider any uniformed enemy soldier a threat.

We should note that we grant exceptions for the wounded, medical personnel, etc. And these exceptions further highlight the nature of combatancy. A wounded soldier is not a threat to us, nor is the medic attempting to render first aid. They are, therefore, not legitimate targets, in accordance with The Means Only Principle (and, of course, the war convention, codified under international law).

Similarly, consider the purpose of banning certain weapons. Christopher observes that the prohibition against certain weapons derives from the fact that they continue to "incapacitate or to prevent recovery after one's status as a combatant ends."[23] One might wonder what difference it makes whether one steps on a clean punji stick or one covered with feces; whether one is hit with a para bellum round or a dum dum.[24] The reason the latter in each case is outlawed is because it continues to harm and inflict damage to the wounded soldier once his status as a combatant is ended. Once I am wounded to the point of incapacitation, I am no longer a combatant. Dum dum rounds are illegal because their purpose is to continue to harm me while I am a noncombatant; this is what it means for a weapon to cause unnecessary pain and suffering.

This might seem like a fine point, and in many instances a moot one: if I am instantly killed by a dum dum or para bellum, it does not really matter which one did the damage. But I am trying to point out the importance of noncombatancy and the essence of its justification. The decisive criterion used to distinguish the class of combatants from noncombatants is the activity of intended direct harming, the adoption of a maxim to harm. The difference between the unwilling enemy soldier and the jingoist enemy farmer might be seen in this way. If, on the battlefield, I happen upon the soldier, we must assume he will attempt to attack me. We assume the opposite about the farmer. Certainly there might be the odd aggressive agrarian who comes at me with a pitchfork. But he is an exception, one, we should note, who is committing a war crime by violating the conditions of his immunity.

And this further underscores the primacy of noncombatancy. A soldier is not a legitimate target for the farmer. The farmer may not attack the soldier. Only a soldier can attack a soldier. Why? Because the soldier is not a threat to the farmer: he is not engaged in harming him. There is no reasonable expectation that the soldier will harm the farmer because the soldier has not adopted a maxim directed at the harm of noncombatants. (Of course this discussion assumes that the soldiers are fighting justly and are not a threat to the civilian population.) The soldier is *in this respect* a noncombatant, which might be a surprising conclusion. But speaking precisely, someone is a combatant (or liable to be harmed) only when he adopts a certain maxim. I am trying to relay the idea that even though he is uniformed and armed, even that in itself does not strip him of his immunity. He must be engaged in harming. And he is engaged in harming only other soldiers. Soldiers can target other soldiers because they pose a real, specific, direct threat to each other. They cannot attack civilians, nor can they be attacked by civilians.

The notion of innocence as used in just war theory is meant to capture this distinction between those who harm and those who do not. As Anscombe says:

"Innocent" here is not a term referring to personal responsibility at all. It means rather "not harming." But the people fighting are "harming", so they can be attacked; but if they surrender they become in this sense innocent and so may not be maltreated or killed.[25]

The "guilty" would be those who are harming. We use the terms innocence and guilt in these senses in order to help clarify and reinforce the distinction between combatants and noncombatants. And our innocence in this sense is ours simply in virtue of our autonomy; noncombatancy is not a role, as I have said. As Murphy says, the guilty are: "all those who can reasonably be regarded as engaged in an attempt to destroy you."[26] Everyone else is innocent. And Murphy asks what moral view would lead to and support this conception of innocence and guilt:

I think it is this: a view which makes primary the status of persons as free or choosing beings who, out of respect for that status, are to be regarded as having the right to be left alone to work out their own lives – for better or worse. This is a basic right that one has just because one is a person. Respecting it is what Kant calls respecting the dignity of humanity by not treating people as a means only. Part of respecting them in this sense is not to use them as a means in one's calculations of what would be good for others. It is fine (indeed admirable) for a person to sacrifice himself for others by his own choice; but it is presumptuous (because lacking in respect for his choices) if I choose to sacrifice him. This is his business and not mine. I may only interfere with the person who, by his own evil actions, has forfeited his right against interference. Innocent persons by definition have not done this. And therefore it is absolutely wrong to sacrifice the innocent, though not to kill aggressors.[27]

Murphy, like Anscombe, envisions a situation where our attacker is doing something evil. We must reject this characterization of the enemy soldier who attacks me using just means, for reasons explained above. Nonetheless, we can use his argument for our purposes. Though we might not call the enemy evil, we can identify certain activities particular to him, ones not engaged in by noncombatants, that warrant our use of force against him. He is engaged in direct harming; we can interfere with him to prevent his interference with us or others.

We can see how the theory of autonomy bears on the distinction and how its features come together in this passage. It captures the notion that noncombatancy is not a role, but rather our basic status as persons. It shows the relevance of rights talk, in that they follow from autonomy; but autonomy itself is the bedrock, ours in virtue of our humanity (as Murphy says, quoted above, something one has "just because one is a person"). We see that as rational beings we are ends in ourselves, never to be treated as means only. And we see the condition under which one loses one's noncombatancy: one forfeits one's "right against interference" through actions that pose a threat to others. When we adopt maxims directed at the harm of autonomous agents, we lose the immunity from attack we otherwise enjoy in virtue of the respect we are owed as ends in ourselves. Combatancy is a role: we lose our innocence because of an activity in which we engage.

I have considered the phenomenon of surrender to indicate how autonomy underscores the relationship even between competing combatants. Now I want to consider surrender with respect to noncombatancy in order to show why it is morally impermissible to attack noncombatants.

I noted how we can understand the use of violence against enemy soldiers as restraining, not simply killing. We want to win, not kill. That is, we want to stop the aggression of the agent threatening us. If the enemy surrenders, we have accomplished our goal. Killing is not our goal. But it seems to be the case that when we attack the innocent, we are simply killing. How can they surrender? What activity is it that they are doing the cessation of which would restore the immunity we are violating? In a sense, they are not doing anything. They are not threatening us, so there is nothing they can stop doing. They are just victims. They are being used as a means only, a means to victory, a means to coerce their government or army. They can gain succor only if *someone else* does something: *we* decide to quit attacking them, or *their government* surrenders.

They have not adopted a maxim that warrants the use of force against them; hence, they cannot give up a maxim to get immunity. In advance, we are excluded from respecting their autonomy since in order to respect it we must be committed to recognizing some action on their part that would restore their immunity. In the case of a combatant, for instance, we understand our use of force against him, in terms of a maxim he has adopted as a soldier engaged in harming us; in accepting his surrender, we recognize that he has given up that maxim. What relevant distinction could apply to the noncombatant? The noncombatant has not adopted a maxim against which the use of force is justified.

We have justified self-defense in terms of resisting a discounting of our agency, or against a maxim of direct harming, or a threat to our capacity to will effectively. But the innocent are not threatening us in these ways such that we have to defend ourselves against them. Since the innocents are not engaged in harming us or threatening our agency, we are aggressors, engaged in unjust activity when we target them. We devalue the agency of the innocent; our action violates principles generated from autonomy; we have used the innocent merely as a means to some end, say the saving of our lives. We are using violence to preserve ourselves.

Even if, by targeting noncombatants, we are trying to stop an aggressor who does threaten us, according to the theory of autonomy, we cannot say we are "stopping aggression with force" employed against the aggression. For example, if we bomb an enemy's cities in order to lower his public's support for the war in hopes that the enemy will capitulate, it would be inaccurate to say we are using force against aggression. In terms of the theory we are advancing, the proper description of our action is that we are using force against the innocent as a means to stop the aggressor. We noted earlier that we can use force against a criminal in reaction to his impermissible maxim but cannot threaten his mother since she has not adopted an impermissible maxim. This notion applies here. We are using the innocent as means only and are using force against those who have neither devalued our agency nor adopted a maxim whereby they intend our harm. In effect, we defile the value we seek to respect.

Presumably we have resisted aggression because it constituted a threat to the autonomy of peaceful people who were not engaged in harming anyone. If, as a means of defense against aggression, we conduct an attack upon noncombatants who are not engaged in harming us, we defile the value out of respect for which we had initially acted. Also note that we have put the noncombatants, paradoxically, in a position much more dangerous than that of combatants. At least potentially, combatants can regain their immunity; their surrender can be accepted and their autonomy respected.[28] Noncombatants enjoy no such possibility; they can only be slaughtered. When we deliberately attack them, we simply refuse to respect their autonomy, and nothing they can do on their part can gain them that respect. We are murderers, they are victims, and only our decision to refrain from evil can save them.

Jus ad Bellum Considerations

Now I want to turn to a problem I promised earlier that I would discuss (Chapter 2), namely, that at some level, when soldiers die in combat, a violation of principles of autonomy has occurred. I have declined to discuss the actions of soldiers in terms of the devaluation of the enemy. In fact, I have shown how combat between combatants can be understood in a way wherein autonomy is respected. But the notion of devaluation does come into play in a very important way. Herman says that our use of violence against aggression is an act of self-respect. We reject actions that manifest a devaluation of our agency. I contend that even though the enemy soldier has not violated principles of autonomy, the principles are violated even when soldiers die or are injured in combat.

That is why I was careful to word the foregoing discussion in terms such that made it clear that the combatant does not violate principles of autonomy, or devalue the other combatant's autonomy while still leaving room to consider whether on some level, a violation has occurred. It is here that we must invoke *jus ad bellum* considerations. When someone starts an unjust war of aggression, he coerces people into roles as combatants. Since our noncombatancy is our status in virtue of our autonomy, an action that forces us into a role we would not and could not choose, especially a role that makes us a legitimate target, is an action that treats us as mere means: we cannot choose the undermining of our capacity to choose, i.e., will; the aggressor who starts the unjust war is the equivalent of a murderer who would use our lives for his purposes and deny us our capacity for any agency whatsoever.

Recall what Anscombe said. For someone to lose his immunity from attack, he must be "engaged in an *objectively* unjust proceeding" (quoted above, my emphasis). I am not sure exactly what Anscombe intends by "objectively unjust," but the phrase provides a way to complete our discussion in a satisfactory manner, one that accounts for our uneasiness if we were to conclude that, because combatants have not done something unjust, an injustice, therefore, has not been done, even in the face of the relentless slaughter mankind has visited upon himself.

When the leader of a regime starts an unjust war and places people into the hell of war, he has violated principles of autonomy by using as mere means everyone who is coerced into this hell. This includes his own soldiers and civilians, as well as those of his enemy. He has made them all victims. He has devalued the agency and autonomy of all concerned. So we can truly say that our self-defense is an act of self-respect, a resistance to being treated in ways that do not respect our status as ends-in-ourselves.

And this characterizes equally the situation of all involved, even that of the soldier of the unjust regime. He has been devalued, he has been coerced into this role. The devaluation occurred at the level of *jus ad bellum*. It does not matter that neither the enemy soldier nor the enemy regime has devalued him. His agency is being threatened, and he resists it. He may not conceive it this way. Soldiers generally see themselves as on the just side and see the enemy as the aggressors. But that he does not see that his own regime is the source of the discounting of autonomy does not deflect the guilt that the regime bears. He has been forced to fight; when he undergoes the horrors of war, his agency has been discounted; he has been used as a mere means.

Has this last discussion blurred the distinction I have labored to make? If even the death of a combatant constitutes in some way a violation of principles generated by autonomy, what is the substantial difference between combatants and noncombatants? What have we gained with the distinction?

When someone starts an unjust war of aggression, he has violated principles of autonomy at the level of *jus ad bellum*. Since the principles have already been violated, the question becomes for us: "What are we allowed to do in response to that aggression?" We are allowed to use force against combatants. We are not allowed to use force against noncombatants. The distinction still matters very much. Someone has committed an injustice, and we are permitted to respond. But we cannot respond in just any way; we must respond only in ways consistent with justice. The reason we see aggression as a crime is that it constitutes an unjust attack against people who are, in virtue of their natural status as human beings, noncombatants. Some of us adopt the role of combatants to resist the evil; we are liable to attack. But the point is that the rest remain noncombatants, and it remains unjust to attack them. From the perspective of *jus ad bellum*, the aggressor is condemned because he uses force against those who are not engaged in harming him. That condemnation extends to the realm of *jus in bello* for anyone who uses force against those who are likewise not engaged in harming. The principles remain in force.

I have argued that the purpose of the war convention is to uphold the distinction between combatants and noncombatants. I have given a philosophical justification for it that does not reduce to convention. My concern here is primarily with *jus in bello* issues, although we see that it operates at the level of *jus ad bellum*. We have clearly marked out the distinction between combatants and noncombatants in a way that will help us limit the horror of war in ways intended by the war convention. In terms of *jus in bello*, a soldier's responsibility, we have marked a path of righteousness, as it were, upon which he can tread and remain free of the guilt that might fall upon his political leaders for their *jus ad bellum* transgressions.

And the contrast between *jus in bello* and *jus ad bellum* is important to bear in mind. I had to have recourse to this brief discussion of *jus ad bellum* issues to help us keep our perspective. Our considered moral judgments tell us that there really is a difference between combatants and noncombatants and that slaughtering the latter constitutes a horror that is different in kind, not degree, from the killing of combatants. We feel combatants have a duty to protect the innocent, that is, noncombatants. So we engaged in an investigation in the realm of *jus in bello* to examine and account for our judgments in these regards. In spite of this, however, our considered moral judgments also tell us there is something horrible about war in general, and that every death in war is morally troubling. When we consider the blood on the hands of the political leader who transgresses *jus ad bellum* proscriptions, we can account for this latter sentiment. Even though we can exonerate soldiers if they fight justly and can charge them with the protection of the innocent, we can nonetheless lament also their plight as victims of evil.

I have presented the theoretical foundation for the distinction between combatants and noncombatants. I have argued that our noncombatancy is not a role, but is a status we enjoy in virtue of our humanity. Combatancy is a role imposed upon us. I have shown how it is possible for combatants to engage each other while still respecting autonomy. I have shown why an attack upon noncombatants is a violation of principles of autonomy. I have provided some insight into the conviction that every death in war is morally troubling, even the deaths of soldiers.

There remains an extremely important issue that I will note here but defer discussion of until later. It is clear from the theory of autonomy that any violation of the principles generated from autonomy is wrong. But is it the case that every deliberate attack upon noncombatants is a violation of principles generated from autonomy? There are circumstances under which it might seem permissible to kill the innocent. There are those who argue that, in order to prevent some horrible evil, say the subjugation of a nation to the rule of violence and hatred, we should be prepared to commit a lesser evil, say, the killing of the innocent. I will examine this critical issue in the chapter on supreme emergency and will consider whether the killing of the innocent in such circumstances follows from a principle that the innocent themselves should accept such that it would not constitute a violation of principles of autonomy.

I have tried to give a compelling justification for the distinction between combatants and noncombatants, and in so doing, provide a firm foundation for the war convention. Since I have argued that one of the primary motivations for the war convention is to uphold this distinction, if I have given a convincing justification for it in terms of autonomy, then I have provided support for my conviction that the theory of autonomy is a better champion of the war convention than its competitors.

Notes

1   Robert L. Phillips, *War and Justice* (Norman: University of Oklahoma Press, 1984), p. 60.
2   George I. Mavrodes, "Conventions and the Morality of War" in *War, Morality, and the Military Profession*, ed. Malham M. Makin (Boulder: Westview Press, 1979), p. 334.
3   Ibid., p. 337.
4   Ibid., p. 328.
5   Ibid., p. 332.
6   Ibid., p. 333.
7   Ibid., p. 337.
8   Ibid., p. 339.
9   Ibid., p. 338.
10 G.E.M. Anscombe, *Ethics, Religion, and Politics* (Oxford: Basil Blackwell, 1981), p. 64.
11 Christopher makes a similar point. p. 162.
12 Christopher, p. 25.
13 Mavrodes, p. 332. Although Anscombe does equivocate here on the meaning of innocent, she does recognize the point of the distinction in a clearer way. See later discussion in this chapter.
14 Ibid., p. 333.
15 Not every theorist makes the same mistake. Walzer realizes the different senses of innocence. He writes: "We call them *innocent* people, a term of art which means that they have done nothing, and are doing nothing, that entails the loss of their rights" (p. 146).
16 Phillips, p. 36.
17 Anscombe, p. 67.
18 I do not contend that we always self-impose a moratorium on combat during religious holidays; I only note that when we do, this is at least one of the reasons. Of course there are other reasons. We might not attack during certain religious holiday periods so that we do not incur the condemnation of other countries with whom we are not at war but who also hold the same holiday sacred.
19 Christopher, p. 126 n23.
20 I will discuss the nature and author of the coercion in greater detail in Chapter 6.
21 Christopher, p. 126 n23.
22 Ibid.
23 Christopher, p. 96.
24 Para bellum rounds are not designed to fragment upon contact; dum dum rounds are. When the latter hit a person, lead fragments can go off in various directions in the body, making diagnosis and treatment much more difficult than in the case of a wound caused by a para bellum round, which usually has a single entrance/exit wound.
25 Anscombe, p. 67. Here Anscombe recognizes the role of direct harming in the ascription of innocence or noninnocence. But there still seems to remain a tension in her thought. Recall her earlier characterization of the noninnocent as being involved in an "objectively unjust proceeding." So by her account, it seems to be the case either that no soldier can fight justly (since they are considered to be acting unjustly whenever they use force), or, if we grant the moral equality of soldiers and recognize that they are acting justly, we have no justification to use force against them (since we would be justified in using force only against those who were "unjustly attacking" us, to use Anscombe's words).

26   Murphy, p. 353.
27   Ibid., p. 361.
28   The sleeping soldier who dies from an artillery barrage on his base camp does not have at that particular time the opportunity to surrender, since no one is there to accept it. Nonetheless, conceptually, since the maxim he has adopted as a soldier makes him a legitimate target at all times, it gives him the potential at all times to surrender.

Chapter 5

Noncombatants

Generally, the class of noncombatants includes civilians, POWs, and wounded soldiers (whose wounds prevent them from carrying on with the fight). The class so described seems relatively uncontroversial: these are the innocents, in terms of just war theory. But problems persist concerning the status of noncombatants. In the last chapter I provided the theoretical grounding for the distinction between combatants and noncombatants. In this chapter I will argue that grounding the distinction as I have in the theory of autonomy gives us clearer, more consistent guidance than other theories do in deciding who is a legitimate target. There are two distinct issues that I will discuss.

The first issue concerns different accounts of the distinction given by other theorists. I want to show that their understanding of the distinction is inadequate and has results that even they would consider undesirable. I will focus on a few representative thinkers, principally Walzer, as I examine this issue.

The other issue I discuss concerns certain problems within the convention itself. I noted that certain provisions in international law, for instance, justify the killing of noncombatants/innocents. The issue here is that the convention authorizes, under certain circumstances, the killing of noncombatants while acknowledging that they *are* noncombatants: the case of reprisals is an example noted in Chapter 2. Because this attitude is so entrenched in the war convention, many theorists embrace it almost automatically. I want to examine this issue and suggest that the war convention, including international law, be revised in terms of the theory of autonomy. I want to challenge what has become, in many respects, accepted dogma. I contend that the clarity provided by a better understanding of the distinction between combatants and noncombatants gives us good reason to revise the war convention in the quest for consistency.

At the Borderlines of Combatancy: Different Accounts of the Distinction

Perhaps the best way to see the different ways the theory of autonomy and other theories see the distinction is to discuss the case of munitions workers. Walzer, for instance, justifies the bombing of munitions factories, saying that somehow the workers have been partially assimilated into the ranks of combatants.[1] On the other hand, food processing plants, and those civilians who work in them, are not considered legitimate targets, even if they produce army rations. Walzer writes: "The relevant distinction is not between those who work for the war effort and those who do not, but between those who make what soldiers need to fight and those who make what they need to live, like the rest of us."[2] He maintains that the people in the food processing plant have done "nothing peculiarly warlike,"[3] but those in, say, a tank factory, are, while assembling the tanks, doing something warlike:

> Those men and women who supply its (the army's) belly are doing nothing peculiarly warlike. Hence their immunity from attack: they are assimilated to the rest of the civilian population. We call them *innocent* people, a term of art which means that they have done nothing, and are doing nothing, that entails the loss of their rights.[4]

In one sense, it is hard to see what is peculiarly warlike about, for example, an uneducated factory worker putting the bolts on the road wheel of a tank. Nonetheless, the distinction has some merits and starts to get at the heart of the temptation to assimilate noncombatants into the combatant ranks. If they are producing something that is threatening and can be used as a direct instrument of war, should we not be able to stop the production of that item at its source, before it reaches the battlefield where it can harm our soldiers and increase the capability of the enemy to attain victory? Should we not be able to target the laboratory and civilian scientists engaged in making a nuclear weapon? Since it will make winning the war easier and might reduce casualties, there is some plausibility to answering "Yes" to both questions. I will argue, that if we do say yes, we are justified doing so only under some important qualifications.

Traditionally, just war theorists have found ways to justify the incorporation of civilians into the class of combatants, and it is important to understand their reasoning in this regard. Jeffrie Murphy says that combatants "are all those of whom it is reasonable to believe that they are engaged in an attempt at your destruction. Noncombatants are all those of whom it is not reasonable to believe this."[5] He makes the further distinction between occupations or actions that bear "contingent connections" to the war effort and those that have a necessary connection to that effort:

> The farmer's role bears a contingent connection to the war effort whereas the general's role bears a necessary connection to the war effort, i.e., his function, unlike the farmer's, is not logically separable from the waging of war. Or, following Thomas Nagel, the point can perhaps be put in yet another way: The farmer is aiding the soldier *qua* human being whereas the general is aiding the soldier *qua* soldier or fighting man. And since your enemy is the soldier *qua* soldier, and not *qua* human being, we have grounds for letting the farmer off. If we think of a justified war as one of self-defense, then we must ask the question "Who can be said to be attacking us such that we need to defend ourselves against him?"[6]

Given such criteria, one could reasonably view a munitions factory worker as involved in an activity directly and necessarily aimed towards our destruction; hence, he becomes a legitimate target. We can make the following further observations that distinguish a farmer from a general or even a munitions factory worker. The farmer, presumably, is engaged in an activity that he has always done and that is independent of the occurrence of a war or even the existence of an army. And his product is needed by both the army and civilians, and it is needed in times of peace as well as war. The munitions worker produces something that is only used by the army and is useful only for the war effort; it is not needed in times of peace. And it is reasonable to assume that the munitions worker would not be engaged in such an activity were there no army or war; it is not reasonable to assume the same about the farmer.

We can see the general lines of argument, then, for targeting certain civilians,[7] who, by virtue of their activities and the products of these activities, lose their noncombatant immunity. The distinctions drawn are important, and their effects offer at least the hope of limiting the horror of war. But the reasoning behind it has led to unacceptable consequences, which are results, ultimately, of the logical implications of just war theory conceived along these lines.

Consider that, for instance, the U.S. military advances four elements of national power: political, economic, informational, military. We assess the strength of a nation by assessing the strength of these pillars. Against our adversaries, we decide how best to target each pillar: they all are considered, in some form or another, legitimate targets. Walzer, for instance, expresses how the process of reasoning proceeds whereby "civilians are, as it were, incorporated into (the) hell" of war[8] by being deemed legitimate targets:

> We shift to the distinction between soldiers as a class and civilians; and then we concede this or that group of civilians *as the processes of economic mobilization* establish its *direct contribution* to the business of fighting. Once the contribution has been plainly established, only "*military necessity*" can determine whether the civilians involved are attacked or not.[9] (My emphasis)

Walzer's description here is representative of the type of reasoning that begins the incorporation of civilians into the ranks of combatants. Usually the justification for either explicitly targeting those who are considered noncombatants or for partially assimilating civilians into the ranks of combatants is in terms of military necessity. It will be worthwhile to examine this concept before we continue.

Christopher explains military necessity in the following way:

> military necessity has been used to refer to a justification for setting aside or overriding the *jus in bello* principles found in the laws of war for the sake of military objectives...expediency receives considerable emphasis under the rubric of military necessity as a justification for violating the sanctity of innocents.[10]

Military necessity, then, is a concept or doctrine soldiers and statesmen appeal to as a justification for undertaking measures in war that would normally be proscribed. That is, given the inherent tensions between "military objectives on one hand and humanitarian principles...on the other hand,"[11] humanitarian interests will often be overridden in order to achieve a particular military objective. The objective is considered so important that we must do whatever it takes to attain it. We can understand military necessity in two primary ways.

The first way is to see military necessity as justifying overriding the rules of war whenever it makes it easier to achieve our military objective. But if we mean this by military necessity, it immediately becomes inconsistent with the purpose of the war convention. If we were justified under military necessity to violate the immunity of innocents whenever it simply made it easier to attain our objectives, then the war convention would provide no protections for noncombatants. There would be no meaningful restrictions on the use of force with respect to noncombatants. Any protections they would have would be simply a matter of expedience. Given the purpose of the war convention, this conception of military necessity cannot be the accepted one.

The other way to understand military necessity is to see it as a justification for doing what is normally proscribed only under circumstances where such a course of action would considerably increase our chance of winning or considerably decrease our casualties. This conception initially seems much more palatable than the first, and not so obviously incompatible with the purpose of the war convention. It would keep protections for noncombatants in place except under the more extreme circumstances. But even this seems inconsistent with the purposes of the war convention. You must be prepared to lose the war, or not fight a particular war if you felt you needed to use impermissible means to win it. To see that this is a plausible point of view, consider the following.

Suppose the U.S. was at war with a small Third World country that had no reasonable chance of winning on the battlefield in conventional combat between combatants. Suppose then, that they bombed Dallas somehow, or used a small nuclear device to destroy the city center. If they appealed to military necessity, saying that their course of action was the only one that offered the least hope of victory, would we therefore exonerate them of their crime? I do not think that we would. That we would not points to a deep recognition that we require more discrimination than military necessity makes in seeking moral justification of our use of force.

I have not discussed all the issues attendant to the concept of military necessity. I merely wanted to give sufficient explanation of it to facilitate the rest of this discussion. I want to point out that if we grant protections to noncombatants based solely on considerations of military necessity, we could get undesirable results – under either version of military necessity I have described. If you are on the weaker side, even under the stronger version of military necessity, there seem to be no meaningful limits to what you can do. If you are justified to do what considerably increases your chance of victory and the only course of action that would do that involves the deliberate targeting of the innocent, then you would be justified in doing so. In the end, military necessity itself only discriminates between actions that are conducive to victory and those that are not. It does not discriminate between combatants and noncombatants. So military necessity would recognize noncombatant immunity only on the basis of expedience; it would grant exceptions to that immunity also on the basis of expedience. In effect, it would not provide any real restrictions on the use of force with respect to noncombatants. We need other reasoned principles to guide us in determining who are legitimate targets. So we must turn our attention to an investigation of what might count as an adequate principle for making this determination and putting proper constraints upon the demands of military necessity.[12]

One of the points to bear in mind is that this conviction – that under certain circumstances civilians become legitimate targets – has more than a little force. And under the pressure of war and desire for victory, the criteria are broadened and the restrictions loosened. Christopher writes:

> Under existing international and national laws the prohibition against harming innocents may be subjectively overridden for the purpose of military advantage, or even military convenience. Moreover, no distinction is made between military necessity in terms of tactical, strategic, or political objectives. Understood this way, military necessity amounts to a claim that certain blatantly immoral acts are justified on no other basis than that they might contribute in some way to military objectives.[13]

This phenomenon is problematic on two levels. The first level concerns application of the theory. There seems to be a certain degree of arbitrariness in deciding what contributes directly to the war effort. Theorists attempt to mitigate the arbitrariness by appealing to certain reasoned principles that are supposed to restrict the exceptions in relevant ways.

Both Walzer and Murphy have given us insights to the standard sorts of principles used for assimilating civilians into the ranks of combatants. Murphy talks of roles that have a necessary connection to the war effort, and Walzer talks about the distinction "between those who make what soldiers need to fight and those who make what they need to live."[14] I think we can capture the sentiment behind both views with Walzer's notion that those who make a "direct contribution to the business of fighting" are assimilated into the ranks of combatants.[15]

We might initially think that such a criterion of deciding whom to target would yield clear guidance and would sanction actions that unproblematically correspond to our considered moral judgments. But consider the case of war in the desert. Can a soldier fight without water, especially in the desert? He needs water as much as ammunition; in fact, he might need it more than ammunition. He can conceivably avoid the enemy for a couple of days through stealth and proper tactics and thereby do without ammunition. But he cannot avoid the heat, and he will surely die within a few days without water.

Reasoning like this, we can justify bombing the Iraqi water purification plants. The civilian workers contribute directly to the war effort, I suppose, by producing water the soldier needs, so they become legitimate targets. Here just war theory will want to say, and should say, that these civilians were not legitimate targets: they were producing something the soldiers needed *qua* human beings, not *qua* soldiers.[16] Further, their activity was the same as before the war, and their product is needed in time of peace as well as war, and is needed by the civilians as well as the soldiers. Many just war theorists (Walzer, for example[17]) condemn the targeting of these plants on several grounds (one important consideration is its collateral effects, which I will discuss in detail in Chapter 6 when I address the Doctrine of Double Effect). Nonetheless, if we use "direct contribution to the war effort" as our criterion to decide whom we can target, we can justify targeting the water plant workers. This is an undesirable result, even for Walzer (see note 17).

In general, this way of thinking, using this sort of criterion, yields unacceptable results. The military strategist can always show how some proposed target contributes directly to the enemy's war effort: in fact, it would be difficult to overestimate the importance of water to the enemy's war effort, especially in the desert. And what if production increased to support the war effort? The strategist could further justify his plan by saying that the extra water was not in fact the same product as produced in peacetime and for civilians also. It was water specifically for the soldier *qua* soldier.[18]

We might say that the strategist has misapplied the theory. But whether we accept his line of argument is not the point. The point is that conventional just war theory at least countenances such argumentation. In this case, our considered moral judgments are not unambiguously in line with the action sanctioned. Murphy is aware of the ambiguity. He says that workers in a munitions factory that makes only bombs can be regarded as combatants because what they make (bombs) bear a necessary connection to the war effort and support the soldier *qua* soldier.[19] But he remains worried about drawing the distinctions this way and granting this first exception to the war convention:

> But what about workers in munitions factories that only in part supply the war effort, e.g. they make rifles both for soldiers and for hunters? Or workers in non-munitions factories that do make some war products, e.g. workers in companies like Dow Chemical, which make both Saran Wrap and Napalm? Or workers in ball bearing factories or oil refineries, some of their product going to war machines and some not? Here, I submit, we do have genuine borderline cases.[20]

And the ambiguity is such that if we carry this line of reasoning a bit further we get results that are even more in conflict with our considered judgments. Consider the civilians in England and the United States during World War II who saved their tin cans for the war effort. Surely this is not generally an activity carried on in peacetime as well. And they saved the cans to contribute directly and deliberately to the war effort. Do they become legitimate targets? There is a way of reasoning available that could justify it, and for reasons like this, cases like these, we need to revise just war theory. The bombing of people who produce water for their countrymen or who save tin cans, even though such activity contributes directly to the war effort, seems to conflict with our moral intuitions.

Perhaps, then, we should say that a combatant is one who puts on a military uniform, bears arms, and goes to meet his enemies in the field of battle. Perhaps it is best to say from the outset that we simply cannot bomb civilians, even those who work in munitions factories. If we rule them out as targets, surely the immunity of the farmer, water purification plant worker, and tin can-saver remains intact. We must consult the theory of autonomy. For instance, are we prepared to treat these civilians with less respect than they are due, even less than that given combatants? As we noted earlier, they cannot surrender, as it were, so these noncombatants, paradoxically, wind up in a situation much more dangerous than that of combatants.

I understand that part of the issue here is that on some accounts, munitions workers are considered combatants. But I have tried to show that the reasoning that incorporated them into the ranks of combatants has undesirable results. We should, then, be suspect of the "direct contribution"[21] criterion. I contend that munitions factory workers are not combatants. The relevant principle to consult here is whether they have adopted the sort of maxim that justifies our use of force against them. Since they are not involved in direct harming, have not adopted this sort of maxim, they are not legitimate targets. They do not threaten the conditions of our autonomy by manifesting the specific, violent expression of willing that devalues our agency. In short, their actions do not meet the conditions that would justify our use of force against them.

Recall Murphy's injunction to "accept...the principle 'noncombatant until proven otherwise'" (quoted earlier). If we consider the munitions workers from this perspective, it becomes increasingly difficult to justify attacking them. We do not conceive their status in terms of rights gained or lost. They are, intrinsically, noncombatants, and they have engaged in none of the activities that would constitute direct harm against us. Even if they are enthusiastic supporters of their government's war, even if they wish us ill will, this sort of ideological commitment does not manifest the sort of devaluation of us that justifies the use of force against them. And, *a fortiori*, workers in water plants and collectors of tin cans retain their immunity.

The notion that it is the adoption of a certain sort of maxim that makes one a combatant warrants some further explanation. Consider the case of the following munitions factory worker. He rabidly hates the enemy with whom his country is at war. He wants to do harm to them. But he is too old to join the military, so he starts working at the munitions factory as the best way of doing harm to the enemy. It certainly appears that he has adopted a maxim of directly harming. But while we can say he has adopted a maxim of harming, it is not a maxim of *direct* harming in the relevant sense and the sense that helps us make clear and consistent distinctions in just war theory.

Think of a paralyzed person who adopts a maxim of harming us. No matter how he might hate us and desire our demise, it is not reasonable to consider him a threat. A maxim is a principle that guides action. Only if an action follows from the maxim, or could reasonably be assumed to follow from a particular maxim, is it a maxim to which we can react. Thus, when we talk about a maxim of direct harming, we are concerned with a maxim from which a certain sort of action typically follows. Actions that result in the production of munitions could follow even from maxims that do not intend our harm in the way that the enthusiastic worker does. It is not part of being a munitions worker that you have adopted a maxim of direct harming. If the action (producing munitions, in this case) does not imply such a maxim, then we cannot legitimately attack those performing such actions.

Furthermore, we cannot probe the depths of people's souls to see why they are working in the munitions factory. Since we are seeking a reasoned principle to give us clear guidance about whom we can legitimately target, it seems appropriate to attach this notion of direct harm to maxims from which follow activities that typically pose a direct threat to us. Soldiers in this respect are clearly different from munitions factory workers.[22]

So I offer this different principle, grounded in the theory of autonomy, as a way of deciding who can be considered legitimate targets. If we restrict our use of force against only those who have adopted a maxim whereby they intend our direct harm, we will have clearer, more consistent guidance. We can still target soldiers and those who pose a real threat to us: we can fight our wars effectively using permissible means. On the other hand, I think we get a clearer picture of who should be counted in the ranks of noncombatants: we more consistently support the purpose of the war convention by making it more difficult to let the pressures of military necessity allow us to assimilate noncombatants into the combatant class. Furthermore, since this principle allows us to reject the sort of reasoning that might allow us to bomb savers of tin cans, it corresponds better with our considered moral judgments.

I want to reconsider the case of munitions factories. What are the negative implications of my stance; is the reasoned principle I embrace for discriminating among possible targets incompatible with some of our general intuitions about how we should be allowed to fight a war? Surely the munitions factory should remain a legitimate target, some will say. A consequentialist argument here might be effective and appealing. If we destroy the munitions plant, we can save many, many more lives on both sides than those lost in the bombing. If the munitions do not reach the field of battle, our soldiers will not be killed by them. Also, since the enemy lacks the needed supplies, they cannot engage in combat. Fewer of them die on the field of battle. Ultimately, surrender or peace terms come sooner, and fewer people are harmed.

I concede that the factory itself might indeed remain a legitimate target, although the theory of autonomy imposes restrictions on us that are not required by consequentialism. We cannot decide whether or not to bomb the factory based on a calculation of total number of possible casualties, thereby subordinating the value of individuals to some conception of general good. If we cannot target it without at the same time targeting the civilians, we are precluded on that account from bombing it.

Nonetheless, we have assumed the justness of some wars, so the principles we generate in our theory must be compatible with at least some of our practical intuitions about war fighting. That is, munitions factories do seem to be particularly important targets. And if a factory remains a legitimate and important target, we must see if there is a way of attacking it that would be consistent with the theory of autonomy and the purpose of the war convention.

Under the theory of autonomy, we could target the factory, but we must be committed to issuing a warning that we are going to bomb it. In this way, we maintain our commitment to the war convention and agent-centered restrictions by recognizing the autonomy of the workers and allowing them the option of not going into harm's way, instead of involuntarily incorporating them into hell. By providing an option for individual workers, we do not include them outright in a calculation of the greatest good by deciding in advance which victims shall die for the benefit of overall welfare. This is not an outrageous suggestion. FM 27-10 says:

a. Treaty Provision
   The officer in command of an attacking force must, before commencing a bombardment, except in cases of assault, do all in his power to warn the authorities. (HR, art. 26)
b. Application of Rule. This rule is understood to refer only to bombardments of places where parts of the civilian population remain.
c. When Warning is To Be Given. Even when belligerents are not subject to the above treaty, the commanders of United States ground forces will, when the situation permits, inform the enemy of their intention to bombard a place, so that the noncombatants, especially the women and children, may be removed before the bombardment commences.[23]

We should extend the protection offered by this provision to civilian workers in munitions factories and other sites involved in endeavors that directly support the war. Note that this provision does not *explicitly* grant munitions plants its protections. In this respect, it points to the tension within the war convention concerning noncombatant immunity. It also indicates a recognition at a deep level of our general responsibilities towards noncombatants.

In terms of the tension, on one hand we stipulate a requirement to warn civilians in proximity of the target area of an impending attack. On the other hand, we consider munitions factories and their civilian workers legitimate military targets, implying that no warning is required before attacking them. They seem to have the same status as any purely military target. This already seems at least problematic since in both cases the victims are acknowledged to be civilians. For those who are not happy with this example and still want to maintain that the munitions workers are not per se civilians, consider the following:

Investment, bombardment, assault, and siege have always been recognized as legitimate means of land warfare....
   Factories producing munitions and military supplies...warehouses storing munitions and military supplies, ports and railroads being used for the transportation of military supplies, and other places devoted to the support of military operations or the accommodation of troops may also be attacked and bombarded even thought they are not defended.[24]

This passage, referencing *Annex to Hague Convention No. IV*, explicitly allows the bombing of "ports and railroads being used for the transportation of military supplies." Now, unless countries build new ports and new railroads specifically for military purposes whenever a war comes about, we must assume these to be the same ports and railroads upon which civilian commerce depends. Furthermore, the workers here must be primarily civilians, plying the trade they plied before the war. In short, we must acknowledge that these sites are primarily or significantly civilian in character.

So if we then conceive the distinction between combatants and noncombatants in terms of an activity of direct harming, the orthodox theory's treatment of the different situations seems conflicted. In one case of planned bombardment, we are constrained to warn civilians, yet in the other (bombing ports and railroads), no such constraint is imposed. And in both cases, the civilians involved are uncontroversially civilians since they have not adopted maxims of intending to harm.

We can, however, resolve the conflict, the tension, by understanding the treatment of the two groups of civilians in terms of the perspective of autonomy. If we must attack a place where primarily civilians work, we must warn them no matter what the target is, be it a neighborhood or a factory. We must respect their status as noncombatants: they are not involved in an activity that makes them combatants. In this way, we are not simply killing: there is something these workers can do such that their immunity would remain intact. We have allowed them to not go to the factory, for instance, thus granting them the moral equivalent of the surrender we allow combatants. The civilian, by having now an option, is not simply a victim; we have recognized him *qua* human being and granted him the respect he is due.

I am neither being callous nor naïve when I say we have provided an option. That is, certainly the choices for these workers will be difficult. They have to feed their families and can probably find very few jobs that are unrelated to the war effort. But at least we have not been presumptuous in making the choice for them. Beyond that, our project is to limit the hell of war; we cannot make sublime that which by its very nature is tribulation. People will suffer; to eliminate suffering caused by war, we must eliminate war. But that is a subject that must wait for a different discussion.

There is another important point to take from the quote above concerning a recognition, deep within the convention, that military necessity does not *void* noncombatant immunity: innocents remain innocents no matter what course of action is deemed necessary for victory. We must warn the enemy of a bombardment "so that noncombatants...may be removed," as FM 27-10 says. We need to bring this recognition to the surface, consciously embrace it, and consistently apply it to just war theory. If we are charged with protecting noncombatants, we should extend that protection to them to the maximum extent, no matter where they reside or work.

There are further unsettling implications of the way I have drawn the boundaries and imposed limitations. Have I tied our hands too tightly and restricted us from attacking targets that must really be attacked? Are we not, in some cases, morally required to attack some targets? And if the only way to attack them effectively is by using the element of surprise, should we not be allowed to attack them without warning? Consider civilian scientists working in a laboratory producing nuclear weapons. Must we refrain from attacking them or must we give them warning? Suppose the enemy had kept the location of the site secret and was unaware that we had discovered its whereabouts. Warning them would allow them to either greatly improve defenses or move critical equipment. I am inclined to say here that we can, and should, attack the site, and do so without warning.

There is an important distinction between what the nuclear weapons developers do and what tank factory workers do. In the case of the tank factory, we can wait till its product gets into the hands of the combatant and attack it on the battlefield. Even if warning the tank factory prevents our successful interdiction, at least we will get the opportunity to engage the tank, combatant against combatant on the field of battle. Of course, in one sense, this is precisely what we wanted to avoid. We want to prevent our enemy from arming himself. But if the choice is between targeting noncombatants or increasing the risk to our combatants, in general, within limitations to be discussed in Chapter 6, we must choose the latter and enforce the war convention in a consistent fashion.

But the case of the nuclear lab is different. There is a meaningful sense in which we can say that, if we do not stop the production of the weapon, we will not get a chance to defeat it on the battlefield, once it gets into the hands of combatants. There will be no intervening battlefield to engage it combatant-on-combatant. In a very real sense it is reasonable to say that the weapon goes from the lab to our backyard. In this sense, the scientists employ the weapon and are, therefore, directly engaged in harming us.[25] We are justified in defending ourselves against this type of threat.

One might argue for an exception in the case of a lab that produces tactical nuclear weapons[26] since these types of weapons are designed to attack armies in the field. That might be so, but can we reasonably determine that the lab produces only tactical nuclear weapons and not strategic nuclear weapons whose express purpose is to attack the heart of a nation, destroying millions of its noncombatants? I think it unreasonable to make, or even ask that we make such a distinction. However, if it were known that a specific lab produced only tactical nuclear weapons, we might consider giving a warning, although the very nature of nuclear weapons makes even this dubitable, as I discuss below. Besides, the technology for one is the same as for the other. Again, given the nature of nuclear weapons, we have good reason to lump all laboratories that produce nuclear weapons into the same category.

There are further distinctions between the tank factory worker and the nuclear laboratory scientist. Indeed, the scientist in many ways is considered as already assimilated into the ranks of combatants. He has to have security clearances equal to those of any military member. He works for the government, or the department of defense.[27] Your average assembly line worker in the tank factory requires minimal, if any, security clearance. He may or may not work for the department of defense: he might, for example, work for Chrysler Corporation, maybe even in the same plant where, a month before, he produced sedans.[28] And, finally, the scientist is working on a weapon that he knows is destined for the civilians of his enemy.

We must reject his devaluation of us, of our innocents. In a real sense, he has adopted a maxim of deliberate harm. We can plausibly argue that he has adopted an impermissible maxim insofar as he intends his weapon to target noncombatants, those not engaged in harming him.

These distinctions are not arbitrary, nor do they set us upon the same line of reasoning that justifies, or tries to justify, targeting water purification plant workers. We can target the lab, and only the lab, and we can do so because there really is no other way to combat its product, and its workers really are assimilated into the ranks of combatants. We cannot wait to engage it on the field of battle because it is never intended to get to the field of battle. Since the weapon essentially goes from the lab to its target – granted, there are a few stops in between, but none of the stops are the battlefield – it is as if the scientists employ the weapon and in this sense, they are combatants. The intention of the weapon itself is to undermine the war convention and obliterate the distinction between combatant and noncombatant.

This discussion raises, immediately, concerns about any nuclear weapons,[29] but that itself is a separate issue I cannot address at this time. I do realize, though, that my argument implies that our own labs are legitimate targets for our enemies (which we must assume they are, to the extent that our enemies know where they are). But there are other factors one must consider when deciding on whether or not to engage a particular target: what is the nature of the regime making the weapons, do they have a stated policy that would suggest they would use the weapon on civilians as soon as they developed it – something like a commitment to the eradication of the Jewish state, for example. In any case, my concern here is with conceptual refinement of the war convention.

But given this is my purpose, some might say that I am capitulating to military necessity, that I am as guilty as any theorist of this concession. I can deflect this charge. My justification rests on the assumption that the scientists are assimilated into the ranks of combatants. But since we have no option of engaging the weapon on the battlefield, it seems plausible to say that the scientists are employing the weapon; they are directly harming. The assumption seems reasonable and forms the basis upon which real distinctions can be drawn. Furthermore, the distinction rests on one of our basic justifications for self-defense, namely, that we use force against those who are directly harming us. This understanding of the issue will strictly limit the extent to which military necessity can influence our decisions.

There are other considerations in terms of the theory of autonomy, but we can accommodate them. For instance, one might ask how it is we respect the autonomy of the scientists. Do we give them the opportunity to surrender? We can offer them the equivalent of surrender. One might reasonably argue that they must see themselves as incorporated into the military machine and involved in directly harming us, given the criteria of our earlier discussion. And we could publicize our policy towards such sites (i.e., that we consider them legitimate targets for the stated reasons) so that the scientists could make their own choices. That is, they could decline their work and regain their immunity. Of course, I have not mentioned the status of the poor janitor who cleans up the lab, or receptionists, etc. Innocents like these pose problems for the theory in every case. It is for these issues that we invoke the Doctrine of Double Effect (DDE).[30]

Military Necessity and the Deliberate Targeting of Noncombatants

Let us turn to our second level of concern: the tensions or inconsistencies within the war convention itself. One can already see the tensions involved in the preceding discussion. The purpose of the war convention is to protect noncombatants, yet under certain conditions, for military necessity, the convention itself authorizes attack against civilians. I am not concerned here with the issue that the war convention incorporates, correctly or not, certain civilians into the ranks of combatants in virtue of their wartime activities, as in the case of munitions workers. Rather, the convention authorizes attacks against civilians in full recognition that they remain noncombatants/innocents. It is not that the convention as a whole endorses its own violation. Rather, certain facets of the convention, such as various international laws dealing with war, seem to conflict with the general purpose of the convention. They at least infuse the convention with ambiguity.

Paul Christopher provides an example of the sort of ambiguous guidance embodied in parts of the war convention. He cites the Nuremberg Principles:

> VI(B) War Crimes: Violations of the laws or customs of war which include but are not limited to, murder, ill-treatment or deportation to slave-labor or for any other purpose of civilian population of or in occupied territory, murder or ill-treatment of prisoners of war or persons on the seas, killing of hostages, plunder of public or private property, wanton destruction of cities, towns or villages, or devastation *not justified by military necessity* [italics added].[31]

It is the caveat captured by the italicized phrase that worries Christopher and is the sort of ambiguity I address. It implies that one can invoke military necessity and henceforth be justified in committing horrible crimes. The ambiguities and tensions have entrenched themselves into the orthodoxy of just war theory in such a fashion that they almost seem to dictate the terms of the debate. Many just war theorists accept the ambiguities and inconsistencies rather than resolve them.

For instance, it seems simply to be accepted that munitions plant workers are legitimate targets, when in fact this should be a topic of considerable debate, as our discussion attests. We begin with a general justification to target combatants, then, given the war convention's military necessity proviso, theorists extend the permission for attack to include those who produce something that can harm us. Perhaps there is justification for this, and we will reexamine the issue below. But the point I make now is that currently many just war theorists, without due reflection, simply assume that munitions workers are legitimate targets. But the case of reprisals will make this point clearer:

> Reprisals are acts of retaliation in the form of conduct which would otherwise be
> unlawful, resorted to by one belligerent against enemy personnel or property for
> acts of warfare committed by the other belligerent in violation of the law of war,
> for the purpose of enforcing future compliance with the recognized rules of
> civilized warfare.[32]

Here is a more explicit example of a theory at odds with itself. I will not engage
the arguments for or against reprisals. The issue here is that the theory itself
expressly says that one belligerent, in order to seek compliance with the law by
another belligerent, can legally perform some action that is normally considered
illegal. This justification extends to the killing of innocents. Christopher tells us:

> (D)uring World War II when the French Forces of the Interior continued to fight
> German occupation forces in France, Germany refused to treat members of the
> French Resistance as combatants – even though they wore insignia, carried their
> arms openly, and were in touch with both the Allies and the French Provisional
> Government in Algeria – and subjected them to summary execution despite
> formal protests by the Provisional Government. The French Forces of the Interior
> threatened reprisals, and when the executions did not stop, they shot eighty
> German prisoners under their control.[33]

This is a problematic example insofar as the law expressly prohibits reprisals against
prisoners. But it is a telling example insofar as many theorists, and much of the
international community, justify reprisals even against prisoners.[34] In any case,
according to the law, a codified part of the war convention, illegal or immoral actions
can be sanctioned under certain circumstances. And one result of this sort of policy is
the enduring conviction on the part of many -- theorists, statesmen, and soldiers -- that
the slaughter of innocents is justified. This is clearly a problem for just war tradition.

But let us remember the issue we are addressing here. I have contended that
the tensions within the war convention have become so entrenched as to dictate the
terms of the debate. They have permeated our collective consciousness. To
support my point here, I refer to Christopher himself. He offers a lucid discussion
of reprisals in which he generally condemns them. They are a dangerous
concession to military necessity and can justify too much:

> When the doctrine of reprisals is coupled with the current doctrine regarding
> military necessity, the potential for "lawlessness" becomes disturbing. If one
> warring faction, the one losing the war, invokes military necessity to justify
> violating the laws of war, then the opposing side is then justified in violating the
> same or other laws in reprisal.[35]

He is aware that reprisals can involve the deliberate slaughter of innocents and
have the potential of reducing "humanitarian laws (to) ideals to be followed just in
case you are winning and your opponent continues to follow them, even if he is
losing."[36] But what is interesting is his ultimate resolution. He justifies reprisals
as long as they are conducted as part of a strategic or national decision. Tactical

commanders could not make the decision. The decision would have to come from the highest political leaders:

> If one adopts our formulation of the doctrine of reprisals, the cases where they might legitimately be conducted can be subsumed under the doctrine of military necessity. If so, then reprisals might be justified using the same criteria that we used to justify military necessity. That is, reprisals are not a military option, but a political one subject to the same *jus ad bellum* conditions as the initial resort to force. In no case may reprisals be authorized as a tactical or an operational decision...Given the circumstances where a belligerent nation employs, as a matter of policy, actions that are illegal and immoral, the nation against whom such actions are perpetrated may employ the same or other illegal/immoral actions in reprisal, provided that such action is a political decision reached in accordance with the traditional *jus ad bellum* criteria.[37]

I applaud Christopher's efforts to refine the war convention and make it more consistent. He sees himself as having refined "the traditional *jus ad bellum* criteria" for the justification of reprisals. But he actually still seems to be in the grasp of the same ideology. He has only transferred the problem, swept it under the carpet only to have it appear as an ugly bulge in some other part of the room. He does not seem to be aware that he is offering the same caveat that worried him earlier (quoted above) where appeal to military necessity could justify that which should not be justified, hence, once again relegating "humanitarian principles to the status of ideals," to use his words (quoted above). His purpose was to provide a means of strictly limiting this particularly repugnant practice. If his solution provides a measure of success, it is only contingent. He has done nothing to correct the fundamental conceptual flaw in the theory as understood now. His method will provide relief only to the extent that the civilian authorities are more reluctant to use such means than their military counterparts or less susceptible to the fear of losing. But from the perspective of the conceptual and moral force of the theory, he is still willing to authorize the same problematic actions.

The problem with Christopher's solution is that it does not seem to offer a principled way to show that the victims (of reprisals, in this instance) become combatants/legitimate targets. If we may not attack a certain class of people on certain grounds, what difference does it make where the decision to attack them is made? If we may not shoot prisoners on the grounds that they are noncombatants, then it would seem that the only way we would be justified in killing them as the result of a political decision is if that decision somehow made the prisoners combatants. But I do not see any way that this could be. Christopher, at least, has not provided an explanation. So, whether the decision to kill the innocent is made at the military or the political level, the innocent remain innocent, and the decision is immoral.

Furthermore, it is not at all clear that soldiers would be exonerated if they killed prisoners on the command of their political leaders. The plea that they were only following superior orders seldom exonerates soldiers from their crimes.[38] I cannot explore this issue in more detail here but merely note it as another problem with the view under discussion.

Christopher's view is representative of these sorts of problems within the war convention.[39] And we can see that these problems are not nuances or obscure facets of the just war tradition. Rather, they are orthodox views, codified into the organon of the theory and embedded into the consciousness of its spokespeople. There are dissenters and critics of the theory: I have quoted some already.[40] They do not condemn the tradition per se, but challenge its inconsistencies and shortcomings. They press the theory to grant the protections it exists to grant. I join this group of reformers in pushing for certain revisions that I think will enforce the purpose of the tradition and further the cause of humanity.

The revisions I propose, informed by the theory of autonomy, put much stricter limitations on military action than those currently recognized under international law. They will also alter the terms of the debate such that the standard forms of argument and accepted ideology must yield to at least a fresh look at old problems and solutions; the accepted dogmas face rejection.

Many of the problems arise when we conceive the tension between noncombatant immunity and military necessity in terms of rights. People – noncombatants and combatants alike – are said to lose their immunity through some loss of rights, or in an exchange of rights. But it is not rights that are at issue, but autonomy. We cannot lose or exchange autonomy for anything.

When we configure the issues in terms of autonomy, we come to a different understanding of the status of persons and the treatment they are due in virtue of that status. The principles generated from autonomy will restrict us from attacking people merely because they are engaged in some set of actions deemed by this or that statesman in this or that war to contribute directly to the war effort of the enemy. The principles will, for example, give a stricter interpretation of what is involved in direct harming such that those who are not engaged in harming us in the relevant ways will retain their immunity. We will be more hesitant, or even prevented from, beginning this line of reasoning because we can now say that noncombatants have immunity in virtue of their autonomy, not their rights. Their status is that they are absolutely valuable ends-in-themselves who cannot be used as means to some goal. This condition does not change because of the advent of war.

Under the theory of autonomy, we consider the maxims adopted by people in order to determine their status. People who have adopted a maxim of intending direct harm are considered combatants;[41] all others are noncombatants. This provides much clearer guidance than criteria focused on direct contribution to the war effort, or necessary versus contingent connection to the war effort. As we have seen, these latter sets of criteria have implications that would be undesirable even for their proponents. That is, even someone who endorses using the direct contribution criterion, for example, might admit that targeting the water plants seems morally problematic. Yet, by this criterion, it would be permissible to bomb them, at least in some cases. Again, at least in some cases, by this criterion, bombing the collectors of tin cans might be justified, and this, even more than bombing water plants, seems unjustified. The principle I propose would unambiguously proscribe bombing either of these targets. If we contend that we cannot bomb water plants or civilians who collect cans, and if my principle supports that contention when others do not, we should see the virtue of the principle.

Now we can reconsider the case of reprisals[42] in light of the theory of autonomy's criterion for deciding who can be legitimately harmed. It seems that the theory of autonomy would enjoin us to condemn reprisals and revise the reasoning implicit in certain parts of the war convention that justifies them. The case for reprisals involves explicit consequentialist reasoning. We justify the doing of evil to stop the doing of evil; in the most extreme case, we justify our murdering of innocents to induce the enemy to stop their murdering of innocents. The similarities to the example of killing the serial killer's mother to prevent further crimes are readily apparent. Let us consider the case Christopher cited concerning the killing of eighty German prisoners of war. Clearly these victims were used as means only. The German prisoners were used by the French as a means of protecting their own (French) people who had been captured by the Germans.

Recall that the conceptual basis upon which enemy combatants can be seen to respect each other's autonomy rests on the willingness to accept each other's surrender. The French had accepted the Germans' surrender. These prisoners were now not engaged in direct harming, and their natural status as noncombatants had been recognized; they had regained their immunity from attack by abandoning the activity by which they had forfeited their immunity. They were innocent, yet the French killed them.

Also consider our discussion of targeting civilians: we condemned this in part because the civilians could do nothing to regain, as it were, their immunity. They could not surrender because they were not engaged in any activity the ceasing of which could constitute surrender. The case under discussion is doubly damned on this account: the Germans *had* surrendered and were killed in spite of this.

Not only do reprisals conflict with principles generated from autonomy, they affront our moral intuitions. It is morally repugnant, for example, to line eighty men up against a wall and slaughter them, men who have committed no crime, innocents who have laid down their arms and have accepted our succor. They have been singled out arbitrarily as victims, simply means to our ends, in a way that should shock our most basic sense of human decency. In this respect, I should point out that, given the repugnant nature of reprisals, it would not be surprising if any number of theories proscribe them, even if in other cases they do not correspond to our moral intuitions. Surely, in fact, using the principle of direct contribution to the war effort, reprisals would be condemned. I am merely here indicating that my theory supports our moral convictions in this instance; further, I am indicating the way we use the theory to reason about such issues.

I want to briefly return to the question of tactical nuclear weapons as a way of transitioning to the subject of the Doctrine of Double Effect (DDE), the topic of the next chapter. Tactical nuclear weapons are relatively low yield nuclear weapons designed for use on the modern battlefield against armies in the field. But modern armies in the field know this, so tactics have evolved to mitigate their effects. One important tactic is dispersal, spreading one's forces over a large area to prevent offering the enemy a lucrative target. So, to get the desired result, a belligerent would have to respond by using more or bigger nuclear weapons. Nuclear weapons are not precision weapons, their effects are not discriminating. Given the nature of nuclear weapons, it is difficult to see how their effects could be limited only to combatants. It is this feature of nuclear weapons that inclines me to say that they should all be lumped into the same category. Their direct effects would harm civilians as well as soldiers. In fact, given that soldiers are trained and have special equipment to protect themselves and decontaminate themselves, it is reasonable to assert that civilians are at greater risk. The distinction between tactical and strategic nuclear weapons borders on the trivial.

But there is a distinction, which is not trivial, between policies that govern their use. A policy that aims strategic nuclear weapons purposely at civilian population centers disregards the combatant/noncombatant distinction; one that would employ tactical nuclear weapons purposely at armies in the field recognizes the distinction and attempts to justify their use by appeal to DDE. We must explore that doctrine and see what it justifies and what it condemns.

Notes

1   Walzer, p. 146.
2   Ibid., p. 146.
3   Ibid., p. 146.
4   Ibid., p. 146.
5   Murphy, p. 351.
6   Ibid., p. 349. We have already seen the problems with making the distinction between *qua* soldier and *qua* human being. Unless we ground the distinction properly, it becomes arbitrary: one could justify almost anything under the proper description.
7   I will say "targeting civilians" to avoid the repetition of cumbersome phrases such as "those who have been assimilated into the ranks of combatants." I do not want to beg the question by calling them civilians. On the other hand, if I say they have been assimilated, I beg the question against my position, since I will argue that they have not been; they do not become combatants. Finally, it is clear that these people are a problematic case since they do not wear uniforms or bear arms: they are not combatants in the traditional sense. So to keep the issue before us, I will call them civilians to underscore that they are a special case. At the same time, I understand that some theorists consider them legitimate targets and in that respect combatants. I also point out that the term "civilian" could be considered a neutral sort of term insofar as it does not track a morally relevant distinction in the way that "noncombatant" does. Civilians are people who are not in the military service; noncombatants are people with special immunity. Not all non-civilians are combatants. Medical personnel in the military, for example, are noncombatants insofar as they have special immunity from deliberate attack. However, just war theory so often uses civilian and noncombatant interchangeably, that to use the terms in special or idiosyncratic ways would be inappropriate. We must rely on the context to determine if a civilian under discussion is clearly a noncombatant or one whose status is in debate.
8   Walzer, p. 147.
9   Ibid., p. 146.
10 Christopher, p. 158, quoted earlier (Chapter 2).

11 Ibid., p. 157.

12 I devote an entire chapter on a special case where military necessity seems to loom large, namely, extreme emergency. Also, I note that military necessity plays a special role in helping discern the morally significant features of the Doctrine of Double Effect, the subject of the next chapter.

13 Ibid., p. 159.

14 Quoted earlier in this chapter.

15 Even if Walzer's and Murphy's criteria do not amount to exactly the same thing, they yield the same sorts of problems that the discussion of Walzer's criterion illuminates. For example, the production of water could be seen both as a direct contribution to the business of fighting *and* as having a necessary connection to the war effort. Yet we do not want to say that the workers in the water plant are legitimate targets. Furthermore, medics who administer to wounded soldiers meet both criteria but are clearly not legitimate targets. So for these reasons, and for clarity of explication, I adopt Walzer's phraseology to account for this general approach to assimilating people into the ranks of combatants.

16 Again, I think it is a mistake from the outset to make distinctions using "*qua.*" I adopt the usage here in order to critique views that seem to be driven by this way of making the distinction.

17 See p. xx of the preface of the second addition of his *Just and Unjust Wars*. He calls attacks against water plants attacks "on civilian society." Although he is concerned here with collateral effects, it seems that if bombing the plants is unjustified, then the deaths of the workers are unjustified.

18 Walzer can more easily address the issue when it concerns a water plant that produces water for both civilians and soldiers. The contribution here seems less direct and it seems to be something the soldier needs *qua* human being, not *qua* soldier. But it seems Walzer would have greater difficulty dealing with a special water plant that produced water only for soldiers. This seems to be a direct contribution to the war effort of a product for soldiers *qua* soldiers. But it still seems as though these workers are doing "nothing particularly warlike," as Walzer says. Furthermore, consider the case of a person who gets transferred from the city water plant to the military one. It seems unacceptable to say that he has become a combatant just in virtue of this transfer. If my intuitions are correct about this, then we have more reason to question the adequacy of Walzer's criterion.

19 I want to make one more point about making the distinction about soldier *qua* soldier. If we understand that the insight behind this way of talking is simply that the soldier has adopted a maxim of direct harm, we might see that the key point is not what the factory workers produce. The only reason we can attack the soldier *qua* soldier is because of the maxim he has adopted. The factory workers, regardless of what they produce, have not adopted a maxim of direct harm and are, on that account, immune from attack. That is, the reasoning that had justified attacking them, when properly understood, actually proscribes the use of force against them. The putative justification to attack them was that they provided something for a soldier in virtue of whatever it is that makes a soldier a legitimate target. But when we understand that the only thing that makes the soldier a legitimate target is that he has adopted a certain maxim, we see that, since the factory workers have not adopted that maxim, they cannot be attacked.

20 Murphy, p. 350.

21 I discuss this criterion because it seems best to capture the standard thinking on the subject. There are other criteria, or criteria stated in different ways, but they all amount to the same way of thinking.

22   Reasoning about this issue in this way is part of the process of trying to achieve a
      reflective equilibrium. There does seem to be something clearly different about a
      soldier and a munitions factory worker or a water plant worker. Although the notion of
      direct harm might not capture all the nuances of intention, it certainly gives us a way of
      drawing finer distinctions, distinctions that align more closely with our considered
      judgments and the purpose of the war convention, than other criteria.
          There are two points I should make related to this issue. The first concerns the fact that
      some might say that a soldier who rigs a booby trap has adopted a maxim of indirect
      harm since he may not be anywhere near the site when the trap harms the enemy.
      While we might question whether this is in fact indirect, let us grant that it is. To say
      that he has adopted a maxim of indirect harm is to conflate the maxim with the action.
      The action may harm indirectly. But setting a booby trap is an activity that we would
      consider typically follows from the adoption of a maxim to harm directly.
          The second issue concerns the reluctant soldier, one who does not want to fight and
      who does not want to harm us. I cannot address all the issues about such a soldier, but
      offer the following thoughts. If he is committed to not harming us, one would think he
      has some obligation to surrender, become a conscientious objector, or perhaps desert.
      Granted, there might be good reasons why none of these options seem reasonable. But
      on the surface, at least, we think some such activities should typically follow from the
      adoption of a maxim not to harm. Furthermore, it would seem that this soldier remains
      a legitimate target for the same reason even the hateful munitions factory worker is not
      a legitimate target. We cannot probe the depths of the soldier's soul to see if he intends
      our harm.

23   *FM 27-10 The Law of Land Warfare*, Department of the Army, (U.S. Government
      Printing Office, 1956) para. 43, p. 20. I am merely suggesting one way we might
      conform to guidelines imposed by a consistent application of just war theory. There
      are other means. A country might have a stated policy, for instance, that it considers
      munitions factories legitimate targets. This would constitute a standing warning. Of
      course, a standing warning does not justify every policy. For instance, just because a
      country had a policy that considered hospitals legitimate targets does not make the
      hospitals legitimate targets. They are protected under international law. In one respect,
      the notion of something's making a direct contribution to the war effort is helpful here,
      since it seems the hospital and the munitions factory are quite different in this regard.
      In another respect, however, this points out the difficulty with using "direct
      contribution to the war effort" as a significant criterion for deciding the legitimacy of
      targets. I say this because one could plausibly argue that the hospital, by treating
      wounded soldiers and returning them to the battlefield, directly contributes to the war
      effort. For reasons like this, the notion of direct harming is a preferable criterion.

24   FM 27-10, p. 19.

25   This seems to be another point in favor of the direct harm criterion. Other ways of
      making the distinction between combatants and noncombatants might count nuclear lab
      workers as merely munitions workers and we would have to address all of the
      ambiguities attendant with such a characterization. But on the account I offer, we have
      a more clear way of understanding why we might attack them.

26   Tactical nuclear weapons are relatively low yield weapons designed to destroy armies
      in the field. Strategic nuclear weapons are extremely powerful, high yield weapons
      that are typically part of a country's nuclear deterrent arsenal. These weapons are to be
      employed against the population centers of hostile nations.

27 Or he works for the department of war, or security... whatever title is appropriate to the nation in question; I feel safe in the assumption that no country allows private, commercial development of nuclear weapons.

28 This same general description might apply to the average soldier, but we must recall the earlier discussion about the specific role of a soldier and the particulars of direct harming. So, there are greater points of disanalogy than analogy between the soldier and the factory worker.

29 On the account I am giving, it is questionable whether there is any way to morally justify the production of strategic nuclear weapons. Given that they are designed for use against those not engaged in harming, there seems to be no principle of autonomy that could be used to justify their use. Hence, their very production is problematic.

30 The Doctrine of Double Effect is the subject of the next chapter.

31 Christopher, p. 159.

32 *The Law of Land Warfare*, para. 497, p. 177.

33 Christopher, p. 181.

34 See Christopher's discussion on pp. 179-87. International law notwithstanding, the recourse to killing the innocent in reprisal is often had or considered. The issue is so controversial that condemnation is rarely forthcoming. The winners particularly, if they have conducted reprisals against the innocent, seem especially immune to prosecution or even moral condemnation.

35 Christopher, p. 180.

36 Ibid., p. 180.

37 Ibid., p. 187.

38 See Walzer's excellent discussion, pp. 309-22.

39 Again, refer to Christopher's discussion, pp. 179-87. He examines the history of the doctrine of reprisals and points out the differing views espoused by statesmen and theorists concerning the doctrine.

40 Anscombe, Murphy, Phillips, Walzer, and Yoder, for instance, all in some measure indicate some of the problems and inconsistencies within the tradition and argue to some extent for revisions.

41 I do not discuss whether civilian leaders – presidents, monarchs, prime ministers, etc. – are to be considered combatants. They are a problematic case insofar as they are the ones who ultimately make the decision to go to war and send soldiers to battle. Nonetheless, they do not seem to have adopted the maxim of direct harm that would make them legitimate targets. If we recall my example of the farmer who would not be considered a threat to the soldier if the soldier encountered him, we might see the politicians in the same light. They are not armed and prepared to kill the soldier. And notice here that in many senses, the political leaders do contribute directly to the war effort; their connection is necessary not contingent. Yet they do not seem to be legitimate targets. Perhaps this is the insight that accounts for our general condemnation of the assassination of the political leaders of our enemies. The case of nuclear war, which I do not discuss at any great length, might be different. If the political leader is the one who commands the nuclear attack, we might consider him as having adopted a maxim of direct harm since he is in many respects employing the weapon. I am undecided here, but note that the nature of nuclear weapons and their manner of employment have a significant impact on our analysis. See the discussion towards the end of this chapter about scientists in a nuclear weapons lab.

42 Again, we should note that not all reprisals are immoral or illegal. Reprisals against soldiers in certain circumstances seems warranted: they are legitimate targets. Such

reprisals involve using weapons we might not otherwise use in order to get the enemy to quit the use of such weapons. What I have in mind is a rejection of the conventional acceptance of reprisals, particularly of the kind represented by the killing of the German prisoners. It is a certain attitude I attack.

Chapter 6

The Doctrine of Double Effect and the Status of Noncombatants

The theory of autonomy says that we cannot deliberately target noncombatants.[1] But this does not solve all of the problems concerning the harm that befalls noncombatants. Given the nature of war, it is almost impossible to shield completely the innocent from war's effects. Often, for example, noncombatants are in danger because of their proximity to a battle between contesting combatants. These innocents are sometimes unintentionally injured or killed by combatants as they (the combatants) conduct their battles. Traditionally, just war theory has appealed to the Doctrine of Double Effect (DDE) to justify the unintended harm that comes to civilians from the legitimate use of force during war.

In this chapter I will investigate DDE and explain how it can give inconsistent or undesirable guidance if not properly understood. Then I will show how the theory of autonomy can illuminate the moral insights behind DDE. I argue that soldiers must adopt a positive maxim to protect noncombatants and that the adoption of this maxim involves a willingness on the part of soldiers to accept risk in order to avoid harming noncombatants. I will examine two wars in order to show how a proper understanding of DDE should inform our decisions and judgments about the use of force.

Overview

The Doctrine of Double Effect, as Walzer puts it, "is a way of reconciling the absolute prohibition against attacking noncombatants with the legitimate conduct of military activity."[2] DDE can help us make important moral distinctions, but it is important to proceed from the correct theoretical perspective in order to understand what DDE will sanction and what it will condemn. DDE in itself does not provide a foolproof formula for making the morally correct decisions.

I will argue for a version of DDE that follows from the theory of autonomy and will show that this version provides the sort of guidance we seek when deliberating on issues in just war. We must apply DDE judiciously, understanding its moral purpose and foundation. If we apply it consistently and properly, we will support the war convention and our efforts to limit the horror of war. This need for consistency and for a correct understanding of the doctrine's theoretical justification becomes more pressing if we consider that we usually invoke it at the extremities. By this I mean that we have recourse to DDE at one of the points where the war convention encounters one of its severest challenges, at the point where we contemplate a military action against legitimate targets/combatants, in full knowledge that innocents may also lose their lives by that same action.

This immediately raises difficulties for the theory of autonomy because any time innocents are harmed as the result of military actions it seems to be a violation of principles of autonomy. At the very least, their harm is morally problematic. In order to more clearly understand the need for some version of DDE, it might be helpful to consider what sort of battles we would be justified to fight without it.

One scenario where it is possible to fight using just means, without fear of collateral effects harming noncombatants, might be a war at sea. If two warships engage each other, there are no noncombatants in the vicinity; there is no worry that innocents will be injured by collateral effects. If all wars were fought entirely in situations where noncombatants were not put in harm's way, it would be much easier to fight the war justly since force would be used only against those engaged in harming.

But one of the particularly ugly aspects of war is that innocents are often in harm's way. If we face an enemy who will not confine his hostile activities to the battlefield, then as long as we remained committed to fighting the war justly, we would not be able to fight him. For example, if the enemy put his defensive positions in cities, and we could not engage him without some collateral damage affecting noncombatants, then it would seem that we would be precluded from conducting any military operations against him. But if we have no recourse against an enemy who refuses to follow any constraints, this seems to conflict with our considered judgments about what means we should be allowed to employ during war against such an enemy.

So if the theory of autonomy does not accommodate some version of DDE, then it does not seem to match our considered judgments. By this I mean that we feel there is some justification for collateral damage in the just conduct of wars lest we be prevented from fighting at all. Even if the harm that might come to the innocent as a result of legitimate military conduct is unintended, if it is nonetheless foreseen, we might be precluded from such conduct. But then, if such harm seems inevitable in war, it might seem impossible to conduct any war justly. If no version of DDE is available to resolve this tension, it might pose a serious objection to the theory of autonomy, even to the extent that it might tend towards pacifism.[3]

To illustrate the extent of the problem we face if we cannot formulate an adequate version of DDE, consider my example of war on the sea. I said that no noncombatants would be in harm's way. But that is not technically correct. Each war ship has medical personnel, as well as chaplains and those who administer to the religious needs of the sailors. These people are not considered combatants; you cannot deliberately target a medic on the battlefield who is giving first aid to a wounded soldier, nor can you target a preacher as he ministers to his flock. Both categories of people are protected under law; under the theory of autonomy, furthermore, we cannot attack them since they have not adopted a maxim of intending to harm us. It follows, then, that even warships could not engage each other on the open seas if no version of DDE were available, since the medical and religious personnel would, undeniably, be in danger of collateral effects.[4]

So it is important to recognize at the outset that DDE amounts to an excusing principle. Consider that we make the distinction between combatants and noncombatants in order to specify that we may not *do* certain things to noncombatants. DDE in a sense has us examine what it means to *do*. There are some consequences for which we do not get held accountable. It is not that we may not harm noncombatants, but that we can only do so under certain circumstances. We get held accountable, blamed, for the deliberate harming of noncombatants, for consequences that obtain from our violating principles of autonomy.[5]

We can generate from my notion of autonomy a conception of DDE that will enable us to make the appropriate distinctions. It will help us understand the justification it provides. But it will do more than this. DDE is not merely a backward-looking doctrine. If understood properly, it will erect moral barriers and constraints. By knowing what it justifies and what it condemns, we will know what actions can be contemplated and what ones are merely contemptible.

I generally follow Walzer's formulation of DDE. He writes:

1)   The act is good in itself or at least indifferent, which means, for our purposes, that it is a legitimate act of war.
2)   The direct effect is morally acceptable –the destruction of military supplies, for example, or the killing of enemy soldiers.
3)   The intention of the actor is good, that is, he aims narrowly at the acceptable effect; the evil effect is not one of his ends, nor is it a means to his ends, and, *aware of the evil involved, he seeks to minimize it, accepting costs to himself.*[6] (My emphasis)

Walzer has a fourth condition that I will not use: "The good effect is sufficiently good to compensate for allowing the evil effect; it must be justifiable under Sidgwick's proportionality rule."[7]

Sidgwick's proportionality rule involves consequentialist analysis and is the requirement that the good achieved is important enough for victory that it outweighs the evil: the benefits must outweigh the costs. For instance, in analyzing a proposed course of action in terms of proportionality, we might be precluded from dropping a bomb on a shed located in a populated neighborhood if the military objective was to destroy a few cases of rations that the enemy had stockpiled. Even if we could use a laser-guided bomb and minimize damage to surrounding structures and people, the potential gain seems disproportionate to the possible harm that could come to noncombatants.

If, on the other hand, the shed contained the compounds necessary to make nerve agent, we might be justified in bombing it. If we had good intelligence that the enemy was planning on producing nerve agent and employing it against our forces and that by destroying the ingredients in the shed we could prevent this, then the good would seem proportionate to the evil. I am assuming here that the explosion would not release nerve agent into the surrounding neighborhood since the ingredients must be combined in a laboratory to produce the nerve agent. If it *would* release nerve agent into the neighborhood, our judgment on the matter gets more complicated. And this highlights what seems most problematic about the proportionality rule: it entails a great degree of vagueness.

What is or is not proportionate will be subject to debate. We might even, for example, justify bombing the rations: we might say that the effect on enemy morale would go beyond the physical distress caused by a mere loss of rations. The enemy might get discouraged if they felt we could strike them anywhere and deny them any sources of comfort. And it seems that the debate will follow along consequentialist lines: we weigh the benefits against the evil. We weigh the tangible loss of noncombatant life with the estimate of the intangible loss of enemy morale. This sort of consequentialist reasoning is incompatible with the theory of autonomy. But even if we could conduct the debate on other terms, we have another reason for dropping this condition: the third condition will do the work.

To see that this is the case, consider the shed example. In the first scenario, the benefit you seek to gain by destroying some rations would be very small. The probable result is that a few enemy soldiers may be hungry and slightly low on energy when you engage them; hence, your fight will be easier, and you might take fewer casualties. If we understand the situation in these terms, it becomes increasingly hard to make the claim that you accepted cost or risk to yourself. In any such example where the benefits of an act are small and the risk of danger to civilians is high, it would seem that condition number three has not been met.

Since condition three seems, at least initially, to provide the sorts of restrictions we seek from an adequate conception of DDE without some of the complications that condition four might cause us, it seems appropriate to drop the fourth condition. In the following investigation, it will become apparent that condition four is not necessary; our initial confidence that we are correct to drop it will be confirmed.[8]

Of course, simply dropping condition four will not eliminate all the vagueness that we face in such situations, since there is still some vagueness involved in the level of risk soldiers are supposed to take. But my analysis of DDE in general will help mitigate the vagueness. Nonetheless I fear it cannot wholly eliminate it. Uncertainty pervades war: uncertainty about the enemy's intent, the risks to ourselves, the risk to innocents, etc. But the theory I espouse will help reduce the uncertainty by more clearly elucidating the moral guidance of DDE.

The highlighted portion of condition three shows Walzer's adjustment to standard just war thinking on DDE, and I think he is correct to make this adjustment, and that it is critical to our reasoning about just war. Some of the grossest mistreatment of civilians during war occurs when belligerents adopt tactics or strategies whose driving consideration is the reduction of risk to their own combatants, such reduction being of paramount importance to victory. We pursue a certain course of action – say a siege – because it greatly reduces the risk to our soldiers. A frontal assault on a city may cost us so many casualties that, even if we win that particular battle, we are likely to lose the war; so we conduct a siege and starve the enemy into submission.

Now, for reasons to be explored later, soldiers are not to be expected simply to sacrifice themselves and accept so much risk that their mission will obviously fail and they will die in a futile attempt to do what they know in advance they cannot do. On the other hand, they must accept a certain amount of risk in order to limit civilian casualties. But this concerns only one of the conditions, and all must be considered and met in order to justify actions that come under the rubric of DDE. I will examine facets of two recent wars to more fully expose the force and limitations of DDE. The two cases I will examine are particularly important because certain features of them seem to represent new ways of doing business in the commerce of wars. If they are paradigms for the future, and I think they are, they provide critical lessons for just war theory. I intend my analysis to lay the groundwork for a reexamination of the propriety of some of our contemporary ways of making war.

The Acceptance of Risk

Before we get to the cases, however, we must provide the theoretical basis, grounded in autonomy, for the distinctions I make. The key to understanding the justification for the use of violence during the just conduct of war, even in cases where harm might befall noncombatants, is seen in the injunction for combatants to accept risk. That they accept risk involves the adoption of a maxim that coincides with principles generated by autonomy. To see this, I borrow an insight from Warren Quinn.[9]

Consider situations involving legitimate projects like the construction of major roads. We must assume that the engineers and planners who design it, and the people who vote to pass a mill levy to finance it, all realize that some construction workers may be injured or killed in the process of building a road. And after its construction, they know that people will be injured or killed in traffic accidents on the road. Even innocent babies might get hurt. In spite of this foreknowledge, we do not feel that the planners and voters are involved with a morally suspect activity; they are not guilty of evil. The reason we do not condemn them is because the maxim of their actions is permissible. However one characterizes the particulars of the maxim – to further progress, to help people get to work and back home more safely, etc. – it is not a maxim that intends the harm of innocents or devalues the agency of others.

We can look at situations involving the use of force during war, where it is known in advance that collateral effects might harm noncombatants, in a similar fashion. If the military mission is directed at a legitimate target and the means used are legitimate,[10] then if noncombatants are hurt, we do not condemn the soldiers who plan or execute the mission. And we do not condemn them in this case because here also the maxim of their action seems permissible. They are not deliberately harming those who are not engaged in harming. And insofar as they do not deliberately aim at the harm of these innocents, insofar as the harm of innocents is not a means to their ends, they are not devaluing the agency of the innocent any more than the engineers who plan the road are guilty of violating the autonomy of those who might get hurt in its construction.

But this is not the end of the story. That is, merely adopting a maxim whereby you do not intend the harm of innocents does not automatically exonerate you from guilt; otherwise, this would amount to a blanket justification for every injury on a construction site and any harm to noncombatants in war. That is why we must consider the injunction to accept risk.

Let us reconsider the construction example. Even if the engineers do not intend that people be injured in accidents, we might condemn them. Suppose that in order to save time and money, for example, they fail to incorporate into their designs certain safety features that will significantly reduce accidents. Under certain circumstances, say that these are features known to work and that the only reason for not using them is to pad an already significant profit, we would generally condemn them. They might even be liable for criminal charges. What is required, beyond the adoption of a maxim that does not intend harm, is the adoption at the same time of a maxim to take positive steps to limit any harm that might result from our actions. Taking these positive steps amounts to a recognition that we are responsible for more than what we directly intend. We have a responsibility to all those who might be affected by the reasonably foreseeable effects of our actions.

The notion that soldiers must accept risk if necessary to protect noncombatants is analogous to the sort of positive care we feel the engineers should take. It is not sufficient for soldiers merely to adopt the maxim not to directly harm noncombatants. They must recognize the potential harm their actions might cause the innocent and accept some costs to themselves in order to reduce the risk to noncombatants. If they are not willing to accept some cost, if they do not adopt this positive maxim, it has the effect of nullifying the original maxim not to do harm. If there are measures they can take to reduce the harm to the innocent, but they fail to take them because the measures involve increased risk to soldiers, it does not seem that the original maxim had any meaningful content. When we say that we do not intend harm to others, there is a sense where we recognize the obligation to avoid harming them. If it simply means that we will not go out of our way to harm them, it is a very weak intention. In fact, it seems to be more of an intention to do whatever is convenient rather than one not to harm. Consider a reckless driver. He may not purposely run down pedestrians: so he might say he has adopted a maxim not to intend to harm them. On the other hand, if he drives blindfolded through a pedestrian mall, it seems preposterous to give any significant credence to his stated maxim. Likewise, if, for example, soldiers say they have adopted a maxim of not intending harm to civilians, yet to reduce or eliminate risk to themselves they rubble an entire apartment building to eliminate a sniper, it seems ludicrous to count as meaningful their maxim of not intending harm.

To understand this point, consider the following.[11] It seems that if the soldier refuses to accept some risk in order to protect the innocent, he acts the same as he would if the innocent had not been there. For instance, suppose the easiest way to attack a building defended by some enemy soldiers is to rubble it with close range artillery fire. Suppose further that there are also many noncombatants in the building. Suppose that it would be feasible, though more difficult, to take the building by having our soldiers conduct a room-by-room clearance. This procedure would accomplish the mission while minimizing civilian casualties; the procedure involving direct artillery would kill or injure almost everyone in the building. If the safest, easiest way to accomplish the mission is the artillery option, then obviously the only reason to prefer the room-by-room clearance is to minimize civilian casualties: if they were not there, then we would use the artillery method. So if the soldiers opt to use artillery, they act as if the noncombatants were not there.

Recall that in the generation of the Principles We Can Reasonably Reject Principle, we examined the notion that each individual life should count as something. We can extend that notion to underwrite the insight we are dealing with here. If we use artillery, we could legitimately claim that we had adopted a maxim of not intending to directly harm the noncombatants, and so be justified under some version of DDE. We could claim justification, for instance, because the noncombatant deaths were not a means to our ends; the target was a legitimate one; and the direct effect was the destruction of the enemy. But there still seems to be something morally wrong with the situation. Every life should count for something, the Reasonable Rejection Principle tells us, and here the lives of the noncombatants seem to have counted for nothing. We have acted precisely as we would have had they not been there. Their presence made no difference. This is the theoretical underpinning to the intuition that we have acted badly, even if we have adopted a maxim that by itself might be permissible. It is not sufficient to simply not to intend to harm. We must adopt a positive maxim to work towards the minimization of harm. This is the insight captured by Walzer's injunction that we must accept some cost in order to limit the secondary effects of our legitimate military operations.

On another level, of course, we could simply say that we have not aimed narrowly, one of the other injunctions of DDE and one that does serious work for us and is clearly applicable in this situation. To aim narrowly means to aim with discrimination, to keep the effects of our force directed as much as possible at combatants. When we aim narrowly, we recognize the obligation to distinguish between combatants and noncombatants and to act in ways that respect that distinction. But I am trying to provide theoretical force to DDE and give an account of why it is wrong not to aim narrowly. The above discussion should help us show how the theory of autonomy coincides with the doctrine, explains our intuitions about the moral force the doctrine should have, and strengthens that moral force. By invoking the Principles We Can Reasonably Reject Principle, I have attempted to infuse the doctrine with the respect for persons that underscores the theory of autonomy. I have introduced the notion that we must adopt both a *negative* maxim not to harm deliberately the innocent and a *positive* maxim to accept risk in order to protect the innocent. This notion, inspired by Walzer's injunction, will provide the sort of guidance we seek when we consult the DDE to resolve just war issues. Without the positive maxim, the guidance provided by DDE remains too ambiguous. In the extreme, when we fail to do this, it is questionable as to whether we have adopted the negative maxim; that is, perhaps we simply are directly harming those not engaged in harming us.

In the discussions that follow, I will sketch how we can apply this version of DDE by indicating what the theory implies in practice. The respect for persons must have practical ramifications that involve recognizing the distinction between combatants and noncombatants in terms related to the effects of our military actions. We want to provide for the maximum appropriate protection for noncombatants while still allowing for the just conduct of military operations. There are ways of fighting that, according to our most considered judgments, seem just even if noncombatants are in harm's way. We must account for these judgments in non-arbitrary ways that follow from the theory of autonomy. Beyond that, we must submit our judgments to the scrutiny of the theory of autonomy in order to see if they are correct judgments.

The Case of the Iraqi Water Purification Plants

I spoke earlier of the bombing of Iraqi water purification plants and condemned it on the grounds that the plant workers should not be considered as having been assimilated into the ranks of combatants. But there are other morally compelling reasons why it should be condemned. First and foremost, this action affects noncombatants as much, or more, than it does combatants, and it affects more noncombatants than combatants – many more, since the entire population is affected. As Walzer says:

> But power and water, water most clearly, are very much like food: they are necessary to the survival and everyday activity of soldiers, but they are equally necessary to everyone else. An attack here is an attack on civilian society. In this case, it is the military effects, if any, that are collateral.[12]

Here one could expect DDE to condemn the action and impose a requirement upon those who would uphold the war convention to refrain from bombing the plants. But it did not have this effect in the first Gulf War. For the purposes of discussion, let us suppose that the coalition invoked just war theory and DDE in deciding what targets to attack.

We can imagine that the water purification plants fell victim to a variation of the line of reasoning explained above, in the chapter on noncombatants. The plants are considered legitimate targets because their product directly contributes to the war efforts of the enemy. And even though many civilians will suffer, they are not the intended target, their suffering is not the intended, direct effect. The direct effect is the destruction of something (water) that is vitally important to the enemy. And with this rationale, we could even justify the plant workers' deaths without conceptually conscripting them into the ranks of combatants, since, if the plant is a legitimate target, we can destroy it as our direct effect, while justifying the plant workers' deaths as an unfortunate indirect, double effect. This is a plausible characterization of how the reasoning might have gone.

My concern is that DDE does not seem to speak forcefully or unambiguously enough against actions like this. But how are we to understand DDE in a way that gives us clearer guidance concerning when foreseen collateral effects are justifiable and when they are not? DDE makes a distinction between direct and indirect effects. But it cannot be the case that it always allows any unintended effect. We want a conceptually forceful way to support our conviction that the water plant cannot be bombed. We need a way of understanding DDE that will help us apply its criteria consistently and will reduce vagueness.

DDE comes into play as a way of justifying actions that might harm noncombatants but that we have little reasonable choice in doing during the legitimate conduct of military operations. For instance, consider a scenario where we are fighting through a city, and the enemy has a machine gun position at a critical intersection. If we are to overtake the position without committing ourselves to a senseless slaughter of our own soldiers, we must use suppressive fire (we must direct a high volume of fire from our machine guns at the enemy position to make it difficult for them to expose themselves enough to engage us effectively). Either some of the suppressive fire or ricochets from it may strike houses in the vicinity. DDE provides justification for this course of action.

DDE provides an explanation for our sense of moral justification. Among other things, we aimed narrowly, and we accepted risk (other considerations, of course, come into play: it was a legitimate act of war and the evil effect was not one of our ends, etc). We can see that we accepted risk to minimize the effect on noncombatants if we consider another option. We could have called in an artillery barrage that would have surely destroyed the enemy position without exposing our soldiers to any risk whatsoever. But, of course, artillery barrages are notoriously indiscriminate and it seems clear that the danger to civilians would have been greatly increased. So by suppressing the target and assaulting the enemy, exposing ourselves to risk, we accomplish the mission in a way that limits the risk to noncombatants as much as possible.

But given that DDE does provide this explanation, we can use it to examine any proposed action to see if it would fall under that explanation. And one problem with the bombing of the water plants is that it seems false to say that we had no choice. We had plenty of other choices. Even if we felt that water was a direct contribution to the war effort, we could wait till it gets to the battlefield: we can interdict military supply convoys. And we will continue to target the soldier who receives the water. Does this expose us to more risk? Yes, it does, but it does not seem to be unreasonable risk, and it does seem to be the price one pays if one wants to maintain the distinction between combatants and noncombatants, that is, if one wants to fight the war justly. If we do not choose this way and take the available option, it becomes increasingly difficult to say that we accepted risk and aimed narrowly. By adopting the appropriate maxim to accept risk in order to minimize harm, we would have made different choices, ones that align better with our moral convictions and the war convention.

I cannot provide an algorithm to perfectly assess what constitutes a reasonable choice, but I do not think this is a serious limitation of my theory. There is a core understanding of what is reasonable or not that seems resilient to the vagueness and arbitrariness I am attempting to limit. When we consider, for example, some military objective, or a political objective we seek with military means, there are several steps we must take. First, we consider the viable options. That is, what are the available means? Can we attack on the ground, through the air, from the sea, etc? We must ask if we have these forces ready. Can we physically perform each option? The ones that we cannot physically perform fall out of the reasonable category. Then we consider whether what we contemplate is legal. Are all the options under consideration legal? The ones that are not legal fall out of the reasonable category. Is the collateral damage reduced as much as possible? That is, have we adopted both the negative and positive maxims? Here moral considerations, not legal ones, will come to bear. This is where vagueness is most likely to intrude. Although vagueness will not be eliminated completely, it can be reduced significantly. The theory of autonomy will provide insight into the realm of the reasonable.

To better understand the role reasonable choice plays, consider another scenario. Let us suppose that the Iraqi regime has placed several SCUD missile launchers on the grounds of the water purification plant and that the missiles are armed with chemical warheads. Suppose further that they are aimed at Israeli population centers and that we have firm intelligence reports that their launch is imminent. In this case we could plausibly appeal to DDE and bomb the SCUDs. If the plant is damaged, it is the double effect, one at which we did not aim. We have not deliberately made war on civilians.

But there are those who would say that we have not deliberately made war on civilians in the original case, that of deliberately bombing the water plants. They contend that their intention was good, they aimed only at the acceptable result of disrupting the supply of this critical soldier need. But intention, specious or sincere, can be given more moral weight than it can in reality bear. In the case of the machine gun position or the SCUDs, we might achieve our aims even without harming civilians: we can aim narrowly. But in the case of deliberately bombing the water plant, we cannot help but harm civilians. There is no attempt at minimizing collateral damage. And by the very nature of the target, it is not possible to minimize the collateral damage: the collateral damage and the intended military target are the same. We do not aim narrowly. The double effect almost collapses into a single effect.

In theory we can separate the two effects: one is a lack of water for soldiers, and the other a lack of water for civilians. But in practice, in this case, they cannot be separated. We might envision a scenario where we somehow provide water to the civilian population, say, through airdrops. Then we might be justified in attacking the water plant. But that we might then be justified does not make the target itself, or the original situation, less morally problematic. We simply have a new situation. In fact, the way we have redrawn the scenario seems to reinforce our conviction that in practice we cannot separate the effects and therefore should not bomb the plant. By recognizing the need to provide an alternate source of water to the civilians, we are implicitly recognizing that to destroy the water plant would be to cause equal or greater harm to the civilian population. This does not necessarily follow, but in this scenario, we could construe it as an admission of direct guilt for their deprivation, an admission that the two effects cannot be separated. And if there is no way to provide water to the civilians, we cannot justify our bombing of the plants.

Let us return to the original scenario of deliberately bombing the water plants. We cannot even *say* we attempted to minimize the effect on civilians in this case. The very fact that we are prevented from even using the vocabulary of just war discourse in this instance should be troubling. And we cannot merely appeal to our intentions in order to seek justification. That is, even if we contend that our intention was good and the evil effect is not one of our ends, the claim lacks credibility. I am not saying that the intention of the actor has no relevance to the moral status of his action; on the other hand, intention on its own cannot make one effect into two. To appeal to intention alone in this instance seems to be mere casuistry. Here the intention seems to be more an instance of wishful thinking. We wish the civilians were not there to be harmed. But we know that they are, and we take aim anyway. Anscombe, writing about the abuse of DDE, captures this way of thinking:

> ...on this theory of what intention is, a marvelous way offered itself of making any action lawful. You only had to "direct your intention" in a suitable way. In practice, this means making a little speech to yourself: "What I mean to be doing is..."
>
> This same doctrine is used to prevent any doubts about the obliteration bombing of a city. The devout Catholic bomber secures by a "direction of intention" that any shedding of innocent blood that occurs is "accidental."[13]

It seems clear that adopting the positive maxim to minimize the effect on the noncombatants would preclude this way of thinking. In spite of this bomber's "direction of intention," he acts as if the noncombatants were not there.

And in the case of the water plants, it is not even as if we aim through civilians who are inadvertently interposed between our enemy and us. We take direct aim; the enemy soldiers and the civilians are united in the target in a way that cannot be severed. There is no chance that the civilians might move out of the way. In this way, such action does not distinguish meaningfully between combatants and noncombatants. And any legitimate use of DDE must make this distinction. It is not enough to simply make the distinction between intended and unintended results.

Viewed in another way, one could even argue that when we bomb a target like the water plants, we fail to aim. We shoot indiscriminately, which is another way of ignoring the distinction between combatants and noncombatants. Even though we intend to harm combatants, we really do not care who else we harm, which is an instance of ignoring autonomy. We act as we would without the presence of noncombatants; by so doing, we do not acknowledge that their lives count: in essence, we ignore their autonomy. We have already discussed how we violate principles of autonomy if we deliberately target noncombatants, if we do not distinguish them from combatants. Now we must consider how we ignore autonomy if the foreseeable effects of our actions do not discriminate meaningfully between combatants and noncombatants, and how ignoring autonomy amounts to violating principles of autonomy insofar as it amounts to a devaluation of agency.

The maxim that we assume sanctioned the bombing of the water plants, looked at from the perspective of autonomy, is morally unacceptable. In the context of DDE, the adoption simply of a maxim not to harm can lead to unacceptable results if it is not directed at the same time by a maxim to accept risk in order not to harm. Warren Quinn tells us that the difference between a terrorist bomber who deliberately blows up innocents and a strategic bomber whose bombs might hit innocents is that the terrorist needs the death of the innocents for his purposes, whereas the strategic bomber does not. The terrorist treats the innocents as means only; the strategic bomber does not. The terrorist harms by "direct agency," the strategic bomber by "indirect agency." He says:

> Someone who harms by direct agency must therefore take up a distinctive attitude toward his victims. He must treat them as if they were then and there *for* his purposes. But indirect harming is different. Those who simply stand unwillingly to be harmed by a strategy – those who will be incidentally rather than usefully affected – are not viewed strategically at all and therefore not treated as for the agent's purposes rather than their own. They may, it is true, be treated as beings whose harm or death does not much matter – at least not as much as the achievement of the agent's goals. *And that presumption is morally questionable* (my emphasis).[14]

I want to say that the presumption is more than morally questionable. For our purposes, it provides the key to understanding what is morally odious about this type of conduct in war.

What I am getting at is that the policy of bombing targets such as water plants is one that does not see the lives of noncombatants as "mattering much." Insofar as we act the same way as we would if the noncombatants were not there, we ignore their autonomy. A policy that ignores them is one that is indifferent to the fate of the noncombatants. As we have said, human beings have absolute value in virtue of their autonomy. Their lives, their presence, must make a difference to us. Their existence imposes limitations upon our actions: they have at least to be considered.

To gain another perspective, let us draw an analogy with the case of the serial killer and his mother. With this example, I want to show how it might be the case that we are guilty of direct harming despite our protestations that we had adopted a maxim not to harm directly. Under certain circumstances, when we are not guided by a positive maxim to minimize risk, the claim that we had acted under a maxim not to harm rings hollow. Suppose the killer has taken refuge in his mother's house and the best way to capture him is to cut off the water to the house. We know that eventually he will surrender, become too weak to resist, or die. We are not aiming our actions at his mother; we are indifferent to her fate.

Nonetheless, we know that an effect of our actions will be that she suffers equally with her son. In this case, depriving her of water constitutes a use of force against one not engaged in direct harming or guilty of adopting an impermissible maxim, insofar as it is an enforced deprivation of something essential to her bodily functioning. Since we cannot separate the effect upon the criminal from the effect upon the mother, and we undertook the action as a form of attack upon the body of the criminal, we at the same time attack her body, the condition of her agency. This is impermissible.

To see this more clearly, consider that the deprivation of water for the indicated purpose is different only in degree, not in kind, from the deprivation of air. Suppose it would be possible to completely seal the house and slowly suffocate the criminal. Of course, this is a ghoulish endeavor in any case and might be proscribed even against the criminal. But for the sake of discussion, suppose we do it. Is it not clear here that the effect upon the mother is the same as that upon the criminal? And do we not readily condemn it? We should view an attack against targets like the Iraqi water purification plants in like fashion. Such an attack is impermissible on grounds similar to those that condemn the deprivation of water from the criminal's mother. Implicit here is that we have other options where there is a legitimate (reasonable) risk we can take. We might get a SWAT team into position to apprehend the criminal without harming the mother at all, for example.

There might be other scenarios where we do not have any reasonable options. Suppose the criminal begins shooting bystanders and our only option would be to use tear gas, even though the gas would also harm his mother. Under these circumstances, we would be allowed to use the gas. I cannot discuss all the possible permutations of this scenario. I merely wanted to indicate how, under some circumstances, the claim that we had adopted a maxim to prevent harm, and that we had not adopted a maxim of directly harming (the mother) seems quite specious.

So even though the intention to bomb the water plants was to hamper the Iraqi military, the action should be condemned because the intention manifests at the same time an indifference or disregard towards the fate of innocents, a disregard that constitutes a devaluation of autonomy. In order to be justified under DDE, we must ask if our actions constitute a devaluation of any of the agents who might suffer their effects. And here it must be possible in principle and practice to separate the effects; otherwise, DDE would provide us very little assistance in unpacking the moral complexities we encounter in war.

Let us look again at the two scenarios, one where we bomb the plants to prevent a SCUD launch, and the case where we take direct aim at the water plants. It is possible to get the SCUDs without damaging the water plant, say, by using laser-guided munitions. So the effects are separable in principle and in practice. We are not indifferent to the fate of the noncombatants. At least, by the fact that the effects are separable, in principle we remain committed to the agent-centered restrictions generated by autonomy.

But in the case of directly aiming at the water plants for the very purpose of destroying them, we foresee the ineluctable inclusion of the noncombatants in the effects and undertake the action even though there is no way in practice to separate the effects. This case is different from the case of the terrorist bomber, but is still condemnable. That is, we do not necessarily need the innocent victims' suffering in order to accomplish our goal. For our purposes, it would be better if the noncombatants would not be harmed. Nonetheless, since there is no way to separate the effects, we devalue them in a way that constitutes a violation of principles of autonomy.

Here we should note that intention does play a role in our determination of the moral rectitude of our actions. Recall that we have no reasonable choice in destroying the SCUDs. Our intentions are acceptable, and we are not indifferent to the fate of the civilians. We would not desire any effects, even collateral ones, to damage the plants. Our actions are a response to the impermissible maxim of the enemy. In that respect, the deprivation of his civilians is his responsibility. On the other hand, our intention when we directly bomb the water plants with the purpose of their direct destruction enjoys no such justification. As we said, we have other choices, we show indifference to the fate of innocents, and the collateral effects are identical to the intended effects.

But this leads to another case that proves more challenging than it might initially seem. I am going to discuss a situation that is part of the larger problem of innocent shields. The problem of innocent shields involves a general scenario where we are threatened by someone who uses another person, who is innocent and does not pose a threat to us, as a shield in order to attack us. And the situation is such that in order to defend ourselves we must harm or kill the innocent shield as a way of getting at our attacker. I am going to describe a possible, though bizarre, wartime scenario to introduce this problem. I do not resolve the problem but will examine features of the issue that would suggest a way it might be resolved.

Suppose the enemy formed a "baby shield brigade." This is a tank brigade that straps babies onto each tank to use as shields. Suppose the enemy knows our commitment to the war convention and its prohibition against deliberately targeting the innocent. The enemy feels that now it can attack with impunity since there is no way we can destroy the tanks without destroying the babies. What are our options here?

Let us suppose that there is no way to cut off the fuel and ammunition supplies to this brigade before it can defeat us decisively and achieve the regime's unjust war aims. For us, it is either destroy the tanks or lose the war. We have already implied that we must be ready to give up certain ends if the means prove impermissible. Recall that we judged that it would be impermissible for some country to bomb Dallas even though doing so provided that country with the only possible means of winning a war against the U.S. We (any country) must be prepared to lose a war if the only way of prosecuting it is through impermissible means.[15] But here we must decide if it would be permissible to shoot the tanks, even though we must shoot through the babies: if the enemy uses babies as shields, are we using permissible means when we destroy the tanks even though we know that the babies will die?

Let us proceed step by step. In the first place, we can say that destroying the tank is a good act, that is, a legitimate act of war. The direct effect is morally acceptable, namely, the destruction of an attacking enemy tank. Our intention is good, we aim narrowly at the acceptable effect, and the evil effect is not one of our ends or a means to our ends. It is the enemy who has placed innocents at risk in order to reduce danger to himself. So he is at least partly culpable for whatever harm comes to these innocents.

So we might think we have a justification by legitimately shifting the blame for the evil to those who put innocents in harm's way. In this respect, this case seems similar to the case involving the SCUDs located in the water purification plant. The enemy has tried to use the plant as a shield; he is adopting illegitimate means. He has put legitimate military targets within the confines of the water plant in an illegitimate attempt to protect them by exploiting the protection normally granted such sites (at least protection that should be granted).

We can perhaps see this more clearly if we consider that it is illegal under international law to use ambulances marked with a red cross or crescent to transport combat troops or ammunition. These vehicles are not legitimate targets since their express purpose is to transport noncombatants, i.e., wounded personnel. To use them to move combat troops is wrong because it undermines the convention and trades illicitly on the distinction between combatants and noncombatants. Any country that would do this gains a double advantage: they use a method their enemies would not; and the effectiveness is guaranteed precisely because their enemy respects the convention.

Of course, once the enemy knows of the illicit use, once the ruse is exposed, it can target the vehicles. If we know that troops, not wounded, are in the ambulance, we can destroy it. If we discover that his policy is to use ambulances in this fashion, we might be justified in adopting a corresponding policy to target any ambulances, even if we did not know for sure that the ambulances had combat troops in them. When the enemy uses illegal and immoral means, the responsibility for the evil that results is his. Walzer gives the following example:

> Consider an example from the Franco-Prussian War of 1870: during the siege of Paris, the French used irregular forces behind enemy lines to attack trains carrying military supplies to the German army. The Germans responded by placing civilian hostages on the trains. Now it was no longer possible to get a "clear shot" at what was still a legitimate military target. But the civilians on the trains were not in their normal place; they had been radically coerced: and responsibility for their deaths, even if these deaths were actually inflicted by the French, lay with the German commanders.[16]

It may be right to lay the blame for innocent deaths on those who adopt such evil means. But the question is whether we are exonerated. Do we not share in the blame?

As it stands now, according to the theory of autonomy, we do share the blame. It would be impermissible to shoot the baby shields. Recall that the version of DDE that we are developing says that the effects of our actions must be separable in practice as well as in principle. There is obviously no way to separate the destroying of the tanks with the killing of the babies. This is one way that the theory of autonomy speaks against killing the innocent shields.

Furthermore, when we shoot the tanks, we act as we would had the babies not been there. It is, hence, difficult to claim that we had valued their autonomy, that their lives had made a difference. We act precisely as we would have acted had the babies not been on the tanks, and this constitutes the sort of ignoring or devaluing of autonomy proscribed by our theory.

And since we act as we would have acted if the babies had not been there, it is very difficult to say that we had accepted risk in order to reduce harm. What was the positive maxim we could have adopted? In the scenario we are considering, it seems that there was only one viable risk-taking option, namely, quitting the field of battle, thus risking defeat. That we did not take that option speaks against any claim that we had adopted a positive maxim to minimize harm. And of course, since we are willfully and knowingly shooting through the babies, any claims that we were attempting to minimize harm to these innocents would be ludicrous in the extreme.

In spite of all this, we seem to have at least some intuition that we cannot grant immunity to those who adopt evil means in order to exploit our own repugnance of evil and our commitment to autonomy. So we feel there must be some way to justify destroying the tanks. I hope there is a way to develop a permissive principle that would allow us to attack the tanks in such situations. Although I have not come up with the principle, I want to examine some features of the baby brigade that might offer hope for future resolution of the problem.

We might gain some insight if we examine the issue in terms of the maxims adopted by the parties involved. The enemy has adopted an impermissible maxim and we react to it. He is using the victim, say the baby shield, as a mere means. We are not using the baby as a means at all; we are not using it in any way. And our maxim is permissible; that is, we intend to destroy a tank. Even though we may have adopted the requisite positive maxim to minimize harm, the enemy has made it impossible for us to minimize the harm and aim narrowly. Our best intentions have been frustrated by the enemy's actions. DDE concerns *our* intentions, *our* options, *our* maxims. It could be that in spite of our own good intentions, we cannot spare noncombatants because the enemy eliminates in advance any of our options to minimize harm.

In some ways, then, it seems to make a difference that the enemy has willfully made it impossible for us to aim narrowly if he uses babies as shields. But it remains unclear *why* it makes a difference or whether the theory of autonomy can account for it. If we examine the nature of the enemy's impermissible maxim, we might gain some initial insight into our intuitions about this case. In the chapter on autonomy, in the discussion of the Means Only Principle, I used a quote from Korsgaard to describe what the use of deceptive methods entails, morally. I want to reuse the quote but adapt it to apply to the impermissible method under discussion:

> ...you must be using some method to achieve your end that not everyone could use to achieve that end. The efficacy of your action depends upon the fact that others do not act as you do, and that in a sense means that others are making your method work...For example, when you tell a lie for a certain purpose, the lie works to achieve the purpose only because most people tell the truth. That is why you are believed, and so why the lie achieves its purpose. In such a case it is not just the person to whom you lie that you treat as a means but all of those who tell the truth. This is because you allow their actions to fuel your method, and that is explicitly treating their rational nature as a mere means: indeed it is making a tool of other people's good wills...you make an instrument of the rational nature of others, and treat them as mere means.[17]

When the enemy uses baby shields, the efficacy of this action depends upon the fact that most people would not do this, that most people consider such an act to be beyond repugnant. If no one generally thought it horrible to use babies as shields or to shoot them, then they would not provide any protection when strapped to the tank. But of course, the enemy is relying precisely on our abhorrence of such methods to generate his success. Hence, he is treating all of us as mere means, not just the babies. It is this maxim that we reject, the enemy's maxim of treating all of us as means only. And this may account, at least in part, for our intuition that it makes a difference that the enemy has willfully made it impossible for us to aim narrowly. In so doing, he is using all of us as mere means.

Of course, this still does not solve the problem of the babies. Nothing about what I have just said gives any reason to say that the babies' lives are forfeit. The fact that the enemy uses them and us as mere means does not translate into a permissive principle that allows us to kill innocent shields. As I have said, this is a very difficult problem whose resolution is outside the scope of my project. In discussing the fact that the enemy makes it impossible for us to aim narrowly and by that fact uses us all as mere means, I have attempted to show how we might formulate an argument that justifies our shooting the tanks of the baby brigade. And we must note that justification may not be forthcoming. Until it is, we must remain committed to the constraints imposed by the theory of autonomy.

That we cannot shoot the tanks on my theory might seem to be an unhappy conclusion to some; they might think it represents a serious problem for the theory of autonomy. I do not think this is so. It is an encouraging fact that not many people use babies as shields. That we might have to hold our fire against a relatively few – if any at all – evil adversaries who would adopt such a tactic does not constitute a major objection to a just war theory that insists on constraints in such rare cases.

Furthermore, considering the many difficult issues attendant to innocent shields, it might be expected that most theories would have problems here and would have to "tiptoe around these incredibly difficult issues," as Robert Nozick says.[18]   And perhaps a solution viable within any theory might be one that the theory of autonomy could use.

I want to return now to the question about risk and will examine it by looking at the recent intervention in Kosovo. I do not contend that the following description of the Kosovo situation captures all the intricacies; it might not be entirely historically accurate. But it is generally correct and, more important, the theoretical issues it raises are important independent of the empirical circumstances.

Kosovo

One way of looking at NATO's air campaign in Kosovo in 1999 is to point out how successful it was in terms of the limited number of NATO casualties. NATO can say it accomplished its mission by getting Milosovic to submit to its demands; and it did so with very few casualties. Whether the West really achieved its goal of preventing ethnic cleansing is debatable: the Serbian forces accomplished a lot of ethnic cleansing and displacement of Kosovar Albanians before they submitted to the demands of NATO.   Michael Evans, a Senior Research Fellow in the Australian Army's Land Warfare Studies Center, writes:

> The air war did not succeed in protecting the Kosovo population. Indeed, it worsened it and accelerated the humanitarian crisis because the Serbs systematically depopulated the province of Albanians. While NATO struck at the heartland of Yugoslavia, Kosovo was subjected to mass terror reminiscent of German SS field units in Eastern Europe during World War II. In trying to prevent genocide, the West used a military method – air power – which accelerated it.[19]

But that NATO suffered few casualties is an indisputable fact. For our purposes, it is a troubling fact. There were many reasons for conducting the campaign in the way we did. But at least part of the reason behind it was to limit friendly casualties. A ground war would have put our forces at tremendously greater risk than that faced with the air campaign.

It is important, morally as well as militarily, to try to limit our casualties. It is also sometimes quite politically expedient to limit them, especially when pursuing a controversial policy. The problem is that in Kosovo, this politically expedient strategy put noncombatants in harm's way *in place of combatants*. The intensity of the Serbian campaign of violence, oppression, and murder against the Kosovar Albanians increased dramatically once we started our air war. And we foresaw this; who would not have predicted it?

Arguably, the only way to have prevented the Serbian atrocities would have been to insert ground forces, to have put combatants in front of noncombatants. These could have protected the civilians directly as an armed protective force, and indirectly by tying up Serbian resources. Some might contend that a ground war would have increased civilian suffering. Given the slaughter that actually ensued, that would be hard to imagine. Frankly, it seems much more reasonable to assume that the Serbian military would have been too busy trying to defend themselves to spend much time on rape and murder.

In any case, we should have been *prepared* to defend the innocents somehow, instead of playing the waiting game and hoping for eventual capitulation while they suffered unimaginable horror. We were not prepared, and these innocents faced the full force of Serbian rage. Were we willing to accept risk to limit harm to innocents? Again, there were many reasons to conduct strictly an air campaign. But if one of them was to limit NATO casualties at the anticipated expense of innocents, then this course of action was morally problematic.

With the advent of new technology, particularly "smart" weapons, we can do war on the cheap, as it were. In terms of our combatants' lives, the cost is relatively low. So perhaps we embark on a course of military action too hastily, simply because we can do so at low cost with relatively little risk. (Yes, Cruise Missiles are expensive, but the public does not raise a hue and cry over such expenditure. It is also a shot in the arm for the defense industry.) It is a much dicier proposition to put combatants on the ground to meet the enemy on the field of battle than it is to hammer away, from a distance or from the sky, at an enemy who is technologically far inferior. We can employ the rhetoric of justification and say that we fight the war justly because we seem to meet the conditions of DDE. After all, the smart weapons limit collateral damage, do they not? But this is one of the subtle, dangerously seductive aspects of this modern phenomenon. Even if these weapons did minimize collateral damage when viewed narrowly, at the specific target area, that does not automatically mean the conditions of DDE have been met. We must look more broadly to find all of the unintended effects, which included the revenge taken upon the Kosovar Albanians by the Serbian forces. This also was a foreseeable and predictable effect, though perhaps an indirect effect.

We must distinguish between *unintended* and *indirect* effects. The shattering of storefront windows near a command bunker is a direct though unintended effect of the bomb whose intended effect was the destruction of the bunker. The suffering of civilians is an unintended though indirect effect of bombing the Iraqi water plants. The civilian population is not directly affected by the explosions that destroy the plant. But they suffer tremendously from the indirect effect of water scarcity, and for this reason we condemn the destruction of the water plants. In like fashion, it is plausible to argue that DDE does not justify many aspects of the Kosovo intervention. We must examine direct and indirect effects as well as intended and unintended effects to decide if our proposed action is justified. As we have seen, DDE is not a blanket permission to perform just any action as long as its intended effects do not harm noncombatants. We must look at all the foreseeable effects, including indirect effects, to see if their impact on noncombatants is acceptable.

To that end, I introduce another distinction. On the *tactical* level, perhaps we were justified under DDE (although some targets, like electrical plants, seem to be in the category of the Iraqi water purification plants and liable to the same condemnation). But on the *strategic* level, we may not be justified. At the tactical level we have narrow concerns, primarily the present battle, the immediate course of action, and the short-term effects. Our concerns on the strategic level encompass the whole breadth and depth of the battlefield, as well as the contribution of each battle to the entire campaign. On the strategic level, we are concerned with how each action on the tactical level fits into a coherent plan aimed at achieving the desired end state of the war. Strategy drives tactics; the tactical objectives we designate are those that contribute to the strategic goals.

Strategy has to do with the ultimate goals of the war and the means for victory. Strategy may also concern effects of our actions and results that are not part of the aim of the war at all. That is, from a strategic viewpoint, we must consider the effect of our actions on the infrastructure of the country with which we are at war. We must consider the state of the social fabric of that nation after the end of hostilities, its ability to rebuild, the long-term health problems the people face as a result of damage to public services (water purification, for example), etc. So, for example, we might be justified at the tactical level under DDE when our Cruise Missile takes out a command bunker in Belgrade even though some of the surrounding civilian facilities incur some damage. But if another foreseeable, though indirect, effect, viewed from the strategic perspective, is retribution visited upon an ethnic minority, our justification is not so readily forthcoming.

In this respect we must recognize that the distinction between strategic and tactical is not simply a distinction between short-term and long-term effects. The Serbian rage vented upon the Kosovar Albanians was a short-term effect. Although it might extend into the long term, it was an almost immediate result of our air campaign. But clearly it is not a tactical concern. The tactical concerns of taking out a command bunker are, among other things, whether enemy command and control will be disrupted and whether we can attack the bunker without too much collateral damage to the immediate area. The effect on Albanians in Kosovo, well-removed from Belgrade, is not a tactical concern.

Nonetheless, it is a very significant strategic concern and one we must consider to assess whether we are justified in attacking the bunker.[20] We *might* be justified, but it is not automatic. We must have unblinkered vision to accurately assess our actions. The tactical level is only the first level we must examine. If we fail to consider the strategic level, we fail to follow the mandates of DDE. If we ignore strategic effects, we may not see the violations of the restrictions imposed under DDE that we actually do commit.

I mentioned earlier that some of the targets of the air campaign should have been precluded from attack. I am inclined to say that destroying electrical plants and other civilian sites that make up the infrastructure of the country constitutes making war on civilians. I want to take a closer look at these actions because they are both symptom and disease, maladies having to do with the very nature of this new way of doing business and the somewhat hidden moral problems associated with it.

They are symptoms of a flawed policy. We could not bring the Serbs to the bargaining table by means of the air campaign alone, as long as we only targeted military targets, which proved harder to find and destroy than we had hoped. To root out the enemy, it is usually necessary to use ground troops. Evans notes:

It also seems clear that the Serb Army in Kosovo escaped serious damage until late May when KLA guerrillas were able to flush hidden Serbian formations into the open where their armor could be targeted and pulverized by American air power.[21]

So, we had to target civilian sites that do not move and are impossible to hide. The hope was to demoralize the Serbian people so that they would pressure the Serbian government to accept NATO's terms. This is what happened, but we must note that NATO achieved its ends by targeting civilians.

Some people contend that the Serbian people themselves are accomplices in the horrible crimes perpetrated upon certain ethnic minorities. But even if this is so, the Serbian people have not become combatants, although we might revile them if it turns out to be true. Justice must come to them through other than military means. I cannot address this issue in detail; I merely recognize the problem and say, for reasons already discussed, we cannot assimilate these civilians into the ranks of combatants.

These actions are also the disease we wish to eradicate, namely the malady of making war on civilians. The bombing of facilities like power plants, which support the civilian population as much or more than the military, is analogous to the case of the Iraqi water plants. We cannot help but harm civilians, and they will be affected more than the military, which has equipment and training to cope with such contingencies. There is no way in practice to separate the effect on combatants from the effect on noncombatants. We have not aimed narrowly. Indeed, this may be a more troubling case since the effect on civilians seems actually to have been intended as a means of pressuring the Yugoslav government. This points to a deeper problem associated with misunderstanding or misusing DDE.

Together, the symptom and disease point to the moral problem, hitherto disguised, of undertaking military action without a proper consideration of DDE and the moral insights it is supposed to illuminate. There is a further stipulation of DDE that this course of action fails to meet, namely that of accepting risk. I have suggested that we simply refused to accept risk at the tactical level and so had recourse to weapons that appeared to eliminate the risk, when they only masked the risk. What I mean by this is that we employed weapons that themselves involved little risk, and this had the effect of making it appear as if there were no risk that *should have been* morally shouldered.

There was a course of action that could have, arguably should have, been pursued that involved more risk, namely, one involving ground troops. But since we had relatively risk-free means available, there was a presumption in favor of their superiority, in moral as well as military terms. Why, one might ask, would we adopt any course of action that put our soldiers at risk when we have an option that would achieve our goals without endangering our troops? A more appropriate question to ask ourselves would be whether there is a course of action we should consider yet have ignored because we do not want to take risk, even if it is the sort of risk we must be prepared to take if we are to follow the moral guidelines imposed by a proper understanding of DDE.

The point is not that we should take risk for the sake of taking risk. The point is that in order to conduct operations within the moral constraints imposed by DDE, it is sometimes necessary for us to accept risk so that noncombatants are protected. The option of using ground troops would have exposed our soldiers to greater risk, but it would have reduced the risk noncombatants faced. And we are morally required to reduce, as much as possible, the risk to noncombatants.

We must consider risk at the strategic level. It could be that we failed to accept risk at the level of policy, the strategic impetus behind the war. As long as we could pursue the war without losing our soldiers, we could maintain support – or at least neutrality – on the home front. For various reasons, NATO leaders sought to gain and maintain popular support for their policies. The cautious approach, then, for leaders more driven by public opinion than justice, is to keep our soldiers out of harm's way. Evans makes this point when he writes:

> This was supposed to be a war of human values rather than political interests, but by ruling out ground forces from the outset, NATO signaled to Belgrade that the Kosovar people were not worth the life of a single NATO soldier...
>
> When General Clark visited Belgrade in early 1999, his delegation was told by Serbian commanders that all the Yugoslav Army needed to concentrate on when confronting the United States was the number 18. Clark's delegation was puzzled – until it was explained that the Serbs were referring to the 18 soldiers killed in Somalia in 1993, whose loss prompted U.S. withdrawal from peace enforcement in the Horn of Africa.[22]

It seems that moral cowardice at the strategic level led to the choice of tactics. The point here is a subtle one and has to do with one of the deep-seated problems with the new paradigm, namely, its seductive force. I am concerned that the question of risk gets masked such that no one asks the question and our (moral) courage does not get impugned, when in fact it should.

In the case of Kosovo, the strategic decision was made not to use ground troops. Then we proceeded with the air campaign, a relatively low risk course of action. So generally people did not raise the issue of whether we were accepting risk to minimize innocent deaths: there was little inherent risk, especially with Cruise Missiles. Also, as I mentioned earlier, we created the illusion, at least before hitting power plants, of following the mandates of DDE. So we seemed to be morally justified: we were seduced by the means we employed into a false sense of propriety. And this is a very important feature of this phenomenon. We want to be able to talk the talk of just war theory, even if we are not in fact walking the walk.

World leaders seek to justify their actions before their own people and the world. One way they could have attempted to justify the legitimacy of the initial strategy could have been in terms of DDE. But this would have been a smoke screen hiding a morally suspect decision. We must be committed to employ the appropriate measures, permissible under the guidance of a well-articulated version of DDE, to achieve our goals. If the goal was the safeguarding of the Kosovo Albanians (and this was the stated goal), then we should have been prepared to do that. Certainly it is acceptable, usually preferable, to start with measures and tactics that risk little. Accomplish the mission with the least expenditure of lives and resources. But if these initial tactics fail, we must be prepared to employ other tactics (or give up the goal).

These tactics did fail, and we were not prepared because *we had decided not to be prepared.* Recall what Evans stated: we ruled out ground forces from the beginning. This was a moral failure, a failure we might have avoided had we followed the guidance that would have come from an adequate understanding of DDE. We can ask, along with Evans: "What price Western values when the deaths of an estimated 10,000 innocent civilians are deemed preferable to the deaths of volunteer professional soldiers?"[23]

That we had decided not to be prepared signifies, in effect, that we had not adopted the appropriate positive maxim to minimize harm to noncombatants. We did not accept the risk required to safeguard those whom we were acting to protect. Our compliance with the conditions of DDE and the considerations of the war convention, informed by autonomy, was inadequate. This moral failure resulted in mission failure on a scale not yet calculated. Prima facie, we failed to stop the persecution of the Kosovar Albanians; we exacerbated the persecution. Evans indicates the magnitude of the failure:

> Professor Michael Mandelbaum…has stated that the yardstick for judging the outcome of the war in Kosovo is simple: Ask the Kosovars if they are better off now than they were four months ago (before the air campaign). This is more than clever rhetoric. Before the air war, there were 45,000 refugees outside Kosovo; after the air war there were 855,000. Even if 80% return, there will still be 160,000 refugees – quadruple the number that existed before the air war. If this is victory, then it is a dark victory.[24]

Beyond this, since we allowed such prolonged, intense violence against innocents, we have set the stage for a protracted era of abject ethnic hatred.

So the ramifications of failing to accept some sort of reasonable risk on the part of combatants in order to limit the threat to noncombatants are many and of profound importance. We must limit war's effects to the battlefield, combatant on combatant, as much as conceivably possible. The theory of autonomy helps us further define the limits of that possibility, and I contend the limits are broader than has been commonly accepted. I have argued for a conception of DDE that incorporates principles generated from autonomy. DDE makes certain distinctions between intended and unintended effects, but we appeal to a certain normative framework – the theory of autonomy – to determine how the distinctions are morally relevant. Autonomy inspires a way of looking at our actions that puts respect for noncombatancy at the center of our decision-making apparatus. I have suggested criteria that help us use the distinctions derived from DDE in ways that enhance and enforce the purpose of the war convention. In the process, I have shown that DDE by itself, independent of considerations inspired by autonomy, might sanction actions that conflict with our considered moral judgments and the purpose of the war convention.

Nonetheless, there are limits to the risk that combatants must endure and limits to the extent to which we can confine war's effects strictly to the battlefield. DDE itself recognizes this. It is the fact of the soldier's autonomy that provides part of the impetus for invoking DDE. DDE justifies some collateral damage, and it does so in part because of a recognition that soldiers are not expected to accept unreasonable risk. They are not required to expose themselves to risks that would doom their ventures to failure or themselves to certain death in order to prevent all harm to noncombatants. DDE constrains combatants to take due care to protect innocents, while at the same time providing moral justification for some types of harm that befall noncombatants because of the actions of combatants. It matches our considered judgments in not making unreasonable demands upon soldiers, as if they were simply expendable assets.

It is not simply a matter of expedience or military necessity that allows soldiers the sort of discretion we grant them under DDE. That we allow for some collateral damage might indicate that we do not think soldiers are mere pawns. DDE implies, in part, that there is a moral limit to the risk combatants must endure, an implication that points to their status as inviolable autonomous agents. We must examine their status.

The Status of Combatants

> ...soldiers who do the fighting, though they can rarely be said to have chosen to fight, lose the rights they are supposedly defending. They gain war rights as combatants and potential prisoners, but they can now be attacked and killed at will by their enemies. Simply by fighting, whatever their private hopes and intentions, they have lost their title to life and liberty, and they have lost it even though, unlike aggressor states, they have committed no crime.[25]
>
> I want to turn now to a recurrent incident in military history in which soldiers, simply by not fighting, appear to regain their right to life. In fact, they do not regain it....[26]

These two quotations, taken together, capture standard just war thinking on the status of combatants. They capture a lot that is important, and one of the reasons for drawing the lines the way these are drawn is to help establish the distinction between combatants and noncombatants. It is true that soldiers have war rights and are the legitimate targets of their enemies. They can legally and legitimately attack and kill enemy soldiers. In these ways they are radically different from noncombatants, and the distinction between combatants and noncombatants, as we have seen, "is the basis of the rules of war."[27]

But there is something fundamentally wrong in this characterization of the status of soldiers. It is wrong to think that they have "lost their title to life and liberty." Walzer says that in certain circumstances, when soldiers are not fighting and seem to pose no threat, they "appear to regain their right to life. In fact they do not regain it."[28] I want to argue that soldiers never lose the right to life and do not need to regain it. Here, again, rights talk is misleading. We are really talking about autonomy, which, I have argued, is something we cannot lose or gain, but is an inherent property of human beings. If we look at this issue from a fresh perspective, we will see how problematic it is to say that a soldier loses his right to life. This change in our conceptual understanding of the status of soldiers may not change their fate much.[29] But it will give us a clearer understanding of the moral status of war. It will also have implications for the magnitude of the guilt born by those guilty in terms of *jus ad bellum* of starting an unjust war of aggression.

Having said this, I will return to and elaborate on an argument I offered in Chapter 4. There I concluded that principles of autonomy are violated in war and that the political leader who starts the unjust war is guilty of the violation. But I will use stronger language now and will make a different point about the status of combatants.

I contend that every death that occurs as the result of a war can be construed in some way as an incident of murder.[30] Even a soldier who dies in a firefight, a legitimate target for his enemy, killed by legitimate means, has been the victim of a crime. The enemy soldier who shot him is not the criminal, for we must grant the moral equality of soldiers. Provided they fight the war justly, using legitimate means on legitimate targets, they are blameless. Nonetheless, a murder has been committed.

The murderer(s) is the leader or leaders of the regime who are guilty under *jus ad bellum* of the crime of aggression, that is, who started an unjust war. We might not prosecute them as murderers after the war, for political and other reasons, but they are guilty of a crime. Soldiers do not lose their autonomy or the right to life that derives from that autonomy. How can the act of, for instance, defending one's homeland, loved ones, and individual life cause one to forfeit one's rights simply because one chose a profession (or was conscripted into one) whose purpose is to defend against an aggression one wished would never occur? Soldiers have been put at risk against their will by he who would force them to defend themselves and others against aggression.

We can return to the police officer analogy. As I pointed out earlier, simply because he has chosen a profession that might require him to put himself in harm's way to stop criminals does not therefore mean that a policeman chooses to be put in harm's way. He is not a legitimate target for a robber; if a robber shoots the policeman, the policeman is a victim of a crime; principles of autonomy have been violated. Of course, the point of disanalogy here is that, in the case of soldiers, the combatants themselves are not normally seen as engaged in criminal activity or violating principles of autonomy as long as they fight justly. But this is accounted for by the notion of the moral equality among soldiers, a relationship that does not obtain between the criminal and the police officer.

But it seems as if I have introduced a tension into the war convention. If all deaths in war, combatant and noncombatant alike, constitute murder, what is the difference between combatant and noncombatant? I have already provided the basis of the distinction and its moral relevance in Chapter 4. Nonetheless, a tension persists when we conceive all deaths in war as violations of principles of autonomy. As we have seen, we resolve the tension by appeal to the distinction between *jus ad bellum* and *jus in bello*. If a soldier targets combatants during the conduct of his battle, he is not blameworthy. Soldiers fight at the behest of their country under the presumption, usually, at least initially, that their side is just. Walzer puts it this way:

> We draw a line between the war itself, for which soldiers are not responsible, and the conduct of the war, for which they are responsible, at least within their own sphere of activity...We draw it by recognizing the nature of political obedience ...by and large we don't blame a soldier, even a general, who fights for his own government. He is not the member of a robber band, a willful wrongdoer, but a loyal and obedient subject and citizen, acting sometimes at great personal risk in a way he thinks is right.[31]

As long as the soldier fights justly, we do not accuse him of murder. Of course, the issue of judgment could get more complex. Consider the case of a protracted war. If a country was prosecuting an unjust war over a long period of time, it might become obvious to all, even soldiers, that the cause was manifestly unjust. Under such conditions, we might withhold justification, or temper it, with respect to combatants. But this is not an issue I can adequately address here. I restrict consideration to cases where the soldiers are ignorant of *jus ad bellum* issues.   On the other hand, if the soldier murders noncombatants, he is blameworthy, he is a war criminal. So the distinction between combatants and noncombatants is morally relevant and, if observed, will do what the war convention would have it do, namely, limit the horror of war.

When we consider the issue from the perspective of *jus ad bellum*, we assign blame to the sovereign of the aggressor state. His crime put people at risk against their will: combatants and noncombatants, both his and ours. He is guilty of the crime of aggression and all the mischief that accompanies it. Walzer says:

> Aggression is the name we give to the crime of war. We know the crime because of our knowledge of the peace it interrupts...The wrong the aggressor commits is to force men and women to risk their lives for the sake of their rights. It is to confront them with the choice: your rights or (some of) your lives!...Every violation of the territorial integrity or political sovereignty of an independent state is called aggression...Aggression is a singular and undifferentiated crime because, in all its forms, it challenges rights that are worth dying for.[32]

Although I would talk in terms of autonomy here, I think Walzer's description of aggression is accurate and compelling. But given that aggression is what he says it is, given that it coerces men and women to give their lives to defend against it, is it not plausible to characterize all these deaths as murder? Walzer is correct to make the distinctions he does, but at the same time we gain a conceptual clarity that gives more force to our theory by acknowledging these deaths for the murders they are. This is why war is so terrible. Human beings are put in the absurd situation where, during the conduct of the war, having to defend their lives and take the lives of other human beings is quasinormalized. We are all conscripted involuntarily into the hell of war; combatants and noncombatants alike are assimilated into the ranks of *victims*.

Why is it not acceptable, then, to send noncombatants into harms way instead of combatants? I have challenged the propriety of our strategy in Kosovo, where innocents bore the horror of war so that our ground troops might be saved. But if all deaths in war are murder, why should we choose one murder over another? In response, we must understand that we do not *choose* either. As I have pointed our, we have been coerced. Just as we do not choose that a policeman be harmed in the line of duty, we do not choose that soldiers be put in harm's way. For that matter, we do not choose that there be a need for policemen or soldiers in the first place.

But there is evil in the world, threats to the agency and integrity of human beings. And we reject the devaluation of autonomy inherent in evil. We have assumed that some wars are just; we assume that we can justly use force to resist evil. So some of our members are put into the role of combatants. They are, we have indicated, coerced into this role. But the adoption of this role constitutes a resistance to coercion. We choose resistance to aggression and coercion. That is the choice we make, not between murders of one class over another.

If we did not identify certain members of our communities as combatants but instead chose for all to remain in perpetual noncombatancy, we would be capitulating to the rule of violence. If we do not choose resistance, then coercion will set its own limits. If all of us remain noncombatants, then we all remain innocents. But in this case, the innocence takes on an ominous feature. Since there is no one now to protect us, we are like innocent lambs led to slaughter. The slaughter stops only at the whim of the butcher. Creating a class of combatants constitutes the essence of resistance to a devaluation of human beings. The existence of the class of combatants, created at the outset of hostilities, is testimony to the primacy of noncombatancy. It shows that innocence is indeed an operative concept because we have designated a class of people who will defend the innocence that is threatened by an unjust war of aggression. We reject a devaluation of our autonomy. Christopher tells us:

> Therefore, soldiers do not attempt to harm enemy combatants because they believe they are guilty, but because they believe enemy combatants must be stopped in order to protect innocent members of their own community.

Even political leaders who order their armed forces into combat are usually presumed to be motivated by a desire to protect their own innocent constituents rather than to harm others. The very act of declaring a state of war begins a chain of events that involves changing the status of active duty soldiers, citizens who are reserve soldiers, and possibly potential conscripts or enlistees, from innocents or noncombatants to combatants who are subject to attack. Thus the act of declaring war entails intentionally putting certain innocent members of one's own community in harm's way…in order to protect other innocents….[33]

In designating a class of combatants, we are not choosing the murder of one class of people over another any more than we choose, by designating a class of policemen, the murder of police officers. In designating the class of combatants we show, instead, a commitment to resist aggression, just as our designating policemen shows a commitment to combat lawlessness. We manifest a deep commitment to autonomy because we will not let go unchallenged threats to the peaceful lives we live. We reject at every turn actions that do not afford the proper respect owed to human beings as ends in themselves.

Notes

1   We must always bear in mind the case of supreme emergency, which might stand as an exception to this prohibition. That is the subject of the next chapter.
2   Walzer, p. 153.
3   I do not devote any discussion to pacifism in this work. Although it is an important issue and, in the minds of many, the correct attitude to have about war, an adequate treatment of it is outside the scope of this investigation. I only note that pacifism is, broadly construed, the view that any use of force or violence is impermissible. This seems a mistaken view because it appears to put the violence used by a criminal against a victim on the same moral grounds as the violence used by a policeman to protect the victim against the criminal, which seems implausible. Analogously, it puts the violence used to resist unjust aggression on the same grounds as the aggression itself. I contend, rather, that the maxims behind particular uses of violence give that violence its moral character. Hence, for example, the criminal's maxim to harm the innocent is morally different than the policeman's maxim to reject coercion.
4   Of course, if failure to come up with a viable version of DDE would bring an end to all wars, this would be a desirable result. I would stop the discussion here. Unfortunately, the most probable result is that only those committed to constraints would be precluded from fighting, and those who are not would have free rein. Also, it is important to note that chaplains and medics are different from civilian noncombatants. They are in the military service and understand that their duty requires that they share in the danger of their fellow service members.
5   Clearly the theory of autonomy is not absolutist with respect to harming noncombatants. It is, however, absolutist with regard to its own principles.
6   Walzer, p. 153 and p. 155. It is important to consider Walzer's use of the word "evil" in criterion #3. "Unintended" might be a better word since otherwise, by this account, we are in some way acknowledging our enterprise to be evil in some respects, and we should reject that characterization of our legitimate projects.

7   Ibid., p. 153.
8   I will revisit, in detail, proportionality and its consequentialist implications in the Epilogue.
9   Quinn, p. 166.
10 I do not mean to beg the question here. The issue is, of course, whether the means are legitimate: that is, we are trying to decide if we can use force when we know that noncombatants may be harmed. Here I am just trying to establish the analogy.
11 This is another insight I owe to Quinn, although he was making a different point. He is examining whether our shooting through an innocent person used as a shield by an assailant would constitute a direct intention to hurt the innocent. He thinks not. See p. 187.
12 Walzer, p. xx.
13 Anscombe, p. 296.
14 Quinn, p. 190.
15 Walzer makes this point about American involvement in Vietnam. See *Just and Unjust Wars*, pp. 194-6. Walzer argues that at a certain point, "the rules of war…become a hindrance to victory." At that point, "(t)he war cannot be won, and it should not be won. It cannot be won, because the only available strategy involves a war against civilians…"
    Yoder says: "At some time (if the doctrine is not a farce) there cannot fail to be cases where an intrinsically just cause would have to go undefended because there would be no authority legitimated to defend it, or when an intrinsically just cause defended by a legitimate authority would have to be lost because the only way to defend it would be by unjust means." (*When War is Unjust*, pp. 74-5)
16 Walzer, p. 174n.
17 Korsgaard, p. 199.
18 Robert Nozick, *Anarchy, State, and Utopia* (New York: Basic Books, 1974), p. 35. It is interesting to note that Nozick also uses the example of people strapped onto the front of tanks to talk about innocent shields.
19 Evans, p. 35.
20 Since one of the strategic goals was to stop ethnic cleansing, failure to consider what would happen to Kosovar Albanians from Serbian retribution was also a military failure. Not only did we fail to meet the mandates of DDE, we failed to accomplish our military mission.
21 Ibid., p. 36.
22 Ibid., p. 35.
23 Ibid., p. 35.
24 Ibid., p. 37.
25 Walzer, p. 136.
26 Walzer, p. 138.
27 Ibid., p. 136.
28 Ibid., p. 138.
29 On the other hand, it could change their fate very much. It is difficult to see all the implications of a given theory when the theory is first developed. Furthermore, this insight about the status of soldiers should have significant impact in the area of military leadership, a topic I had initially intended to include in this project but must leave aside for another investigation.
30 I leave aside considerations of accidents. For example, a soldier who, while deployed in a combat zone, gets drunk and drives his jeep into a tree, might not be considered a murder victim. Of course, had he not been forced to deploy to the area, this might not

have happened. In any case, my focus is on those who die as the more or less direct result of hostile actions.

31   Ibid., pp. 38-9.
32   Ibid., pp. 51-3.
33   Christopher, p. 163.

Chapter 7

Supreme Emergency

In this chapter I will investigate the question of whether we can be justified in deliberately targeting noncombatants under the extreme conditions of supreme emergency. I will examine what constitutes a supreme emergency, whether it is a question of sheer numbers of lives to be saved or lost, or whether other conditions must obtain. I will argue that we face a supreme emergency when we face what we could plausibly describe as a fate worse than death; furthermore, I will argue that we can only target noncombatants if they share with us the same worse-than-death fate. And if they share that fate no matter what, their sacrifice (our targeting of them) might be permissible as following from principles they (the noncombatants) could not reasonably reject. I will also offer a description of what a fate worse than death might be. Finally I will indicate the problems certain rights-based theories encounter when attempting to deal with supreme emergency, and I will point out how the theory of autonomy avoids these problems.

The Problem

Supreme emergency concerns the situation when we are faced with imminent defeat by the type of horrible threat posed by Nazi Germany, what Walzer calls "evil objectified in the world."[1] Walzer succinctly expresses the argument for overriding the war convention, when faced with a supreme emergency, in the following terms:

> ...there is a fear beyond the ordinary fearfulness (and frantic opportunism) of war, and a danger to which that fear corresponds, and that this fear and danger may well require exactly those measures that the war convention bars.[2]

Walzer justifies the deliberate targeting of noncombatants when nations or civilizations face such a threat. He does not exonerate us completely from guilt if we deliberately kill the innocent when faced with supreme emergency. The innocents who die have been victims of a crime; we override their rights, according to Walzer, but the rights remain all the same. We have done something wrong. We have violated justice for the sake of justice.

Furthermore, Walzer does not justify the killing of innocents merely to prevent the killing of other innocents. The situation he envisions for a supreme emergency seems to be one where no one's life would be worth living if we suffered a defeat. As in the case of the threat posed by Nazi Germany, if we were to lose the war to them, the very conditions of a life worthy of the dignity of humanity would be undermined. Walzer says, "it is possible to live in a world where individuals are sometimes murdered, but a world where entire peoples are enslaved or massacred is literally unbearable...."[3] As he explains:

> For such calculations need not be concerned only with the preservation of life. There is much else that we might plausibly want to preserve: the quality of our lives, for example, our civilization and morality, our collective abhorrence to murder, even when it seems, as it always does, to serve some purpose. Then the deliberate slaughter of innocent men and women cannot be justified simply because it saves the lives of other men and women.[4]

Walzer contends that there is a "positive role (for) utilitarian calculation: to mark out those special cases where victory is so important or defeat so frightening that it is morally, as well as militarily, necessary to override the rules of war."[5] Supreme emergency is the special case.

The problem for the theory of autonomy is that so far we have not seen a way for the theory to accommodate the deliberate targeting of noncombatants, yet supreme emergency seems like a case where it might be, as Walzer says, morally as well as militarily necessary to do so. And we must note that the problem for us is not just that Walzer and other theorists seem to relent at this point. The most difficult issue is that they seem to relent because many of our considered moral judgments are unclear in this case. Whereas throughout this work I have argued that the theory of autonomy coincides with and supports our moral intuitions, we encounter in supreme emergency a case where the theory of autonomy might conflict with some of our deep moral convictions.

I have described supreme emergency as a situation where, if the evil regime wins, life for the survivors would not be worth living; in some sense we could say that the survivors would be better off dead. The conditions necessary for living a life worthy of autonomous human beings would have been undermined. That was the threat posed by the Nazi regime, a regime so rooted in evil and hatred, in everything dark and inhuman, that life under its power would be literally unbearable. So we must consider whether, faced with this real possibility, we could deliberately kill the innocent if doing so would prevent defeat at the hands of this sort of evil.

It is necessary to understand supreme emergency in terms such as these, to understand that the essence of supreme emergency is not a matter of sheer numbers. That is, some views of supreme emergency see it simply in terms of a scenario where we might be faced with the option of killing a relatively small number of innocents in order to save a vastly greater number of other people. But in this scenario, the survivors do not face a fate worse than death: they are not faced with a Nazi-like regime. Rather, we are concerned with the weight of numbers. We kill a few to save many, and the justification for killing the innocent derives from the greater good that is achieved by saving an even greater number of innocents. This seems to be a fairly straightforward consequentialist calculation. I have rejected consequentialist approaches throughout this investigation, and I reject it here. In such a scenario, it does not seem that mere numbers makes a difference from the perspective of autonomy; it is impermissible to kill the innocent to save other people, even if the numbers involved are extremely high.[6] I want to examine this conception of supreme emergency, defined fundamentally in terms of the numbers of people involved, so that we might more fully understand the way autonomy speaks on the subject and to underscore how this conception of supreme emergency differs from the conception I have described.

A Question of Numbers?

Consider the following situation. Suppose we were going to conduct an attack and have estimated that two of our soldiers would be killed during the battle. Suppose also that we knew that if we kidnapped the enemy general's daughter and killed her, the general would be so grief-stricken that he would lack the will to further prosecute the battle. We would then be able to achieve our objective with no losses.

It seems clear here that if we kidnap this girl and kill her, we are treating her as a mere means. We are coercing her, using her as a tool to save the lives of two other people. We are not directly using force only against those engaged in harming us, who have adopted a maxim aimed deliberately at our harm. This girl has done nothing to warrant our use of force against her. The theory of autonomy condemns such an act in a way that corresponds unproblematically with our considered moral judgments.

But if we change the numbers involved, will it change our conclusions? Could we come up with another permissive principle, consistent with the restrictions imposed by the Means Only Principle, that would allow us to deliberately kill some people to save many more? Suppose we could save an entire battalion of 600 soldiers by killing the girl. Some might initially think the killing of the girl justifiable here, since so many would benefit from the action. But such a judgment does not hold up under scrutiny. Nothing about the status of the girl has changed whatsoever; hence, nothing about the status of our action has changed. If killing her is unjust in the first scenario, it is unjust in the second. If we were using her as a means in the first scenario, surely we are doing so in the second.

It seems that any attempt to work out a permissive principle here would be incompatible with the Means Only Principle. Moreover, there does not seem to be anything in the principle that says, if the numbers are high enough, you would not be treating people as mere means if you kill them to save a (much) larger number of people. There does not seem to be anything in the principle that could be used to derive a principle that permits us to deliberately target the innocent after we reach a certain threshold based merely on the numbers of people affected. We may not make exceptions to the principles. We have generated these principles from a conception of humanity as the source of value and, as such, unconditionally valuable. As following from autonomy, the unconditioned value, these principles themselves are supposed to be unconditional and may not be justifiably overridden.[7] From this it follows that if we conceive of supreme emergency as a situation that justifies deliberately targeting the innocent, we must conceive of it along different lines than those involving simply the weight of numbers.

Sharing a Fate Worse Than Death

So the notion of supreme emergency we must consider concerns a situation where, if we should lose the war, we would face a fate worse than death. If we all face the same threat and some of us, by being sacrificed, could save the rest from such a fate, should we, whose sacrifice would rescue the others, consent to being sacrificed? Could we reasonably reject a principle that permitted our sacrifice under such conditions? Bear in mind that if we do not consent to the sacrifice, we, along with everyone else, face a fate worse than death. We must consider whether it would be indecent[8] of those whose sacrifice would save us all to refuse to be sacrificed. Should they accept the sacrifice out of respect for autonomy? There is a concomitant consideration. I have stated that every violation of principles of autonomy is unjust. Is it the case that every deliberate killing of the innocent constitutes a violation of principles of autonomy? Could it be just to kill some innocents to save many others from a fate worse than death?

It seems that it would not be reasonable to reject a principle that allows some to be sacrificed in order to save others under the circumstances described. Consider the analogous example of a sinking ship, for example, the case of the Titanic. There were not enough lifeboats for everyone. Either some people would have to go down with the ship, or everyone would: presumably, if everyone fought for the lifeboats, it could have prevented anyone from boarding them. Hence, everyone would have perished. The sacrifice of a few really could save many others: if no one sacrifices, everyone will die. Those who could save the others but refuse to do so gain nothing from their refusal. They are going to die anyway. It would seem indecent for people to object to a principle that would permit the saving of some by volunteering for a fate they are doomed to anyway.

Of course, in the case of the Titanic, the selection of those to be saved seemed somewhat arbitrary. But we can construct a scenario that eliminates the arbitrariness. Suppose that on a certain ship, only one person could possibly save the ship from capsizing and killing all on board. Because of his weight and location on the ship, either he jumps into the stormy seas to certain death, or the boat capsizes and everyone, including him, dies. This seems to be the situation that obtains in the case of supreme emergency as we have described it.

We have traded on the notion of consent throughout this work and have stated that what it is to treat someone as a mere means is to treat him in ways to which he could not possibly consent. In the situations about the ship that I have described, it seems that not only *could* the people to be sacrificed consent, but they *should* consent. If we sacrifice people under such circumstances, it appears that we are not using them as mere means, and are not therefore violating principles of autonomy. If this is the case, then we are justified, under these extreme circumstances, in killing the innocent.

In supreme emergency, either some die or all face a fate worse than death. To that extent, we all really are in the same boat. It would seem indecent of anyone, if he were going to suffer the same fate either way, to refuse to sacrifice so that others would be spared the fate. The insight here is that under these conditions, to refuse the sacrifice would be to manifest a complete indifference to other people's lives. We can reason from the Reasons We Can Reasonably Reject Principle in the following manner.

We had noted that when faced with a choice between saving two people or one person, we should save the two, all things being equal. Each person's life must count for something, and any principle that was indifferent between saving fewer as opposed to more could be reasonably rejected. In this instance, if we are the ones to be sacrificed, we face, in effect, that sort of choice. The only difference is that we ourselves belong to both groups. Still, it is a choice between saving a smaller or larger group. We would reasonably reject a principle that justified each choice equally, that is, was indifferent. We could not reasonably reject a principle that required us to save the larger group, given that each person should count as something.[9]

In fact, it might seem that the theory tells us that we have a duty to kill the innocent since not to do so under these extreme circumstances would seem to manifest the sort of impermissible indifference towards others that we have proscribed. If we consider the ship scenario, suppose the person who must jump ship in order to save the rest is either unwilling or unable to jump. It seems plausible to assert that other crewmen have the responsibility of throwing him overboard. This scenario actually seems closer to the sorts of cases we envision for supreme emergency. What we generally envision is not that some group of innocent people will actually volunteer, or can volunteer, to put themselves in harm's way to save us all. Rather, we envision a case where we must decide to put them in harm's way and, as it were, throw them overboard. This is how it went with the German civilians who were victims of Allied terror bombing during World War II, for instance, during a situation of putative supreme emergency.

As unpalatable as it might seem to have to toss the sailor overboard or deliberately bomb innocents in supreme emergency, we must remain focused on our fundamental question of whether those to be sacrificed could reject a principle that, under these circumstances, permitted their sacrifice. It will be helpful to recall that in Chapter 3 we noted that the Reasonable Rejection Principle has much of its force in its forward-looking character. We noted that of two groups in danger, the members of the smaller group whom we do not rescue in favor of saving the larger group might, at that time, object. Nonetheless, in advance, people could not reject a principle that, *ceteris paribus*, permitted us to save the larger group. So even though we face the unenviable task of sending a man into the stormy seas or targeting noncombatants, we must see these courses of action as consistent with principles to which those who are sacrificed could (and should) consent. It is not that they necessarily *would* consent; rather they could not reasonably reject the principle that allowed their sacrifice.

We are left with the uncomfortable position that in extreme emergency it is justified to deliberately target the innocent. We *must* feel uncomfortable with this result; moral anguish here seems to come with the territory. In terms of throwing a person overboard, clearly only a ghoul would relish the act, even if it turns out to be a duty. In terms of our just war scenario, even if it turns out to be our duty to do so, we are still killing the innocent. We are engaged in harming those who are not engaged in harming us.[10] Understanding this, it will be worthwhile to reexamine the nature of supreme emergency. What conditions must be met for some threat to qualify as having put us in supreme emergency?[11]

The Conditions That Must Be Met to Invoke Supreme Emergency

First we should examine the notion of a fate worse than death. One obvious example would be the following.[12] Suppose someone was captured by a particularly evil sadist who intended to preserve this person for the pleasure he (the sadist) received from torturing his victim. The person's life consisted in being tortured hideously until the very brink of death. But the sadist would stop just short of killing his victim and would revive him so that the torture could renew. The victim is never without pain but knows only brief periods when the pain is less than excruciating. The sadist has the means to keep this person alive for the length of his natural life. So implied in this characterization of such a fate is that there is little hope of rescue, or that, if rescue arrives, it will be a long time coming. This counts, I contend, as a fate worse than death. And our deepest intuitions seem to tell us that anyone would beg for death rather than endure such a fate. This is the sort of fate we must face to qualify as a supreme emergency. Other people may have different conceptions of such a fate, but if we are going to call something a fate worse than death in order to justify actions under supreme emergency, this seems to be the sort of thing we should have in mind.

Of course this does not mean that only physical pain would count as constitutive of a fate worse than death. For example, the psychological torture of living at the complete mercy of arbitrary power might count. One's life might be so hopeless and debased under such conditions that it would be worse than death.

Second, it must be the case that killing innocents is necessary to prevent such a fate. We cannot kill them to make winning easier or to speed the end of the war against an enemy that poses such a threat as that described above. Rather, killing them must be necessary: it must be the case that there are no other possible measures to prevent defeat that themselves do not involve the deliberate targeting of noncombatants.

Finally, we must be reasonably certain in all of this: reasonably certain that we face such a horrible fate and that killing the innocent is the only way to defeat the threat. What reasonable certainty amounts to is not completely clear. Certainly, though, we cannot require absolute certainty: it is dubious that such certainty is possible. The sort of certainty we require is the sort the people on the Titanic had that the ship was going down.

Having outlined the sorts of requirements I think we must meet before we can invoke supreme emergency to justify the slaughter of innocents, it becomes doubtful if the conditions ever have been met or ever will be met. Obviously, much of this is an empirical question. It is not within the scope of this project to do extensive historical research. But it is at least plausible to assert that even the situation involving the Nazis did not meet these conditions. Did humanity really face a fate worse than death: was there no hope of eventual rescue or respite, and was the potential misery of the nature necessary to qualify? Was the slaughter of German civilians really necessary: was it the only recourse available? Did we have the appropriate level of certainty that these conditions were met? I contend that few, if any, of the conditions were met.

I acknowledge that my position is controversial. It probably is the case that the first condition was met. The Nazis represented the sort of abject evil that certainly threatened everything decent; life under them would have to be characterized as bleak and hopeless. Furthermore, had they been victorious, it seems probable that they would have remained in power for quite some time. What length of time meets the criterion is difficult to specify precisely, but surely the span of a generation would count. But even if this condition was met, it does not seem that the others were met. Nonetheless, I could be convinced otherwise. If they were met, then the bombing of the German civilians would have been justified.[13]

Again, people can argue as to whether these conditions were met; they might contradict my conclusion. My main purpose in this discussion was to lay out what I think are the sorts of criteria that must be met before we can cite supreme emergency and deliberately target the innocent. If the theory of autonomy justifies deliberately targeting noncombatants, it does so only under such conditions that render remote the possibility that we ever have or ever will face such a threat.

Autonomy, Consequentialism, and Rights-Based Theories

From the perspective of autonomy, we are justified to deliberately target the innocent only if they themselves could consent to the sacrifice, only if their refusal would be impermissible as constituting a gross indifference to the lives of others. We do not kill them for the greater good; rather, we act from the perspective that each life must count for something.

We have seen that consequentialism would permit actions that conflict with our considered judgments and would permit actions that conflict with the very purpose of the war convention. The theory of autonomy, on the other hand, has provided guidance consistent with our considered moral judgments and the purpose of the war convention. And here, at the extremities, the theory of autonomy grants an exception to the prohibition against killing the innocent only if the exception follows from the principles themselves, that is, only if the exception follows from a respect for autonomy. Only if the innocent themselves must consent, out of respect for humanity, can we contemplate deliberately targeting them. Each individual *does* count for something; human beings are not reduced to communal property.

Rather than subordinating the worth of the individual to some general good, it is respect for individuals that justifies the exception. It is respect for a value, not a result we wish to bring about, that motivates our actions. By maintaining a fundamental respect for humanity, yet offering us a principled account of why we might sacrifice the innocent under conditions wherein their refusal would be indecent,[14] we show how autonomy aligns with our considered judgments. For we do think that people act impermissibly when they show utter indifference to the lives of others; and only at the point where we feel they are shirking their duty – a duty of a particularly important kind – do we feel justified in insisting that they do it.

And this last point gives us insight as to how the theory of autonomy can provide greater clarity and more consistent guidance in just war theory, even in the very hard cases, than rights-based theories. Consider the following argument from Paul Christopher, like Walzer, a rights theorist:[15]

> Once one accepts that there may be scenarios where the outcome is so important, the alternatives so heinous, that the intentional expenditure of human life is justified in order to gain a particular result, then one has already committed oneself to some type of consequentialist analysis.[16]

Christopher and Walzer are committed to some type of consequentialist analysis, and its attendant vagaries, because they misconstrue the nature of justification for response to aggression. We do not act to gain a particular result; the recourse to consequentialist reasoning is never taken since it is ruled out in advance. We react to a certain devaluation of our agency; we reject impermissible maxims; and we act out of respect for a value. This seems to be the proper attitude to adopt towards the use of violence in response to aggression. Indeed, as I have argued, it provides the most consistent, defensible justification for our resort to violence.

The fundamental point of departure between my approach and theorists like Walzer and Christopher is that they *do* adopt consequentialist reasoning to ground at least some of their conclusions about supreme emergency. So their theories have problems in terms of consistency. A theory should be able to account for the guidance it renders using its own resources; at least, if it uses other sources, it should show how they are consistent with its own perspective. In the case of at least these two rights-based theorists, they adopt as a ground for their conclusion a theory that is generally at odds with their overall projects. They argue for the protection of individual human rights against the claims of the general welfare. Yet at the point of supreme emergency, they argue for the general welfare at the expense of individual rights. This is at least problematic.

But according to the theory of autonomy, the principles of autonomy ground the decision to kill the innocent. It specifically rejects consequentialism and looks to its own resources to see if there could be any possible way to justify such an act.

Before concluding, we should examine one last view about supreme emergency and the justification for deliberately targeting noncombatants. This view has it that citizens of a thoroughly evil regime become legitimate targets just by the fact that they remain in the country. The reasoning is that anyone who stayed as members of such an odious community must be seen as having adopted an impermissible maxim we could justifiably resist. There is some credibility to this way of thinking, especially if these civilians know about and endorse the evil aims of their government. If they actively participate in the persecution and exploitation of disenfranchised members of their own community or members of conquered lands, it becomes increasingly more plausible to attribute to them the adoption of maxims to harm. Moreover, these seem to be impermissible maxims to harm.

But we should resist this line of thought. For surely the babies in this country have not adopted maxims that justify our deliberate targeting of them.[17] We would have to have a way of singling out only those adults who were involved in the evil. It also seems unreasonable to think that all of the civilians had knowledge of the evil machinations of their government. And, even if they did, is it reasonable to expect people to leave their country? Furthermore, do we believe it is even possible? The sorts of regimes we are considering here are the sorts that do not generally have liberal emigration policies. For example, does anyone really believe that the average Iraqi citizen could have left Saddam Hussein's Iraq whenever he (the citizen) wanted?[18] Finally, to expect open revolt in most of these circumstances is unrealistically self-righteous. A theory that expects people to openly resist an evil regime when the cost would surely be their lives and perhaps the lives of their families seems unreasonable.

This is obviously not an exhaustive treatment of this view. But it seems clear that using as the criterion to justify the deliberate attacking of noncombatants the mere fact that they remain in their country has undesirable implications.

The theory of autonomy accounts for our ambivalence about supreme emergency without capitulating to consequentialism. It accounts for our intuitions that we should not have to succumb impotently to the rule of abject evil. Yet it characterizes that evil in such a way, and permits the deliberate targeting of innocents only under such conditions, that ambiguities about supreme emergency are greatly mitigated. In a sense, we have demystified supreme emergency, heretofore conceived as a situation of moral conflict where we could not do right. The description I give more accurately captures the true character of supreme emergency. There may never have been or ever will be a true supreme emergency. But if we are faced with one, at least on the theory of autonomy, we *can* do right. We have an option, consistent with the principles of autonomy, that permits targeting noncombatants.[19]

Finally, I briefly note, that even though we have not violated principles of autonomy if we kill the innocent in times of supreme emergency, the principles have nonetheless been violated. We should not forget, as we learned, explaining how even the death of a soldier is morally wrong, that he who starts the unjust war of aggression violates principles generated by autonomy. He has made victims of us all.

Notes

1   Walzer, p. 251.
2   Ibid., p. 251.
3   Ibid., p. 254.
4   Ibid., p. 262.
5   Ibid., p. 132, quoted earlier.
6   Of course, that the theory of autonomy will reject such consequentialist reasoning might itself pose a problem for the theory in the eyes of many. There are those who think that any theory that prevented us from killing a small number of people in order to save many other people is flawed. But to debate the issue on this level merely brings us back to the fundamental debate between consequentialism and theories informed by a Kantian perspective, which is not the focus of my project. Nonetheless, I must recognize that even under this description, our intuitions are not clear as to what to do: do we refuse to kill the baby in order to save the world? This is why supreme emergency is such a difficult issue. But here I am concerned with showing how the theory of autonomy can guide us on the issue. It might well be that the conclusions autonomy provides are unacceptable to many people.
7   I understand that this is not a decisive argument. But it shifts the burden of proof to those who say the numbers make a difference to articulate a reasoned principle that accounts for the difference. I do not see any such principle at this time.
8   I borrow the term "indecent" from Warren Quinn. He says there are certain circumstances where it would be indecent of people to refuse to accept great personal sacrifice. He does not specify what those circumstances could be, but notes that "...noncombatants are not morally obligated to serve the right side by accepting the role of demoralizing civilian casualties..." (p. 191). In the case of supreme emergency, of course, the noncombatants are not, or should not be, targeted for demoralizing purposes.
9   Of course it follows that, in some circumstances, the morally correct course of action might require sacrificing a *larger group to save a smaller group*. This is clear when we consider a situation similar to that of the Titanic. Suppose that there are enough boats to save only a very small minority of passengers. If people clamor and fight for the lifeboats, no one will be saved: the lifeboats will either capsize or be destroyed. We can put all sorts of stipulations on the scenario, but the general idea is that we presume there to be a way of designating some people, a minority, who could take the boats and be saved. The majority would willingly have to accept their fate. In such a scenario, since the majority faces the same fate either way, we would see their failure to accept that fate as indecent. If they doom everyone to a death that they cannot avoid in any case, they show the sort of profane indifference towards the lives of others that should elicit our general opprobrium.
10 I acknowledge the tension here. What exactly is it about the man on the ship, for instance, that lifts his immunity and allows us to throw him overboard? I cannot completely resolve the issue here. Nonetheless, there are features of the situation that might point the way to a satisfactory resolution. Insofar as he manifests a gross indifference for the lives of others, he seems to have adopted an impermissible maxim. As such, our use of force against him seems morally similar to our response to unjust aggression. But it is not exactly like this. And even if it were, it would not answer the question for noncombatants whom we deliberately target in supreme emergency. Unlike the man on the ship, they are not now manifesting indifference towards the lives

of others. That is, it is not as though they are in a position to see and understand our shared peril and then choose to jump or not jump into the breach, as it were. And it is because the issue is so complex and morally problematic that I will stipulate the conditions necessary to constitute supreme emergency in terms that make it unlikely that there ever has been or will be a true case of supreme emergency wherein we would be justified in deliberately targeting noncombatants.

11 The conditions I will outline seem implied in the way we have characterized supreme emergency; they seem to follow from Walzer's depiction of the Nazi-threat. Nonetheless I must acknowledge that others may conceive it differently and consider my criteria too severe. They might "set the bar lower," as it were. But given what we want to be able to justify by invoking supreme emergency, I think we must insist on the most stringent criteria. In order to respond in detail to those who differ, I would have to examine their criteria.

12 I owe this example to Sergio Tenenbaum.

13 We must remember that one criterion that must be met is that the German civilians faced the same fate. Would life for them be a fate worse than death? If not, we would be precluded from targeting them since the only justification to do so would follow from the sort of consequentialist reasoning I reject.

14 Perhaps our judgment that their refusal would be indecent rests on a notion that somehow their maxim is one of deliberately harming. If they object to a particular course of action that could save others even though that course of action costs them nothing (they are going to die either way), we might plausibly describe their maxim as one of deliberately harming: they are, in effect, obstructing those who otherwise could be saved. It is as if they say, "Because we cannot possibly live, we coerce you to share our fate, even though there is no reason at all for you to have to die." Of course, the insight here requires far greater development, but if this turns out to be a plausible account of their maxim, it might point to the reason why we judge as indecent the refusal to accept certain sacrifices.

15 I take Christopher to be a rights-based theorist. Christopher argues from two moral truths which seem to assume human rights, particularly the right of noninterference and the right to render aid against aggression; see pp. 162-3. See Walzer, pp. 134-7 for the articulation of his rights-based views.

16 Christopher, p. 172.

17 No plausible account of DDE could justify the deaths of babies from terror bombing; certainly the conception of DDE that I have outlined would condemn their deaths.

18 I use the Iraq example because some people hold the opinion that the Iraqi people deserved the misery they suffered from the effects of economic sanctions since they had chosen to remain in Iraq, not because I equate Iraq to a Nazi-like regime, in spite of the fact that Saddam was a malevolent ruler. It is necessary to point out that it is absurd to think that the average Iraqi citizen could leave his country or revolt (the next point in my discussion). These types of oppressive regimes are precisely the sorts where it is exceedingly difficult to openly resist. That is why I think it is a mistake to conclude that people become legitimate targets simply because they remain in their country. At least, we should have a very strong presumption against it.

19 Obviously there are those who would reject my assertion that we can do right, that we can avoid moral conflict. But they owe us an alternate theory. Furthermore, I have provided an argument to show that the theory corresponds to our moral intuitions in this regard.

Epilogue

Just War Theory, Law Enforcement, and Terrorism: A Reflective Equilibrium

This epilogue was written after 11 September. Since then, given the nature of the current struggle against worldwide terrorism, some have called into question the relevance of just war theory. I contend that just war theory remains viable, indeed remains as important as it has ever been. In this epilogue I will show how the theory of autonomy provides ample and consistent moral guidance in the fight against terrorism. Once we understand the deep principles that justify the use of force in general, we can apply them consistently and lucidly to any particular case. I seek a reflective equilibrium between just war theory and principles of domestic law enforcement in order to present a coherent picture of the nature of the struggle against terrorism. In the process, I must examine the standard *jus ad bellum* criteria in reference to the so-called war on terrorism in order to address misconceptions about the morality of our response to terrorism. Many people apply these criteria and conclude that our response to terrorism has been unjust or that just war theory is obsolete; hence, they come to feel uneasy at the prospect of having no consistent theoretical way to justify the war against terrorism. And without the conceptual apparatus to justify the war, they fear that we may lose our moral bearings as we face this pressing challenge to our deepest human values.

Such fears are unfounded, for there are deep principles that can and do justify and guide our use of force in the war against terrorism. Just war theory is not obsolete, and understood properly it can provide appropriate moral guidance to us. The problems of justification have arisen in attempting to apply the just war theory template in inappropriate ways. We are engaged in a conflict that conceptually, in many important respects, resembles law enforcement. But the enemy is so arrayed, armed, and organized that the forces and tactics required to combat him make our struggle look like conventional war. Hence, at times the appropriate model to understand the situation in a moral sense is the model of domestic law enforcement; at other times, just war theory is the appropriate model.

I will articulate a reflective equilibrium between principles of just war theory and principles of law enforcement and show how the theory of autonomy grounds both. Neither model – just war nor law enforcement – adequately captures the moral reality of the war against terrorism independently. But if they are taken together, using moral insights from both domains, a new and relevant model emerges that can provide moral guidance in the war against terrorism. I do not claim that what follows is an exhaustive treatment of the issues. More analysis is required, but I offer a moral framework with which to direct the analysis so that we can yield more satisfactory results than are perhaps possible using other conceptual apparatuses.

The Domestic Analogy

Michael Walzer describes the domestic analogy in the following way:

> The comparison of international to civil order is crucial to the theory of aggression.... Every reference to aggression as the international equivalent of armed robbery or murder, and every comparison of home and country or of personal liberty and political independence, relies upon what is called the *domestic analogy*. Our primary perceptions and judgments of aggression are the products of analogical reasoning. When the analogy is made explicit...the world of states takes on the shape of a political society the character of which is entirely accessible through such notions as crime and punishment, self-defense, law enforcement, and so on.[1]

As Walzer points out, just war theory owes much of its moral force to analogical reasoning about domestic law enforcement. But there is a notorious point of disanalogy, namely, that there is no world sovereign or world police force. Hence it is often considered difficult, even illegitimate, to traffic back and forth between the two domains in attempting to resolve the more intractable problems we face concerning the use of force, particularly in the international arena. But despite the points of disanalogy between the international and civil realms, between war fighting and law enforcement, the justification to use force in either realm follows from deep moral principles, having to do with resisting unjust coercion or rejecting threats to our capacity to will, that transcend the civil/international distinction. The theory of autonomy provides the link between the domestic analogy/law enforcement and just war theory and accounts for the moral force of the analogy. When we examine any use of force along the lines I have discussed throughout this work, we can see a common moral thread. We use force justly to uphold our deepest human values, and justice is defined in terms of respect for humanity as outlined in the theory of autonomy. As such, the pursuit of a reflective equilibrium, informed by the theory of autonomy, will greatly aid our understanding of the current struggle against terrorism.

Seeking the Equilibrium

As I have said earlier, just war theory is often considered from two perspectives: *jus ad bellum* and *jus in bello*[2]. In this epilogue, I will focus on *jus ad bellum* but will have occasion to address some relevant *jus in bello* issues.

There are several ways to articulate the various components of *jus ad bellum*. I will discuss the following: *just cause, right intention, proper authority, reasonable chance of success, no precipitous use of force (last resort), and proportionality*.[3] I will examine their applicability to the war on terrorism, incorporating insights from domestic law enforcement, in order to arrive at a coherent, satisfactory, and morally compelling understanding of the war on terrorism. I understand that the war on terrorism takes many forms. My discussion here is primarily informed by the sorts of conflicts typified by the war in Afghanistan and the American experience since September 11. I believe the insights ultimately have a more general application.

Just Cause

Defense against aggression represents the paradigm of just cause to use force. When one nation invades another, unprovoked, absent an offense to be redressed, the invaded nation can use force to defend itself. As we have seen in the Walzer passage above, we understand this insight in terms of the domestic analogy. The relationship obtaining between states is analogous to that obtaining between individuals within states; both states and individuals are considered in this context to be rights-bearing agents, and nations have the right to political sovereignty and territorial integrity. Any violation of these rights in the international sphere is analogous to robbery or murder in the domestic sphere. Brian Orend states:

> The key principle here is the defence and vindication of fundamental rights, and
> the protection of those who have them from serious harm. From these general
> considerations, three just causes, in particular, can be deduced: 1) self-defence
> from aggression; 2) the defence of others from aggression; and 3) armed
> intervention in a non-aggressive country wherein grievous human rights
> violations are occurring.[4]

There is a presumption that the use of force against such threats is justified. In general, we have just cause to use force in self-defense, to protect the innocent, and to vindicate human rights: we do all of these in our fight against terrorism. Such justification aligns with the Means Only Principle and the Rejection of Unjust Aggression Principle.

In the case of terrorism, the US can claim just cause. Especially with regard to the terror network responsible for 9/11, we are using force against murderers, those who deliberately targeted and killed innocents. Furthermore, the 9/11 attacks violated the territorial integrity and political sovereignty of the US.

But the incursion into Afghanistan requires some sorting out. It is not as if the 9/11 attacks exactly resembled an attack undertaken by a sovereign nation, analogous to the Japanese attack on Pearl Harbor in 1941. That is, the attacks did not appear to be a national effort on the part of Afghanistan. Nonetheless, the terrorists used Afghanistan as a sanctuary in which they planned and from which they launched their attacks. If the Afghanistan government was unwilling to control the terrorists and unwilling to hand them over, our attacks there seem roughly analogous to a police raid into the home of someone who is harboring a criminal. On the other hand, if the Afghanistan government was unable to prevent or hand-over the terrorists, our actions might resemble a police raid intended to secure a neighborhood victimized or held hostage by a criminal gang. In any case, I do not see the justification here as conceptually that difficult. We do not grant criminals impunity on the grounds of the supposed inviolability of their sanctuary. In both the domestic and international domains, principles of justice permit the pursuit of criminals wherever they go. There are limitations as to what can be done, and justification is clearly required. But the point is that justification is also *possible* within the context of principles that both protect the rights of individuals and states yet permit the pursuit of criminals.

The principle of just cause, then, seems to work in very similar ways in both just war theory and law enforcement. In both arenas, just cause derives from notions of human dignity. We are justified in rejecting actions that coerce human beings and treat then as mere means; we are sometimes justified in using force in the defense of human rights.

Right Intention

Even if we have just cause, we cannot use it as a cloak for other aims. For example, it would be impermissible to use our legitimate claim of just cause for attacking Al Qaida (as a war of self-defense or law enforcement) as a cloak to hide another intention, say, the eradication of the opium trade. If the latter did provide just cause in itself, it would have to be justified independently (an unlikely prospect).

This principle includes the requirement to abide by *jus in bello* proscriptions.[5] The primary injunction of *jus in bello* is discrimination: nations engaged in conventional war or war against terrorism must discriminate between combatants and noncombatants. As the theory of autonomy emphasizes, we must take great care in minimizing harm to noncombatants. The distinction between combatants and noncombatants translates further into the distinction between legitimate and illegitimate targets, an important clarification for issues attendant to the war against terrorists. For example, even though we are using conventional soldiers to fight Al Qaida in Afghanistan, we do not automatically consider those terrorists to be legal combatants in the sense that they merit POW status and all that goes with it in terms of the Geneva and other conventions. They are suspected criminals who typically will be prosecuted in accordance with due legal process. Nonetheless, they *are* suspected criminals, and insofar as they are engaged in harming us, they *are* legitimate targets. And although they do not have POW rights, they generally acquire the legal rights of the accused. And under any description, if they attempt to surrender, we must accept their surrender and follow due process after that. It is worth noting at this point that, through the process of reflective equilibrium, we are able to arrive at a better understanding of the status of terrorists.

In some way, right intention and just cause are two sides of the same conceptual coin. To have a right intention is to be committed to vindicating human rights, rejecting evil, and abiding by the terms of the justice that warranted our violent response to evil in the first place.

Proper Authority

This is an oft cited yet little understood principle of just war, and it holds great importance for our understanding of the fight against terrorism. On some level, we could view this principle as fundamental to civil or international order. This principle addresses issues concerning the legitimate authority to declare and wage war. It is generally acknowledged that only viable political communities, in the person or persons of their leaders, can legitimately declare and prosecute war. This immediately implies that private persons, ordinary citizens, are denied the right to wage war, and the denial of this right accounts for the essential criminality of terrorism.[6] This criterion has, then, a permissive and a restrictive aspect. It is permissive insofar as it grants to the sovereign the authority to wage (just) wars, restrictive in that it denies this authority to ordinary citizens. Although the permissive aspect is often highlighted, the restrictive feature may shoulder more of the moral work, at least in the context of an analysis of terrorism.

Insights from social contract theory inform our ideas with regard to proper authority. In the state of nature, everyone is empowered to enforce the law of nature. Once the community is formed, however, the power of enforcement is transferred to the body politic and the people's representatives who have been designated to perform the law enforcement function. Except under extreme circumstances, ordinary citizens are precluded from law enforcement activities. *A fortiori*, they are prohibited from mounting personal violent campaigns against states. Those who transgress this prohibition or do not acknowledge its force remain in the state of nature with respect to everyone else. Hence, the rationale behind this principle is *sine qua non* to the possibility of civil and international society. Those who prosecute "private wars" put themselves in the state of nature with respect to all of humanity. And we should specify that this is a Hobbesian state of nature, a lawless, anarchical condition where the very concepts of morality, justice, and injustice do not exist.

Terrorists proclaim by their actions their unwillingness to abide by the sorts of laws or social conventions that make society possible. At the very least, they reject pluralist society, and we are justified in saying that the coercive measures they adopt put them in the state of nature with respect to the communities they target. They recognize no proscriptions or constraints or any authority over them such that it would bind them as members of communities committed to a cooperative quest for justice. It seems that, to them, their cause defines whatever justice they recognize; it might even be more accurate to say that they deny the relevance of commonly accepted notions of justice. Every value, including the value of humanity, is subordinated to their cause. The struggle against them is in this respect like domestic law enforcement against depraved, violent criminals who violate state law.[7] Understanding this conceptual framework properly will pay big dividends as we investigate the connection of just war concepts to the war against terrorism. Terrorists represent a rejection of community. In a very deep sense, their ideology is logically incompatible with the idea of a cooperative human venture, either in its civil or international forms. It is not simply that they do not act under the aegis of proper authority, they deny the relevance of the principle. In so doing, they deny the legitimacy of states, they deny the rights of people to carve out a shared life, they deny the unique importance of individual human beings, and ultimately they deny morality. They are like predators with whom coexistence is unthinkable. As Locke says, they have "declared war against all mankind, and therefore may be destroyed as a lion or tiger, one of those wild savage beasts with whom men can have no society nor security."[8]

This just war principle includes the following requirement (an insight which again I borrow from Brian Orend). A country engaged in a just war must remain committed to maintaining and securing the civil liberties of its own citizens. For instance, we witnessed an alarming call for the curtailment of civil liberties in the U.S. after 9/11. This call was made more disconcerting by the attempt in some quarters to legitimize racial profiling, reminiscent of the treatment of Japanese Americans during World War II. Countries who are committed to justice should eschew reactionary measures that violate the rights they are fighting to defend. Furthermore, in some sense, if we impinge our own civil liberties, the terrorists have won insofar as they seek to threaten our way of life. If we in essence coerce ourselves as a response to their coercion, they have achieved their ends. This is not to say that we cannot take measures that make our lives more inconvenient (e.g., airport lines). But inconvenience is not prohibition; our rights remain intact. It merely takes a little longer to get what we want. And note that the inconvenience itself is noncoercive; the security is something we freely choose as a people to safeguard our rights. The lines at the airport take on the same moral dimensions as speed limits – agreed-upon measures that protect us from the reckless and the criminal.

Reasonable Chance of Success

In the context of just war, this principle enjoins nations to decline the resort to war when it seems clear that the effort would be futile. For example, a small nation invaded by an overwhelmingly superior force should not resort to war. To resort to war with no chance of success manifests gross indifference to the lives of those who would die in the futile effort, an effort whose result is foreseen. It represents a waste of human lives and a decadent abuse of power by those who frivolously spend the precious national resource that the citizenry is. For nations faced with this trying situation, there at least remains hope of diplomatic resolution some time in the future; but for those wasted dead, all hope is lost. Although capitulation to evil violates our sense of justice on one level, complicity in senseless slaughter is a far deeper violation of justice.

However, there is one circumstance where, even in the face of certain defeat, resistance might nonetheless be preferable to standing by and doing nothing. If the invading force represents a certain level of evil and malevolence, such that life under them would be nightmarish, a fate worse than death, then it might be best to resist. If death or enslavement is inevitable whether you resist or not, it seems best to resist. Such resistance might be consistent with respect for humanity and represent consent on the part of the citizenry, since all would reasonably be assumed to prefer to fight and die rather than live such an existence. As Chapter 7 indicated, the Nazis represent the sort of evil that might warrant such a response. When we face death or enslavement whether we resist or not, it seems at least permissible, if not preferable, to resist with force.

In any case, this principle comes to bear on the war against terrorism in the following way. There are those who say that we have no reasonable chance of success in eliminating terrorism; hence, they argue, we should not take up the fight. Or they argue about the difficulty in identifying an end state, and they hesitate to resort to force in those cases where force is the most appropriate response. But the confusion here arises because detractors are trying to apply this just war concept to a problem that is much better understood in terms of the law enforcement model. Consider it this way. We can never reasonably hope entirely to eliminate robbery or murder. Does it then follow that we should not pursue and bring to justice this particular robber or that particular murderer? It seems implausible to think so; we endeavor to bring to justice all evil doers even in the face of the fact that evil will nonetheless persist.

We are forced to reevaluate our conception of what an appropriate end state would be. Yes, we would like to eliminate all terrorism and bring every terrorist to justice. But falling short of that does not mean we have failed. We gain some measure of success with each terrorist we bring to justice. Furthermore, we are successful if we reduce the threat, just as domestic law enforcement agencies are successful if they reduce crime. The notion that success is intrinsically tied to the unconditional surrender[9] and the complete eradication of the enemy is as inappropriate in this war as it is in most conventional wars. Justice is met, perhaps only met, when less comprehensive conditions are set.

A conceptual error results if we do not seek the reflective equilibrium. If we follow this line of analysis, we will develop some reasoned principles to guide us in non-arbitrary ways in conducting a just campaign against terrorism.

No Precipitous Use of Force

Just war literature often refers to this principle as "last resort"; it requires nations to resort to war only as a last resort to resolve problems. But to call it last resort is problematic. Hence, I prefer (following Orend again) to capture the essence of this principle in terms of the precipitous use of force. The principle conceived under the description of last resort is not very helpful in war or in law enforcement. For one thing, we can never know what constitutes lastness, as Michael Walzer says:[10] there always will be one more negotiating session or one more concession that we can make. Furthermore, by waiting for the so-called conditions of last resort, we might unwittingly concede the victory to the enemy. Witness the war in Kosovo. The longer NATO refrained from the resort to force, the longer the Serbs had to commit their ethnic cleansing. We could argue that, under these circumstances, justice demands a resort to force sooner rather than later.

What is required, then, is for nations to consider judiciously the circumstances and certainly seek peaceful resolution before any resort to war. On the other hand, nations should recognize that hesitancy to use force in the face of certain forms of evil fails the test of justice as much as the unnecessary, precipitous use of force. Consider an example in law enforcement. If a criminal is engaged in harming his victim, we do not require the police to first negotiate with the criminal to have him stop. The "last resort" criterion does not come to bear here in the same way as it does in the arena of conventional war. The immediacy of the situation and the unambiguousness of the evil intent/action minimize or eliminate the requirement for lastness. Of course, if the police can get the criminal to cease and desist by simply yelling "halt" or some such thing, we would call for such a course of action. It is circumstance dependent; we could make the same point about circumstance with respect to war. But in the case of law enforcement, the presumption in favor of using force is different than that in the case of war. We recognize the exigencies involved with *hot pursuit* and do not impose last resort requirements under such conditions. Perhaps we feel that we have already met the last resort requirement when involved in hot pursuit against a criminal who is presently engaged in harming. But that is only to recognize that negotiations, the use of measures other than force, are sometimes not appropriate; indeed, they are sometimes impossible unless one sacrifices the victim.

So in response to a criticism about precipitous use of force in response to terrorism – for example, Operation Enduring Freedom in Afghanistan – we can plausibly offer the domestic analogy. We are involved in hot pursuit against criminals who have harmed and are actively engaged in harming. Like a policeman, we should not negotiate with murderers who have indicated by word and deed that they will not negotiate; in fact, we cannot negotiate. Negotiation is not logically possible with those who reject the very principles that ground the possibility of negotiation. Hence, if the only way to stop a criminal or terrorist is by force, then the resort to force is not precipitous. Indeed, as the only feasible course of action, precipitousness is not logically possible; there is only one acceptable recourse, and that is force. It is not, and cannot be, precipitous: any other course of action might fail the demands of justice.[11]

Proportionality

I am going to approach the issue of proportionality a little differently than the other criteria and offer a perspective somewhat different than that encountered in much of just war orthodoxy. In the end, my discussion suggests at least the plausibility of eliminating proportionality as a just war criterion, and this is consistent with the account of the Doctrine of Double Effect that I have already presented in Chapter 6. I am concerned that consequentialist reasoning gets smuggled into any theory that has recourse to proportionality as one of its fundamental moral notions. I must begin with its *jus in bello* application.

In the context of just war theory or law enforcement, proportionality must be considered a normative, not a descriptive term. By this I mean that if we condemn a particular action on grounds of proportionality, it must be because some normative standard has been violated, not because of a violation of some descriptive standard understood along something like mathematical lines. In other words, it cannot be about numbers and ratios of forces, otherwise we would get absurd results. If we are justified in using force to resist evil, we are justified in using as much force as necessary to win, as long as we do not ourselves commit evil in the process. And since at least part of what is impermissible with the evil we are facing, especially when facing a violent criminal or conducting a war, is that it coerces us to face the risk of bodily harm or death, then it is permissible for us to do not only what is necessary to win, but also what is necessary to reduce our risk to the bare minimum. Hence, we are morally permitted to achieve overwhelming force, if possible. That is, when we resist a threat, say a criminal who attacks us, our just end is to eliminate that threat. It cannot be the case, then, that we are morally required to endure risk proportional to the amount we seek to impose on the criminal, as if he were entitled to fair odds. Hence, we are not restricted to the use of means proportionate to those available to our attacker. We may use a bigger stick than he does, for example, and we may enlist help from as many people as are available and willing to aid us.

This does not mean that we are permitted to do whatever would be required to secure victory or reduce risk. When facing our attacker, we may not snatch a baby out of the arms of a bystander and use it as a shield. Furthermore, once we have subdued the criminal, once he can no longer threaten us, we are no longer permitted to harm him – we may not beat him or abuse him, although we can continue to restrain him, put him in jail, and bring him to trial.

Consider a scenario from domestic law enforcement. Suppose a drunkard is causing a disturbance in a public place by starting fights and attacking people. When the police are called, do we feel their response is disproportionate when they arrive with several officers to subdue the man? Hardly. We do not expect the police officers to fight a "fair fight" and go one-on-one with the criminal just in order to meet some bizarre proportionality requirement. It does not matter if they surround him with 100 police officers; no rights of the criminal will have been violated simply by the force of numbers. His being gravely outnumbered does him no injustice. He is committing a crime, and it is permissible to stop him. And that is the appropriate, permissible goal of the officers. They can subdue the criminal and use force if required. So our moral concerns about proportionality cannot be simply descriptive in nature; we are not concerned, per se, that law enforcement officials, for instance, overwhelm the criminal.

But granting this point does not resolve the more complicated issues about proportionality. It still seems to make sense to say that even if we allow the police greatly to outnumber the criminal, their response must be proportionate, understood in some normative sense. If they must beat the criminal in order to subdue him (say he is struggling violently), they must stop beating him once he is subdued. Moreover, they must not beat him more severely than is required to subdue him, which seems to be a requirement for proportionality and is the most pressing problem we must solve.[12]

There is also an important sense in which we feel that the punishment must "fit" the crime and that even the means of enforcement must be proportionate to the offense. We should neither incarcerate jaywalkers for life, nor should police shoot people for spitting on the sidewalk. Such draconian measures would be condemned as disproportionate, and it is from consideration of such examples that we see the normative dimension of proportionality.

Deeper analysis will give us a different understanding of proportionality. My primary target here is the conception of proportionality as a tradeoff of good and evil, especially with regard to the use of force in the domestic or international arenas. Typically, when we demand proportionate force, we demand that the good outweigh the evil, as if an evil component were necessarily connected to the use of force. I reject the idea that evil necessarily attaches to any use of force; it is an incoherent notion, and it has disastrous moral results if reasoned to its logical conclusion. Look more closely at a domestic scenario. We do not judge our use of force against a criminal along a spectrum, with good and evil on its opposite ends vying for preeminence in one and the same act of violence, both intimately involved. The act's moral character is not defined arbitrarily according to the amount of good or evil produced, as if somewhere along the spectrum a mysterious transmogrification takes place, changing good into evil. Kant makes a similar point when decrying the shortcomings of virtue ethics:

> [it is]...the most objectionable...because it bases morality on sensuous motives which rather undermine it and totally destroy its sublimity, inasmuch as the motives of virtue are put in the same class as those of vice and we are instructed only to become better at calculation, the specific difference between virtue and vice being completely wiped out.[13]

When a police officer struggles with a criminal, it does not make sense to say that he is doing something that is both good and evil but that we condone his use of force because the good outweighs the evil. He is doing something right in rejecting unjust aggression. We do not judge him on a scale. On the other hand, if he shoots the jaywalker or continues to beat the criminal after the criminal is subdued, we do not think that his use of violence is wrong because the evil now outweighs the good. Rather, we feel he is simply doing something evil in its own right. It is not evil because it is disproportionate; to think so reverses the order of our judgment. I contend that our judgment that such an act (i.e., shooting the jaywalker) is evil is prior to our designation of it as disproportionate and is based on principles that form the general grounds for the justification to use any force whatsoever. Putative violations of proportionality violate more fundamental notions having to do with human dignity, as outlined in the theory of autonomy. We can use force against criminals only as a response to a threat they might pose.

Once a criminal is subdued, it is impermissible to continue to beat him. I will not work out all the implications here of the theory of autonomy for law enforcement, but it should be clear that judgments about the legitimate use of force are based on notions more fundamental than proportionality. Once a particular threat is thwarted, no further warrants follow – except for, of course, those that follow from civil codes having to do with appropriate punishment for transgressions.[14] But these are all meted out within the context of recognizing the criminal's autonomy in spite of his crimes and thus granting him protection from the sort of *unjust* coercion that police brutality represents.

Given the foregoing discussion, we can see how *jus in bello* charges of disproportionality in war, understood normatively, become absurd, as if one side should give up its advantage over the other in the interests of fairness. As a normative term, it has no meaning here. Any victory is marked by disproportion in some respect: more supplies, more men, more weapons, more will or courage. If we had to meet some criterion of proportionality, viewed normatively, in order to justify our actions in war, then it would be impossible to fight the just war justly – at least it would be impossible to win the just war justly, and this is a preposterous conclusion, resulting from confusion about proportionality. Proportionality can only be applied with meaning in a descriptive sense, and nations are permitted to attempt to overwhelm their enemies. We expect them to achieve an advantage, a disproportion in training or weaponry, in order to vanquish their foes, and we do not attach moral significance to the attempt. We do not, for instance, begrudge countries for developing better tanks than those of its enemies. If, however, they use means that deliberately harm noncombatants, they fail the moral test of discrimination, not proportionality. If they use means that cause unnecessary suffering to enemy soldiers, it is the same sort of failure, since, as discussed earlier, the proscription against "unnecessary suffering" requires us to avoid the use of weapons designed deliberately to cause injury that continues to harm after a soldier's status as a combatant has ended. Furthermore, they must accept the surrender of those who would lay down their arms in submission. So, countries that fail to abide by these sorts of limits are like police who continue to beat a criminal after he has been subdued; the evil is not in lack of proportion but in the violation of the sorts of rights the protection of which justified violent response in the first place. Other principles more fundamental than proportionality do the moral work.

Note that this conception of proportionality coincides well with our more considered judgments about just war and the purpose of the laws of war. We fight a just war to safeguard human dignity and to protect the innocent: autonomy imposes the moral limits we must follow. Once we see that our use of force is not inevitably a tradeoff of good for evil, we will see the inherent evil in some actions, say, the deliberate targeting of noncombatants, and will be prohibited from taking such actions. This is an important result of this analysis of proportionality. We rule out in advance the notion that we can do evil to prevent evil, as if somehow the real blood of the few innocents whom we deliberately kill can be washed from our hands by the imagined blood of the many innocents we allegedly save. Our understanding here reinforces the notions of constraint that must govern our response to terrorism. The theory of autonomy provides moral illumination.

In terms of *jus ad bellum*, proportionality traditionally plays out in two ways. First, nations must consider whether the resort to war for a given offense is a proportionate response. Not every violation of territorial integrity or political sovereignty constitutes aggression; hence, not every such violation justifies war as a response. Nations are not justified in going to war against their neighbors simply because of inadvertent border crossings. Such violations of borders do not constitute a threat to fundamental states' rights and so would not constitute just cause. Even if we conceive such border crossings as violations of fundamental rights, there are clearly other measures we could take short of war. We could and would pursue diplomatic solutions, for instance. The sense is that we would resort to war only when it became apparent that other solutions were not reasonable and that the offensive practice promised to continue and increase in magnitude such that it would represent a real threat to sovereignty or territorial integrity. Under such circumstances, war might be considered a *proportionate* response. But all we are saying, ultimately, is that we now have *just cause* to use force. A resort to war in the first instance would violate the principles of just cause and precipitous use of force. Proportionality would not be the real issue; all the normative work is done under a consideration of principles other than proportionality.

The second way, closely related to the first, in which proportionality is said to figure in just war analysis has to do with the weighing of consequences. As Orend writes:

> A state must, prior to initiating a war, weigh the expected universal good to accrue from its prosecuting the (otherwise just) war against the universal evils expected to result. Only if the benefits, such as rights vindication, seem reasonably proportional to the costs, such as casualties, may the war action proceed.[15]

I disagree with Orend's analysis here in that it involves us in a conceptual error. It makes it appear as if there is something intrinsically evil in the recourse to war, as if we must admit that dirty hands are somehow inescapable on the part of those who would resist aggression with force. As we have seen, the domestic analogy provides some insight as to the inadequacy of this conception of proportionality.

There is nothing inherently evil with the policeman's doing of his duty. We do not think that there is an evil aspect of his use of force against the criminal that is justified only if outweighed by the good results. In the terms of this discussion, the policeman has adopted a permissible maxim – in itself there is no evil aspect. This is not to say that no action on his part could be impermissible. For example, it would be impermissible for him to throw a baby in front of the vehicle of an escaping criminal in an attempt to get the criminal to stop. But this course of action is ruled out because it is so grossly rights violative; it is not an issue of proportionality. The policeman has been commissioned to protect the innocent, and this commission imposes the just limits on the actions he can take. He must not hurt the innocent in the pursuit of the guilty; he must not violate justice in the name of justice.

It is the protection of rights that imposes limits, not a principle of proportion. When we view the underlying principles that justify our resistance to evil in the first place, we see that justification is not based on principles of proportionality but rather on principles of human rights, which we have accounted for in terms of autonomy. We are committed to rejecting unjust coercion and must eschew means that themselves violate the principles in whose name we act.

We must consider the enterprise of war in a similar light. We should not consider it as an inherently unjust endeavor for the same reasoning as we reject such a conception of the situation in the domestic sphere. When coerced to protect ourselves, using force against evil, it is inaccurate to characterize our use of force as involving an inherent aspect of evil. Undeniably, bad things happen in war. We would be grossly remiss if we did not acknowledge this and anticipate the ugly consequences of war. But the foreknowledge of unfortunate results does not itself implicate us in evil. We must resist this line of thinking because if we were to conceive our enterprise as in some respects evil, it could permit the contemplation of actions that violate the principles of justice that warranted our violent response: we would, in the end, involve ourselves in a contradiction. The worry is that if we see ourselves as already committing evil in a general sense by going to war, then we might justify particular acts of evil within the conduct of the war (such as deliberately targeting noncombatants) in order to bring the general evil, the war, to an end. What would be involved is a simple tradeoff of good and evil. In effect, it would open the door to the sort of consequentialist reasoning the war convention is meant to forestall and against which I have been arguing throughout.

It is not the case, then, that police brutality or wartime atrocities are condemned on the grounds that they are disproportionate. What we will find, ultimately, is that actions that have historically been condemned as disproportionate have in fact violated other principles. And if my account is correct, we might consider dropping proportionality as a standard just war criterion.

Conclusion

Terrorism is a menace that will not soon leave us. It threatens our lives in pervasive ways. Such a threat assails even our moral bulwarks, and it is at times of gravest extremity when we must guard and cherish our integrity most zealously. For in the end it is our integrity that is under the severest assault. We face a challenge to our deepest values, and we cannot capitulate in the face of such moral coercion. Firing a volley in defense of our profoundest human ideals, I have offered a conceptual apparatus that both explains and proves legitimate our deep intuitions about the justness of our response against this most heinous of evils. My hope is that a clearer understanding of the moral reality of the war against terrorism will yield consistently appropriate and ethical responses to this grave threat to humanity.

Notes

1   Walzer, p. 58.
2   Some theorists see *jus post bellum*, justice after war, as a separate category; some include it in a discussion of *jus ad bellum* issues. I will not address it other than to note here that it has to do with setting legitimate ends of war and seeking a better state of peace. Wars can end too soon or go on too long: justice itself must dictate the goals of a just war.
3   I borrow much of this particular list from Brian Orend's work, *War and International Justice: A Kantian Perspective*. Furthermore, much of the discussion follows his insightful approach to the issues. Anyone with a serious interest in just war theory should read Orend's excellent book.
4   Orend, p. 268.
5   I follow Brian Orend in this discussion. His way of elaborating the issue is very insightful, helpful, and clear.
6   Some might think we trivialize the evil of terrorism by characterizing it in terms of criminal activity. But there are crimes of varying degrees of malevolence, and terrorism resides on the very limits of the spectrum of evil. Furthermore, the criminal model is most appropriate for our conceptual analysis.
7   As highlighted earlier, an important just war concept is the moral equality of soldiers. As long as they are fighting justly, obeying the laws of war, soldiers on all sides of a conflict are considered moral equals, fighting for their own country (a proper authority) in a cause they think is just. That is why they are given POW rights if captured and are repatriated after a war. Terrorists are not considered moral equals with those who combat them, anymore than the criminal in a shootout is considered a moral equal of the policeman trying to apprehend him. This insight further reinforces the appropriateness of the law enforcement model in understanding certain aspects of the war against terrorism.
8   John Locke, *The Second Treatise of Government* (Bobbs-Merril, 1952), p. 8.
9   Just war theory generally rejects as unjust any demand for unconditional surrender as being violative of the political sovereignty of a people. Except against a Nazi-like nation, the just goals of war must be more modest. See Walzer's excellent discussion, *Just and Unjust Wars*. esp. pp. 110-17, 266-8.
10   Ibid., p. xiv.
11   An important point to ponder is that, in many cases, nonviolent responses might be far more morally troubling than violent ones. Consider the evil effects on the Iraqi people of the sanctions that have been imposed on the Iraqi government. The sanctions are indiscriminate, and their effects are more widely felt by the innocent than by the guilty.
12   I owe this insight to Richard Schoonhoven.
13   Kant, p. 442.
14   There might be room for a consideration of proportionality when it comes to deciding punishment for crimes: we want to have the punishment *fit* the crime. But it is also possible that some deeper principle of rights is involved, having to do with the rights of the criminal *vis a vis* the rights of his victims or the nature of the societal values he has profaned.
15   Orend, p. 269.

Select Bibliography

Anscombe, G.E.M. *Ethics, Religion, and Politics*. Oxford: Basil Blackwell, 1981.

Axinn, Sidney. *A Moral Military*. Philadelphia: Temple University Press, 1989.

Christopher, Paul. *The Ethics of War and Peace*. New Jersey: Prentice Hall, 1994.

Donagan, Alan. *A Theory of Morality*. Chicago: University of Chicago Press, 1977.

Herman, Barbara. *The Practice of Moral Judgment*. Cambridge: Harvard University Press, 1993.

Kagan, Shelly. *The Limits of Morality*. Oxford: Clarendon Press, 1989.

Kant, Immanuel. *Groundwork of the Metaphysic of Morals*. Trans. H.J. Paton. New York: Harper and Row, 1948.

——. *Perpetual Peace and Other Essays*. Trans. Ted Humphrey. Indianapolis: Hackett Publishing Company, 1983.

——. *The Metaphysics of Morals*. Trans. Mary Gregor. Cambridge: Cambridge University Press, 1991.

Korsgaard, Christine M. *The Sources of Normativity*. Cambridge: Cambridge University Press, 1996.

Locke, John. *The Second Treatise of Government*. Indianapolis: Bobbs-Merrill Company, 1952.

Nagel, Thomas. *The View From Nowhere*. Oxford: Oxford University Press, 1986.

Nozick, Robert. *Anarchy, State, and Utopia*. New York: Basic Books, 1974.

O'Neill, Onora. *Constructions of reason: explorations of Kant's practical philosophy*. New York: Cambridge University Press, 1989.

Phillips, Robert L. *War and Justice*. Norman: University of Oklahoma Press, 1984.

Quinn, Warren. *Morality and Action*. Cambridge: Cambridge University Press, 1993.

Scanlon, T.M. *What We Owe to Each Other*. Cambridge: Belknap Press, 1998.

Scheffler, Samuel. *The Rejection of Consequentialism*. Oxford: Clarendon Press, 1994.

Soelle, Dorothee. *The Arms Race Kills Even Without War*. Trans. Gerhard A. Elston. Philadelphia: Fortress Press, 1983.

Wakin, Malham, M. ed. *War, Morality, and the Military Profession*. Boulder: Westview Press, 1979.

Walzer, Michael. *Just and Unjust Wars: A Moral Argument with Historical Illustrations*. 2nd ed. USA: Basic Books, 1977.

Yoder, John, Howard. *When War is Unjust: Being Honest in Just War Thinking*. Minneapolis: Augsburg Publishing House, 1984.

United States Government Publications

U.S. Department of the Army. *Your Conduct in Combat Under the Law of War*, Field Manual 27-2. U.S. Government Printing Office, 1984.

——. *The Law of Land Warfare*. Field Manual 27-10. Washington, D.C.: 1956.

Articles

Anscombe, G.E.M. "War and Murder" in *War, Morality, and the Military Profession*, ed. Malham M. Makin (Boulder: Westview Press, 1979): 285-98.

Cummiskey, David. "Kantian Consequentialism" in *Ethics*, 100 (April 1990): 586-615.

Evans, Michael. "Dark Victory" in *Proceedings*, U.S. Naval Institute. Sept. 99, Vol. 125/9/1, 159: 33-7.

Geddes, Leonard. "On the Intrinsic Wrongness of Killing Innocent Persons" in *Analysis*, Vol. 33-34, Oct., 1972-74: 93-7.

Korsgaard, Christine. "Kant's Formula of Humanity" in *Kant Studien*, 77 Jahrgang, Heft 2, 1986.

Movrodes, George I. "Conventions and the Morality of War" in *War, Morality, and the Military Profession*, ed. Malham M. Makin (Boulder: Westview Press, 1979): 327-42.

Murphy, Jeffrie G. "Killing the Innocent" in *War, Morality, and the Military Profession*; ed. Malham M. Makin (Boulder: Westview Press, 1979): 343-70.

Otsuka, Michael. "Killing in Self-Defense" in *Philosophy and Public Affairs*, Vol. 23, 1994: 74-94.

Index